ALFONSO II AND THE ARTISTIC RENEWAL OF NAPLES 1485–1495

Yale Publications in the History of Art, 19

Vincent Scully, *Editor*

ALFONSO II AND THE ARTISTIC RENEWAL OF NAPLES 1485-1495

by George L. Hersey

New Haven and London, Yale University Press, 1969

Library of Congress catalog card number: 69–15446

Designed by Marvin Howard Simmons,
set in Garamond type,
and printed in the United States of America by
Connecticut Printers, Inc., Hartford, Connecticut.

Distributed in Great Britain, Europe, Asia, and
Africa by Yale University Press Ltd., London; in
Canada by McGill University Press, Montreal; and
in Latin America by Centro Interamericano de Libros
Académicos, Mexico City.

Preface

In the 1480s, when he was still Duke of Calabria, Alfonso II of Naples began to refurbish his capital. His plan was to straighten the ancient streets and erect triumphal gates on the main east–west thoroughfares. A new set of walls was built, and Francesco di Giorgio re-fortified the Castel Nuovo and the Castel Sant'Elmo. A restored aqueduct brought water to new fountains throughout the city. Giuliano da Maiano created two splendid villas; churches were built or remodeled—one as a royal pantheon—and a vast palace of justice was designed by Giuliano da Sangallo. Sculptured chapels and a group of exquisite portrait busts were further expressions of Alfonso's intent. While only parts of this ambitious plan exist today, these fragments, together with documents that record the rest of the scheme, can help us reconstruct the whole.

A study of Alfonso's artistic renewal has a number of uses. One of his villas, Poggioreale, was probably the earliest rigorously symmetrical, cross-axial secular building of the Renaissance, and had important offspring in designs by later architects. Moreover, Poggioreale and the projected palace of justice were apparently planned in accordance with a novel overall grid by means of which an architect could lay out abstract and geometrical buildings that included both very large and very small spaces. Another important part of the renewal was Francesco di Giorgio's fortifications, which were built up from the interlocking polyhedral forms that had come into vogue for this purpose. Their enormous scale and emphasis on volume anticipated High Renaissance urban space. In other ways Alfonso's projects add to our knowledge of royal and civic imagery—the coronation portrait, the triumphal arch, the tomb, and even the city itself as an anthropomorphic image.

Figure 1 attempts to show how the city's cavea-shaped topology would have looked had Alfonso's plans been completely realized. The old Greek sector is restored as a set of narrow blocks, and clusters of new buildings and walls appear around each of the triumphal gates. New roads were built from each of these gates to a more distant new structure: on the west to Castel Sant'Elmo, and on the east to Poggioreale.

Within this civic context, like characters on the stage, some of the great works of Quattrocento sculpture played their roles. For example, portrait busts of the Neapolitan princesses by Francesco Laurana acted as ambassadors in matrimonial negotiations, and Guido Mazzoni's Lamentation in the Church of Monteoliveto became a tableau of death and vanished hopes after Alfonso's abdication.

A somewhat different drama involved the roles played by Alfonso's artists and by the iconographies and styles they brought to the renewal. Within the program as a whole, each style or image acted expressively, so that a medieval-looking seated king, his connotations of age and eternity intact, was carved by Benedetto da Maiano in a setting of consciously active contemporary figures; a boldly "modern" set of fortifications re-presented, as a symbol and

v

heirloom, the older castle within them; a specialist in naturalistic sculpture was called on to express uncontrollable grief.

Against this same theatrical setting, too, we can witness the stages of Alfonso's own life, first as condottiere, then as Maecenas, and finally as penitent. Again, these three stages well fit the succession of artists he employed: first the Maiano brothers and their solid, graceful work; next Giuliano da Sangallo with his colossal Palazzo dei Tribunali and Francesco di Giorgio with his even more immense fortifications; and finally Mazzoni with his neurotic passion and naturalism.

Behind the shifting fortunes of such personal and political dramas, however, the renewal expressed certain constant ideas: the legitimacy of the Aragonese house, the power of the Crown over the barons, and the need for a Florentine alliance to keep up Naples' political momentum. Pontano's eclogue *Lepidina* also provided a unifying metaphor, of the city both as theater and heroine, and as a recumbent stone goddess, Parthenope, who is awakened, cleansed, and impregnated with new life by Alfonso's act.

Despite these generalizations about the renewal I have not attempted a complete picture of it. That would be impossible since so little has survived. Instead I have constructed seven linked studies which range through the literature, the portraits, the urbanism, the chief buildings, and the funeral sculpture. I hope the conclusions that emerge from these individual studies will stimulate other students to seek further answers to the questions they raise.

Many people have helped me with this book. My profoundest thanks go to Charles Seymour, Jr., who has been sympathetic and inspiring in all my endeavors. He and the editor of the series, Vincent Scully, have read the entire manuscript and I have greatly benefited from their criticisms. For more specific favors I thank Alois M. Nagler, J. D. Hexter, William L. MacDonald, Edgar Munhall, John F. Oates, Perry B. Cott, John Pope-Hennessy, Graham Pollard, Leopold Ettlinger, Roberto Weiss, John Moores, G. K. Jenkins, J. B. Trapp, Otto Pächt, Françoise Gavoty, Oliver S. Kapsner, Philip Foster, Thomas F. Reese, Walter Langsam, David Summers, Janet Smith, and Frances Robb. In Italy I have been encouraged over many years by Roberto Pane and Giancarlo Alisio; and I also thank Ottavio Morisani, Alfonso de Franciscis, Raffaello Causa, Iole Mazzoleni, Ulrich Middeldorf, Ugo Procacci, Erwin M. Auer, Maria Fossi-Todorow, Hartmut Biermann, and C. L. Frommel. At the Yale University Press Anne Wilde and Vivien Silverstein have been extremely patient and helpful.

I have obtained photographs through the kindness of Guido Spinazzola and Alberto Cotogni. Two grants have assisted me: one in 1965 from the American Philosophical Society and the other in 1966 from the Morse Fellowship Committee at Yale. Parts of Chapter 3 were read before the Society of Architectural Historians in New York in January 1966, and part of Chapter 6 appeared in *Napoli nobilissima,* whose editor, Roberto Pane, I thank for permission to reuse the text. In descriptions of churches, compass points are meant ecclesiastically, elsewhere, geographically.

New Haven, Connecticut   G. L. H.
1968

Contents

List of Illustrations

Faustus. Then up to Naples, rich Campania,
Whose buildings fair and gorgeous to the eye,
The streets straight forth, and pav'd with
     finest brick,
Quarter the town in four equivalents.
                   Marlowe, *Doctor Faustus*

Chapter 1: THE POLITICAL AIMS AND ARTISTIC SETTING

HISTORICAL BACKGROUND Aragonese rule in Naples began in June 1442 with the happy victory of Alfonso I, Il Magnanimo, over forces representing his rival for the throne, René of Anjou. The dynasty continued for fifty years, its path marked by frequent military successes. But these could only rarely be exploited satisfactorily. Camillo Porzio, the sixteenth-century historian, put the case thus: "The kings of Naples, so long as they possessed no other states, were in such low and despicable condition that not only foreign powers, but even their own barons, plotted against them."[1]

This was even truer of Alfonso I's son Ferrante, who reigned from 1458 to 1494, than it had been of Il Magnanimo; and Ferrante's position had other weaknesses as well. On his accession the Angevins vigorously revived their claims to Naples and led the local barons in revolt against the Aragonese.[2] These wars kept Ferrante from his capital for eight years. Ferrante's second problem was his illegitimacy. In Italy bastardy was not morally offensive but it could be a legal problem, especially with a king who ruled a fief of the Church such as Naples. Finally, Ferrante's birth could well have been secretly offensive to himself if not to his Italian subjects, for he was Spanish born and bred and was called "el bastardo" by his Spanish relatives.[3]

One goal of Ferrante's policy was therefore a system of foreign alliances as a step toward the "other states" he needed for political equilibrium against Anjou. Another was the establishment, politically and psychologically, of his own legitimacy. These goals were clearly expressed in the artistic renewal undertaken in the 1480s by Ferrante's son and heir, Alfonso of Calabria.

Alfonso was born in Naples on November 4, 1448.[4] His mother was Isabella of Chiaro-

---

1. "I re di Napoli, mentre non possedettero altri Stati, in si basso luogo e si disprezzabile sedettero, che non solo a' Potentati esterni, ma ad ogni loro Barone dettero animo di macchinar loro contro . . ." *La Congiura dei baroni del regno di Napoli* [1565] in G. Gravier, ed., *Raccolta di tutti i più rinomati scrittori dell'istoria generale del regno di Napoli*, 5 (Naples, 1769–72), 2.

2. L. Volpicella, "Un Registro di ligi omaggi al re Ferdinando d'Aragona," *Studi di storia napoletana in onore di Michelangelo Schipa* (Naples, 1926), 305–29; E. Gothein, *Il Rinascimento nell'Italia meridionale*, tr. and ed. Tommaso Persico (Florence, 1915), pp. 3–30.

3. Pontieri, in "La Giovinezza di Ferrante I d'Aragona," *Studi in onore di Riccardo Filangieri*, 1 (Naples,

1959), 537–39, tells us that his mother was variously described as the daughter of a barber, as a nun, etc., but that she was in fact Giraldona Carlino, who was or became the wife of Gaspare Revertit of Barcelona. Despite his birth, however, Ferrante had been made Alfonso I's heir at the barons' own request, on February 28, 1443 (ibid., p. 563). Cf. also G. J. E. Martínez Ferrando, "Consideraciones en torno la exposición documental sobre Alfonso el Magnánimo organizada en el Archívo de la corona de Aragón," in Antonio Torraja, ed., *Estudios sobre Alfonso el Magnánimo* (Barcelona, 1960), pp. 213–32, esp. pp. 228–29.

4. For Alfonso of Calabria see G. A. Summonte, *Historia della città e regno di Napoli*, 5 (Naples, 1749); L. Volpicella, ed., *Regis ferdinandi primi in-*

monte, a daughter of Tristano, Prince of Rossano, and her marriage to Ferrante had been an attempt to cement relations between throne and barons. The birth was not without its unpleasant accompaniments: we are told that a beam of fire, seen as a sign of Alfonso's future terribilità, filled the heavens.[5] Nonetheless there was plenty of reason for optimism. The prince was educated by famous humanists, among them Antonio Panormita and Giovanni Gioviano Pontano. From early youth he distinguished himself as a warrior and loyal supporter of his father. Indeed this intense loyalty, and the resulting identity of interests between father and son, have led later generations to confuse the physiognomies of the two men.

Alfonso's first exposure to battle came in 1462 at the age of 14. Later, in 1478–79, supported by Genoa and Sixtus IV, he was put in charge of the war against Florence occasioned by the Pazzi conspiracy.[6] Vasari suggests that Alfonso's siege of Castellina (June 26–August 3, 1478) was fundamental in the history of modern warfare, for here the giant new field artillery pieces showed that medieval curtain walls were no longer adequate protection.[7] The Duke's successful siege of Poggio Imperiale in the same year is recorded in a beautiful medal by Francesco di Giorgio (Fig. 33). On the obverse is a portrait of the young condottiere in profile, with his sharp, pouchy features and squinting eyes, and on the reverse a scene of Roman military sacrifice, a tribute to Mars before the conquered city.

Largely owing to Alfonso's successful campaigning, Lorenzo de' Medici was forced to sue for peace. It was then, 1479, that he made his famous and perilous voyage to Naples. As a result, a new alignment of interests occurred, with Florence, Naples, and Milan in opposition to the Papacy and Venice.[8] Many of Naples' later grandeurs, especially the artistic ones, were to be direct expressions of the Florentine connection, as her misères were of the Milanese.

Another mode of influence was matrimony, or, more precisely, protracted matrimonial negotiations. Ferrante was lucky in this, for the Aragonese womenfolk were most of them intelligent and good-looking, at least if we can judge from the works of art made to express this point. The first stroke of nuptial policy occurred in 1465 when young Alfonso married Ippolita Maria, daughter of Francesco Maria Sforza, Duke of Milan.[9] Later on Ferrante

structionum liber (Naples, 1916), pp. 225–65; Benedetto Croce, "Antonio de Ferrariis, detto il Galateo," Humanisme et Renaissance, 4 (1937), 366–82, esp. 373–80; Alessandro Cutolo, "La Nascita di Ferrandino d'Aragona," Archivio storico per le province napoletane [hereafter ASPN], 67 (1945), 99–108; Ernesto Pontieri, Per la Storia del regno di Ferrante I d'Aragona, re di Napoli (Naples, 1946); and idem, "La Giovinezza," pp. 531–601.

5. Anon., Dell'Istoria del regno di Napoli d'incerto autore, in Gravier, Raccolta, 4, 227.

6. See Angelo di Costanzo, "Istoria del regno di Napoli," in Gravier, Raccolta, 1, 570–72, 586; Summonte, Historia, 4, 432–35; Pontieri, Per la Storia, pp. 117–277; and Warman Welliver, L'Impero fiorentino

(Florence, 1956), pp. 75–101.

7. Giorgio Vasari, Vite de' più eccellenti pittori scultori ed architettori, ed. Gaetano Milanesi (Florence, 1906) [hereafter cited simply as Vasari], 4, 269 and n. 1.

8. Pontieri, Per la Storia, pp. 211–31; and Welliver, L'Impero, pp. 99–101.

9. For this marriage, see G. F. De Lignamine, "Inclyti ferdinandi regis vita et laudes" [1472], excerpted in Pontieri, Per la Storia, p. 59; also Alfredo Baccelli, "Ippolita Sforza Duchessa di Calabria," Rassegna nazionale, 52 (1930), 21–32. Ippolita, whose mother was Bianca Maria Visconti, was born on April 18, 1445, in Pesaro during the reign of Bianca's father, Francesco Maria Visconti.

planned other marriages, which would have formed alliances between Naples and, respectively, Castile, Burgundy, and (again) Milan; but these came to nothing. However, in 1473 Alfonso's sister Eleonora married Ercole I d'Este, Duke of Ferrara. It was one of the few Aragonese matches that turned out well.[10] In 1476 Beatrice, Alfonso's other, more troublesome sister, married Matthias Corvinus, King of Hungary.[11] In the following year, having mourned Queen Isabella di Chiaromonte for more than a decade,[12] Ferrante married his first cousin, Giovanna d'Aragona, sister of the man who in two years would be Ferdinand the Catholic of Spain and eventually King of the Two Sicilies. A matrimonial web was now woven between Naples and Ferrara, Hungary, and Spain. All that was lacking were similar alliances with Florence and Milan. The latter came in 1489 with the long-announced marriage between Alfonso's daughter Isabella and Giangaleazzo Sforza, heir to the Duchy of Milan and, for the moment, protégé of Lodovico il Moro.[13] Only Florence was never included in the network; but perhaps it is not too fanciful to think of the artists and works of art that Alfonso imported from Lorenzo's republic as surrogates for the Florentine princesses who did not exist.

With the Tuscan war over, the second challenge to Alfonso's military prowess met with even more satisfying results. In 1480 the Turks, under Mohammed II, had begun to occupy the Province of Otranto.[14] Sustained by the other members of the alliance, however, the Neapolitan forces won a decisive victory. The main battle was at the town of Otranto and took place on September 10, 1481. A contemporary account by a Neapolitan chronicler named Ferraiolo tells us:

> The day of the battle the Duke was among the earliest to expose himself to danger on the walls of the city, and his strong heart led him to despise death; he rode about on

10. C. Corvisieri, "Il Trionfo romano di Eleonora d'Aragona nel giugno del 1473," *Archivio della società romana di storia patria*, 1 (1878), 475–91, and Riccardo Bacchelli, *La Congiura di Don Giulio d'Este* (Milan, 1931), pp. 83–96.

11. Albert Berzeviczy, "Les Fiançailles successives de Béatrice d'Aragon," *Revue de Hongrie*, 2 (1909), 146–65. Beatrice had been offered to G. B. Marzano, son of Marino, Duke of Sessa and Rossano, in 1463 and to Filiberto, Duke of Savoy, in 1473. The latter match was prevented by Louis XII so that Beatrice would be free to marry the Dauphin, later Charles VIII (a third negotiation that proved abortive). In 1464 Ferrante had meanwhile offered Eleonora's hand to Matthias Corvinus, but the Hungarian rejected her, apparently because of her looks. See also idem, "Rapporti storici fra Napoli a l'Ungheria nell'epoca degli Aragonesi (1442–1501)," *Atti della Accademia Pontaniana*, 58 (Naples, 1928), 180–202; idem, *Beatrice d'Aragona*, ed. Rodolfo Mosca (Milan, 1931); and Tiberio Kardos, "Mattia Corvino, Re umanista," *La Rinascita*, 3 (1940), 803–41 and 4 (1941), 69–83.

12. Isabella di Chiaromonte was niece to Giovanni Antonio del Balzo Orsini, Prince of Taranto, and cousin to the Duke of Andria. One should mention, as another Neapolitan link for the family, Alfonso's brother Federigo's marriage in 1487 to Isabella del Balzo, daughter of the Prince of Altamura and another niece of Orsini's. Meanwhile Alfonso I's daughter Eleonora had married Marino Marzano, Prince of Rossano (later a leader in the Baron's Revolt), who had been proposed as a husband for Beatrice. Cf. Pontieri, "La Giovinezza," pp. 569–74.

13. Cf. Robert de la Sizeranne, *Béatrice d'Este et sa Cour* (Paris, 1920), pp. 87–115; and Achille Dina, "Isabella d'Aragona, Duchessa di Milano e di Bari," *Archivio storico lombardo*, 48 (1921), 269–457, esp. p. 292.

14. Pontieri, *Per la Storia*, pp. 232–57. For sources and documents, see Giovanni Albino, *De bello hydrundino*, in *De gestis regum neapolitanorum*, Gravier, *Raccolta*, 5, 22–35, and E. Perito, "Uno Sguardo alla guerra d'Otranto e alle cedole di tesoreria aragonese di quel tempo," *ASPN*, 40 (1915), 313–35.

his horse, and when he saw that the infantry was unwilling, he jumped to the ground among his soldiers and encouraged them like a lion. In that hour they climbed the great city wall with the Duke, with the artillery bombardment continuing all the while, and he urged his forces forward not only with words but with his very body; and things went well because of his justice and good faith.[15]

The triumph of Otranto is commemorated in a medal of 1481 by Andrea Guacialoti (Fig. 32). On the obverse is a three-quarter view of the Duke, in armor and wearing a cloth cap; on the reverse, the congested triumphal procession.

During the 1480s the financial and political ties between Florence and Naples became even closer. To a great extent Florentine loans and contributions had made Otranto possible, and in the succeeding years, as Pontieri points out, Ferrante's letters substitute all sorts of heartfelt cordialities for the normal diplomatic style. "Lorenço," he calls him, and "Lorenço mio amato amico."[16]

Now peace was temporarily established abroad, but there was war at home. In 1485 the famous revolt of the barons began, instantly followed by renewed hostilities with the new Pope, Innocent VIII.[17] Again Ferrante's control of his kingdom was threatened, and again Florence came to the rescue. This support was not just a matter of friendship but of Florentine financial investments and banking activities in the south (e.g. those of the Gondi and Strozzi families), and perhaps even of Alfonso's future military usefulness.[18] We are told it was Alfonso's incredibly bad manners, his crudity and ferocity, that especially kindled the hostility of the barons. At any rate, he proved a singularly bad diplomat with them, some of whom were governors of the seggi (i.e. the municipal districts, Capuana, Nilo, Montagna, Porto, and Portanova). The issues were not well resolved until 1486, when Alfonso was able to take to the field and march the Neapolitan army to the walls of Rome. Innocent's forces collapsed and, on December 27, 1486, for the third time, Alfonso entered Naples as a triumphator. He rode through the whole city, says Ferraiolo, his captured Neapolitan rebels shuffling behind.[19]

If tradition is to be believed, Alfonso later showed more than bad manners to his captives:

15. Riccardo Filangieri, ed., *Una Cronaca napoletana figurata del quattrocento* (Naples, 1956), p. 42.

16. E. Pontieri, *Per la storia*, pp. 261, 268–69; idem, "La Dinastia aragonese di Napoli e la casa de' Medici di Firenze," *ASPN, 65* (1940), 274–342; *66* (1941), 217–273; Giulio Grimaldi, "Bernardo Dovizi alla corte d'Alfonso II d'Aragona," *ASPN, 25* (1900), 218–37. In a speech to Bernardo Dovizi [Cardinal] da Bibbiena, Alfonso speaks of himself as being "mezo fiorentino" (ibid., p. 220).

17. Cf. Enrico Perito, *La Congiura dei baroni e il conte di Policastro* (Bari, 1926), also Pontieri, "Camillo Porzio Storico," *ASPN, 75* (1957), 127–61; *76* (1958), 121–79; idem, "L'Atteggiamento di Venezia nel conflitto tra Papa Innocenzo VIII e Ferrante I d'Aragona (1485–1492)," *ASPN, 81* (1963), 197–324, esp. 197–204.

18. Pontieri, *Per la storia*, p. 269. Such considerations, I am sure lay behind the trading of honors, as on July 15, 1483, when Lorenzo became Gran Camerario of Naples (ibid.), when Alfonso had been made Condottiere of the Republic of Florence (Welliver, *L'Impero,* p. 100), or when in 1486 Ferrante gave Lorenzo the palace he had seized from Francesco Coppola, Count of Sarno and a leader of the Barons' Revolt (Irma Schiappoli, "Il Conte di Sarno," *ASPN, 61*, 1936, 15–115).

19. R. Filangieri, *Cronaca figurata*, p. 70.

he incited the King to issue a wolfish invitation to the Count of Sarno and his family, and others, to a party at the Castel Nuovo celebrating the peace.[20] During the festivities, as music played and wine was drunk, the Count was arrested. Later, other leaders of the revolt were taken, and many were executed. But Ferrante did well out of the party, both financially and politically: it at once deprived his rivals of power and diverted their revenues to him. This money helped finance the renewal, just now getting under way; not surprisingly one of its main messages was one of admonition to baronial power.

On January 25, 1494, with the words, "Figliuoli, siate benedetti," Ferrante died, his family tenderly gathered around him. The funeral took place on February 2 in San Domenico Maggiore. His body still lies, unburied, in a coffin in the sacristy of that church. Summonte's panegyric is typical of the court's flavor. He says Ferrante was gracious in reason, modest, long-suffering, universally loved, and an excellent dissimulator.[21]

ALFONSO'S REIGN   The coronation of Alfonso II was the gayest and most sumptuous ever held in Naples—the confident fanfare of what was expected to be a great reign.[22] It took place in the cathedral on Ascension Day, May 8, 1494. In the church an apsidal "theatrum," hung with golden draperies, was set up in the choir. Around it, says Summonte, sat 53 prelates and ambassadors representing new or renewed alliances. Afterward a spectacular procession wound through the city (Fig. 34) ending at the Castel Nuovo to the tune of artillery salvos—"a stupendous thing to hear."[23]

Summonte continues, however, that daily one also heard about the preparations of the King of France to invade Naples. Indeed, well before Alfonso's coronation signs of disaster had begun to appear. The Angevin claims to Naples had by this time been assumed by the French king, and in 1492 the ambitious Charles VIII attained his majority.[24] Innocent thereupon declared Ferrante deposed and planned to summon Charles to Rome to invest him as King of the Two Sicilies. Fortunately Pontano convinced the Pope to change his mind, but in 1492 the new Pope, Alexander VI Borgia, threatened again to revoke Ferrante's investiture. Now it was Lorenzo de' Medici who intervened—one of his last kindnesses for Ferrante before Lorenzo died that year. Earlier, meanwhile, in 1490, Matthias Corvinus had also died, and his successor, Ladislas II, refused to take over Beatrice as his queen. Then, on October

20. Cf. Pontieri's edition of Porzio, *Congiura* (Naples, 1964), pp. xliii–l, and Pontieri, "L'Atteggiamento di Venezia."

21. G. A. Summonte, *Historia, 4,* 624–25.

22. The usual source is the diary of Jean Burchard, master of ceremonies at the event, which has been published by L. Thuasne (Paris, 1884, *2,* 154–64). However this is not as complete as the account in G. A. Summonte, *Historia, 5,* 3–20, which is longer and which unlike Burchard quotes copiously from the actual liturgy used. See also Tristano Caracciolo, *Opuscula historica de Ferdinando qui postea rex Aragonum fuit,* etc., in Gra-

vier, *Raccolta, 6,* 146–47; G. Passero, *Giornali,* ed. M. Vecchioni (Naples, 1785), pp. 60–61; and the *Diurnali* of Giacomo Gallo, p. 7. For modern accounts see Erasmo Percopo, "Coronazione di Alfonso II d'Aragona," *ASPN, 14* (1889), 140–43 (where the wrong date, February 8, is given), and Gothein, *Il Rinascimento,* p. 189.

23. G. A. Summonte, *Historia, 5, 4,* 20.

24. Pontieri, *Per la storia,* pp. 362–81, 348, and Emilio Nunziante, "Il Concistoro d'Innocenzo VIII per la chiamata di Renato duca di Lorena contro il regno (marzo 1486)," *ASPN, 11* (1886), 751–66.

21, 1494, came the death of the ineffectual Giangaleazzo Sforza, heir to Milan, whereupon Lodovico il Moro, the new Duke, welcomed Charles as his ally against Naples. Thus not long after Alfonso II's coronation almost all of Ferrante's carefully built alliances had been broken or weakened, and France was an immediate enemy.

In order to stop Charles VIII, Alfonso sent two armies north. His brother Federigo sailed to meet the French in Liguria, and Ferrandino, an excellent soldier, marched against the Milanese in the Romagna. But with Alfonso in Naples instead of in the field, the campaigns were disastrous. Federigo was decisively beaten at Rapallo and Ferrandino driven back to the Neapolitan frontier.[25]

The new king now began to give way to superstition and hysteria. The fearful prognostication at his birth was coming true. Paying little attention to the elaborate defense measures he had called for, he spent his time weeping, praying, and washing the feet of paupers. His doctor told him of someone's dream, in which Ferrante's ghost had appeared saying that Alfonso had no hope of resisting the King of France, and that the House of Aragon must lose its kingdom in return for the enormities it had committed, and become extinct. Summonte even suggests that defeat and death were Alfonso's unavoidable fate: the King had suffered all his life from a deformity of the eyes and was known as "Il Guercio"; and it was said that people with such deformities were intrinsically evil: "Si guercus bonus est, inter miracula scribe."[26]

Late in 1494, in this atmosphere of fear and retreat and even of occult threats, Alfonso was persuaded by Alexander VI and Pontano to abdicate in favor of Ferrandino. On January 23, 1495, two days before the first anniversary of his father's death, Alfonso II left his throne and shortly afterward sailed for Sicily with several boatloads of treasure and works of art.[27] He went to live in the Olivetan (White Benedictine) monastery at Mazara del Vallo, where, according to Summonte, he was preparing to don the habit of a monk when he contracted a fever. An abscess developed in his hand, and he died in Messina on November 19, 1495, at the age of 47. He was buried in the cathedral there. His tomb, which no longer exists, bore this epitaph:

> O Death, long didst thou flee Alfonso when he was armed. Now that he has laid by his weapons, for what glory, pray, dost thou kill by deceit?[28]

Only a month after Alfonso's abdication, Charles VIII entered Naples, having again defeated Ferrandino's forces, and sent the young ruler with his uncle Federigo and the navy to

25. M. Sanudo, "La Spedizione di Carlo VIII in Italia," ed. R. Fulin, *Archivio veneto*, 2 (1873), Supplement; H. F. Delaborde, *L'Expédition de Charles VIII en Italie* (Paris, 1888); Erasmo Pèrcopo, "Per l'Entrata solenne di Carlo VIII in Napoli," in *Studi di storia napoletana in onore di Michelangelo Schipa* (Naples, 1926), pp. 347–52; and L. Pastor, *History of the Popes*, 5 (London, 1898), 420–523.

26. Summonte, *Historia*, 5, 28–29; Porzio, *Congiura*, in Gravier, 5, 3.

27. Notar Giacomo (*Cronica di Napoli*, ed. P. Garzilli, Naples, 1845, p. 185) mentions five galleys "plus una fusta con due bargie"; cf. also Passero, *Giornali*, p. 64.

28. Summonte, *Historia*, 5, 28. See also Francesco Guicciardini, *La Historia d'Italia* (Venice, 1563), 1, fols. 14, 15.

Ischia. The French held the city until July 1495, when Ferrandino entered his capital on the east through the Porta del Carmine. The French were still holding the Castel Nuovo on the west. In November, however, they were driven out by an exploding mine—the first on record. Soon afterward the remainder of Charles' forces left for France; on this occasion even more Neapolitan art was removed. The departing occupiers took boatloads of precious objects by sea, wagonloads by land, and two of Alfonso's artists in person, Fra Giocondo and Guido Mazzoni.[29]

Ferrandino's triumph was short-lived: he died (of natural causes) on October 7, 1496, only ten months after he had cleared the French out of the city. His successor was his uncle Federigo, who assumed the throne with the motto RECEDANT VETERA, putting away old hostilities. But soon Federigo too was deprived of the throne. In 1498 France renewed its claim through Charles VIII's successor, Louis XII, while the Spanish claims were taken up by Alfonso I's nephew, Ferdinand the Catholic. He and the French ruler planned to share the Italian kingdom, but they fell out in 1502 and, in the ensuing war, Gonsalvo de Cordoba, the legendary Gran Capitano who had driven the Moors from Granada in 1492, was victorious at the River Garigliano. Naples was established as the Spanish Viceroyalty it remained for 231 years.[30]

The remnants of the House of Aragon led sorrowful lives. Giovanna, Ferrante's second queen and widow; her daughter the Infanta Giovanna, who had become Ferrandino's wife; Isabella del Balzo, wife of Federigo; and Beatrice, wife of Matthias Corvinus, were the subjects of lachrymose poetry as "les quatre tristes reines de Naples."[31] Cariteo put this apostrophe in the mouth of Parthenope herself:

> Four excellent queens! . . . What stone can keep itself from weeping? How sorry I am that I cannot die![32]

At the same time Pontano (who had disloyally delivered an oration of welcome to Charles in 1495) and Sannazaro were committed to new causes and patrons, while Federigo was an exile in France.

URBANISM   Alfonso of Calabria arrived on the scene in the midst of artistic conflicts as vigorous as his political and military battles. The important developments in urbanism took place not in Florence but in the work of Florentine and other Tuscan architects who traveled outside that city. Four centers are particularly relevant to Alfonso's renewal: Rome, Pienza, Urbino, and Naples itself.

29. Pontieri, Per la Storia, pp. 347–96; Sanudo, "La Spedizione," pp. 193–95; and Lud. Lalanne, "Transport d'oeuvres d'art de Naples au Château d'Amboise en 1495," Archives de l'art français, 2 (1852–53), 305.

30. G. A. Summonte, Historia, 5, 31–112. See also Paolo Negri, "Studi sulla crisi italiana alla fine del secolo XV," Archivio storico lombardo, 50 (1923), 1–135; 51 (1924), 75–144, and G. Coniglio, Il Regno di Napoli al tempo di Carlo V (Naples, 1951).

31. F. Scandone, "Le tristi Reyne di Napoli, Giovanna III e Giovanna IV di Aragona," ASPN, 53 (1928), 114–55; 54 (1929), 151–205.

32. Benedetto Gareth, Rime, ed. Erasmo Percopo (Naples, 1892), 2, 308.

In Naples, in 1443, when Alfonso I began to rebuild the Castel Nuovo (Figs. 1, 4),[33] the area around the castle, the so-called "coda" between San Giovanni Maggiore and the Angevin fort was also rebuilt.[34] The new castle, tall and five-towered, trapezoidal in plan, was set between gardens at different levels that recalled (and perhaps restored) a famous park built by Robert the Wise. Alfonso's classical triumphal gate stood at the northwest corner, facing a towering hill crowned with a second castle, Belforte, now Sant'Elmo. The gate also stood at right angles to a new boulevard leading up the northern margin of the coda to the heart of the city, the Strada dell'Incoronata (now in part via Medina). Looking at a detail of the Tavola Strozzi (Fig. 4), one sees also the rectangular arcaded glorietta, on the left, the observation balcony that jutted from the rear of the Castel Nuovo, providing its occupants with a panorama of the bay and islands. In these ways the Castel Nuovo, far from closing itself off from its surroundings in the normal military manner, was linked openly to them.

With the construction of the Castel Nuovo, its parks, and the Strada dell'Incoronata, the main part of Alfonso's urban achievement ended. Ferrante contented himself with developing his father's ideas. In 1465–66 he built a square, later surrounded by shops, in front of the Castel Nuovo. In 1472 Jacopo della Pila added fountains to the northern park. Ferrante also erected a barbican in front of his father's arch, and other outer walls and defenses.[35]

During these same years, according to some, Alberti was working out a scheme for Rome which included rebuilding the Borgo Leonino, the area linking the Vatican and St. Peter's with the Castel Sant'Angelo.[36] There were to be three wide parallel avenues leading to the rectangular square in front of St. Peter's. One would lead to the Vatican Palace, and the other, on the south, to a palace for the canons of the cathedral. In the center of the square was to be Nero's obelisk on a base including statues of the four Evangelists and topped by a statue of Christ with a golden cross. The side of the square running across the front of St. Peter's, which was already built up into terraces, would be backed by a continuous portico

33. Giuseppe Russo, "La Città di Napoli dalle origine al 1860," in Mario Napoli, *Contributi allo studio della città* (Naples, 1960), pp. 61–70, republished in G. Russo, *Napoli come città* (Naples, 1966); R. Filangieri, "L'Architetto della reggia aragonese di Napoli," *L'Arte, 31* (1928), 32–35; idem, *Castelnuovo, reggia angioina ed aragonese* (Naples, 1964). But the standard study by Filangieri is still his "Rassegna critica delle fonti per la storia di Castel Nuovo," *ASPN, 62* (1937), 267–333; 63 (1938), 258–342; 64 (1939), 237–322. See also Ottavio Morisani, *Letteratura artistica a Napoli* (Naples, 1958), pp. 25–32.

34. G. A. Summonte, *Historia, 1*, 29–30; R. Filangieri, "Rassegna critica," *ASPN, 62* (1937), 267–33.

35. Morisani, *Letteratura artistica*, pp. 30–32. Ferrante built the Church of San Vincenzo Ferrer (later San Giovanni dei Fiorentini) for Isabella di Chiaromonte, restored the Duomo and San Domenico Maggiore, and laid out the Piazza dell'Olmo in 1468. See also De Lignamine, "Ferdinandis . . . vita" in Pontieri, *Per la Storia*, p. 64; R. Filangieri, "Rassegna critica," *ASPN, 63* (1938), 260, 277, 285; and Sanudo, "La Spedizione," pp. 238–40.

36. For Alberti's urbanism in general see W. A. Eden, "Studies in Urban Theory. The 'De Re Aedificatoria' of Leon Battista Alberti," *Town Planning Review, 19* (1943), 10–28; and Hermann Bauer, *Kunst und Utopie, Studien über das Kunst und Staatsdenken in der Renaissance* (Berlin, 1965), pp. 29–62. For the work in Rome see the life of Nicholas V in Vespasiano [da] Bisticci, *Vite de uomini illustri del secolo XV*, ed. P. d'Ancona and E. Aeschlimann (Milan, 1951), pp. 21–47, esp. p. 41; Vasari, 2, 538–39, 546–47; Georg Dehio, "Die Bauprojekte Nikolaus V und L. B. Alberti," *Repertorium für Kunstwissenschaft, 3* (1880), 241–57; and Torgil Magnuson, *Studies in Roman Quattrocento Architecture* (Rome/Stockholm, 1958), pp. 65–97.

two stories high. The three avenues were also to be flanked by porticoes, with shops on the lower floors and housing above.[37]

For all its classicizing sound, this proposal very probably made use of the important existing features of the site, e.g. the atrium of old St. Peter's, with its terraces, and the two avenues that led up to it from the river. If so, Alberti was not calling for the removal of an agglomeration of old forms and the substitution of abstract geometry but for the adaptation of what existed, the straightening, widening, and improving of an irregular topography, and then the addition of regularizing elements. And not only this—Alberti's classicized circulation space was to be wrapped in an impenetrable set of walls, an irregular perimeter for the re-formed city, so high, we are told, that only birds could get in without permission. Indeed, Alberti's proposed scheme was in all probability a stylistic mixture, a juxtaposition of the empirical and the theoretical, of the existing and the new, and therefore of the medieval, the antique, and the Renaissance. If so, in all these qualities it anticipated Alfonso's less abortive renewal of Naples.

Shortly after the death of Alfonso I in 1458, Pius II, who had spent time at Alfonso's court, contributed another element to the prehistory, or at least to the general atmosphere, of the renewal. This was the transformation of his birthplace, the little town of Corsignano near Siena, into the model Renaissance town of Pienza.[38] Pienza is laid out along a tall ridge above the Tuscan plains (Fig. 2). To its south Mount Amiata rises grandly from groves of chestnut trees into a series of arched crests. Like Naples, Pienza exploits a sloping site, though more dramatically, and a mountainous panorama. Here, in 1459, Bernardo Rossellino began a new civic center. This consisted of an open trapezoidal piazza, expanding toward the south, surrounded by large separated palazzo blocks. The centerpiece was the new cathedral. The interior of this building is a classicizing version of a South German Gothic hall church, but its facade is a two-story, three-bay classical triumphal arch. The axis leads to a polygonal apse that plunges over the cliff at the town's edge to retaining walls below. The cathedral is flanked by palaces, echoing the arrangement of Nicholas' Vatican plan: on the left, the bishop's palace and canons' residence and, on the right, the palace of Pius himself. The facades of the latter are modeled on that of Alberti's Palazzo Rucellai in Florence, the only significant alteration being that the proportions of the stories are lower, so that the arches completely fill the rectangular bays.

Perhaps as a further result of Alberti's influence, the urbanistic effects in Pienza are more pronounced and controlled than in Naples. The bishop's and canons' palaces are neutral

37. The existing arrangement, for which these modifications were planned, is illustrated in a 1493 view by H. Schedel, reproduced in F. Ehrle and H. Egger, *Piante e vedute di Roma e del Vaticano dal 1300 al 1676* (Rome, 1956), pl. ix. Nicholas' planned third street was eventually created by Sixtus IV as the Via Sistina. According to some it was on Ferrante's advice, and for military reasons, that this was done (Stefano Infessura, *Diario della città di Roma . . .* [1475], ed. Oreste Tommasini [Rome, 1890], p. 79).

38. Ludwig Heydenreich, "Pius II als Bauherr von Pienza," *Zeitschrift für Kunstgeschichte*, 6 (1937), 105–46; Enzo Carli, *Pienza, die Umgestaltung Corsignanos durch den Bauherrn Pius II* (Basel/Stuttgart, 1964).

stylistically, while the town hall, farther to the left, might be described as Romanesque and Gothic Revival. The discontinuous siting of the buildings means that glimpses of the vista are constantly being caught as one moves through the square; and, in turn, the square itself can be seen from the narrow, jagged streets that approach it. There are thus continual transitions from closed to open, from shadow to sun, from irregular to regular, as one proceeds. Then, by standing near the northeast corner of one of the northern existing structures (now the Palazzo Ammanati), one is directly on axis with the cathedral facade and, as Heydenreich has shown, one can see both wedges of vista framing the building (Fig. 2). The axial qualities inferred from the Vatican layout are here integrated with asymmetrical elements similar to those found in Naples, and with an equally "Neapolitan" stylistic mixture to boot.

The Pope's palace is in itself unusually axial and symmetrical for its period; according to Weber, it may be the first such Renaissance domestic building.[39] The main axis runs directly through the building, whose portals form a series of prosceniums or diaphragms leading the visitor out to the horizontal tiers of loggias at the back. The loggias, significantly called a theatrum by Pius (Fig. 5), are focused on a small formal garden that spreads to the edge of the cliff, framed on the left by the cathedral's towering apse. The cliff itself functions as an immense ha-ha and one sees, after the bright geometric foreground, a distant panorama, the inner surface of the great orb of hills and sky. This sudden juxtaposition must be the spectacle for which the theatrum was built. As a whole, Pius' palace takes the irregular sequence of the Castel Nuovo—frontispiece, courtyard, glorietta—and recasts it in terms of geometrical regularity. The same process will continue with the even more abstract plan of Alfonso of Calabria's villa, Poggioreale.

Another citadel-building program, for the castle of Federigo da Montefeltro at Urbino, was a third variation of these ideas.[40] It was begun in 1465. As in Naples a fortress-palace focuses on two panoramas (Figs. 3, 6). Inside the building, also, is a closed trapezoidal courtyard, while outside it a stack of arches forms a belvedere or glorietta. There is also a big open piazza leading to an arterial road; and, as in both Naples and Pienza, there is the piquant juxtaposition of asymmetrical and symmetrical forms. The loggias at Urbino follow the Neapolitan suggestion, combining the narrow projecting stack on a scarped base, which is seen on the eastern side of the Castel Nuovo (Fig. 4), with the decorative arches and flanking towers on the west (Fig. 7).

At Urbino, however, everything has changed in its inner psychology. The volumes of the building are expansive and horizontal, and the individual features—towers and windows—are dainty. Their shapes suggest symbol or paraphrase, even heraldry. Whereas the Castel Nuovo stands up from the sea, slowly and massively rising, its towers gathering the thick planes of the walls upward with them, Federigo's palace spreads across a valley, blocking its

39. Henny Weber, *Achsialität und Symmetrie im Grundriss des italienischen Prafanbaus von der Frührenaissance bis zum Frühbarock* (Berlin, 1937), p. 12.

40. Pasquale Rotondi, *Il Palazzo ducale di Urbino* (Urbino, 1950); and G. Marchini, "Il Palazzo ducale di Urbino," *Rinascimento,* 9 (1958), 43–78. The Neapolitan connections are brought out by W. R. Valentiner, "Andrea dell'Aquila in Urbino," *Art Quarterly,* 1 (1938), 275–88; and by R. Filangieri, "L'Architetto," pp. 32–35.

axis like a majestic aqueduct. It also seems to stretch down no less than up, its strength encased in fragile volumes, to integrate itself with the town. The trapezoidal courtyard is lifted to the level of the first floor and two piazzas flank it: the Piazza Mercatale lies far below on the floor of the valley; the Piazza Duca Federigo is nestled symmetrically between two palace wings.

All three of these urban centers were conceived around wide arteries, large trapezoidal voids, and a new combination of defense and residential features. In Naples and Urbino, moreover, there was the exploitation of panoramas through raised belvederes rather oddly (from a defense viewpoint) combined with military towers. Their progress toward daintiness and axiality, and their orientation to selective segments of garden and panorama, will reappear in Poggioreale. The larger sensibility these novelties betoken, for a sort of architectural control of stretches of landscape, will in turn reappear and be developed in the great western wall system, with its two castles, undertaken by Alfonso II.

ARCHITECTURE   In the design of individual buildings much the same thing was happening as in urbanism, i.e. outside Florence the new ideas of humanist art and classical revival were developed positively along with medieval ones, often in the same monuments. One instance is of course the Arch of Alfonso I (Fig. 7) with its internal stylistic contrasts and strong overall classicism, all the more forceful in the "medieval" setting of the towers. The inner part of the Arch (Fig. 8) can be seen as a second triumphal gate, on axis, and built in a kind of forced perspective. The two would thus be a marble version of the forced-perspective theatrical arches of a slightly later time, which created in a limited depth the effect of plunging tubes of space, articulated by arches forming a series of diaphragms or templates. The same effect, achieved with real space, is found in Pius' palace at Pienza and other axially planned buildings of the period. (We can also compare Pietro's intentions, though alas not his achievement, with Bramante's perspective apse in Santa Maria presso San Satiro, Milan.) Again, too, we have the juxtaposition of classicizing and medieval, for Ferrante's gate leads to a tall, rib-vaulted Catalan Gothic vestibule that is coeval with it. At the same time, Ferrante's arch is more Albertian than the outer one, and a more orthodox anticipation of the High Renaissance. The stubby engaged columns and the broken entablature may reflect what was happening in San Sebastiano, Mantua. The broad, coffered barrel vault in the upper niche is equally Albertian, while the upper niche as a whole—if we can read the upper hemisphere as a large dome in relief—recalls the plans for the Tempio at Rimini.

The third exterior Renaissance portal in the Castel Nuovo is the narrow, dainty gate of the Chapel of Santa Barbara, 1474. This, like the outer arch, is part of a stylistic contrast, for it stands directly beneath an elaborate flamboyant rose window (1469–70) by Matteo Fortimany (Fig. 9).[41]

41. On March 26, 1475, some money was paid for a Madonna and Child which "has been placed" over the chapel door. Cf. Gaetano Filangieri, Documenti per la storia le arti . . . , 6 (Naples, 1891), 53; Nicola Barone, "Le Cedole di tesoreria dell'Archivio di Stato di Napoli dal 1460 al 1504," ASPN, 9 (1884), 227, and

Other buildings erected in Naples at this time reveal more of the same juxtaposing process, and of Alberti's manner. Thus in 1466 Alfonso I's friend, Diomede Carafa, Count of Maddaloni, began a palace at 121 via San Biagio dei Librai (Figs. 10, 11).[42] It is a tallish, heavy block, with facades rusticated in the manner of the Rucellai Palace in Florence. The fenestration, though irregular beyond the bounds of normal Florentine practice, consists of classical edicular openings. Large oculi, possibly derived from Brunelleschi's Palazzo di Parte Guelfa or even from the Tempio, appear in the upper story. There is more certain Albertian influence in the portal which, as Pane has pointed out, resembles that of San Sebastiano, Mantua, presumably designed around 1459.[43] But inside the Palazzo Carafa, especially in the courtyard, medieval elements come to the fore. Clustered Gothic piers support the vestibule vault on its inner side, which consists at this point of a typical stilted segmental Catalan form. Yet at the same time, in the inner part of the courtyard, the stair vault is carried on a Composite column with a tall pedestal, very much like the columns on Ferrante's inner arch; one is even tempted on this basis to assign the building to Pietro da Milano.[44] In any case, the solid essentials, visually neutral, are Catalan Gothic, e.g. the vestibule and the arches on the right in Figure 11, while the self-conscious, presentational, and novel parts are classicizing—the portal, the facade, and the inner courtyard pier.

The second important Renaissance palace in Naples roughly coincides in date with the facade of Santa Barbara. This is the Palazzo Sanseverino (1470), home of the princes of Salerno and ascribed to an otherwise unknown architect named Novello de San Lucano.[45] In 1584 this building was transformed into the Gesù Nuovo, and in 1685 its facade was enlarged and embellished (Fig. 12). The facing and the inner part of the portal frame, however, remain Quattrocento. In its prime it was the most splendid house in the city. Even today in its mutilated state it rises with a cold, magnificent rush, tingling with gray light when seen across the sloping square in front of it. It must have been what we would call a fully Renaissance facade, the first in a Neapolitan palace. It was probably as impressive as any of the royal castles in Naples, and yet it suggested a more private, less military way of life.

Lodovico de la Ville sur-Yllon, "La Chiesa di Santa Barbara in Castel Nuovo," *Napoli nobilissima* [hereafter *NN*], 2 (1893), 70–74, 118–22, 170–73, esp. 73.

42. Carlo Celano, in *Notizie del bello dell'antico e del curioso della città di Napoli* [1640], ed. G. B. Chiarini, 3 (Naples, 1858), 686, says that Diomede Carafa merely remodeled the building in 1466 (Chiarini disagrees). Cf. L. Catalani, *I Palazzi di Napoli* (Naples, 1845), pp. 9–12; Ceci, "Il palazzo dei Conti di Maddaloni poi di Colubrano," *NN*, 2 (1893), 149–52, 168–70; and G. Tesorone, "Una porta del rinascimento a Napoli," *Arte italiana decorative e industriale*, 11 (1902), 61–62.

43. Roberto Pane, *L'Architettura del rinascimento a Napoli* (Naples, 1937), p. 107.

44. Jacopo della Pila had not yet appeared on the scene, Laurana was in France between 1458 and 1474, and Domenico Gagini, another sculptor who at this time was important for Naples, was in Sicily. Pietro da Milano was engaged on the main royal commission of the period, Ferrante's portal. He had worked in Dalmatia and may well have known the similar portal on the "Temple of Jupiter" at Spalato. On the palace of Antonello Petrucci, i.e. the Palazzo Penna, in Piazza San Domenico, is a c. 1470 copy of the Palazzo Carafa's portal (Pane, *Architettura*, p. 113).

45. Pane, *Architettura*, pp. 43–47; G. Ceci, "Il Palazzo dei Sanseverino principi di Salerno," *NN*, 7 (1898), 81–85; and Carlo De Frede, "Il Palazzo dei Sanseverino, principi di Salerno," *Partenope*, 2 (1961), 19–28.

Above all, its owner after 1474 was Antonello Sanseverino, one of the ringleaders of the Barons' Revolt.[46] On the eve of the renewal, therefore, the Palazzo Sanseverino could have been seen by the Duke of Calabria as a combined hint and challenge.

One attempt to take such a hint is indicated by the Palazzo Como on the via Duomo (Fig. 13).[47] This was built out of earlier structures for Angelo Como. Work was begun in 1488 and finished about 1490, during the climax of the renewal. Its use of quarry-faced masonry on the ground floor derives from the Strozzi and Gondi palaces in Florence—both, interestingly, built by families who had been active in Naples. There are also Albertian features to the Palazzo Como: the dainty sill course, the light, sharp cornice, and the smooth-faced masonry of the two upper floors. The Croce Guelfa windows are more ambiguous. Flat, sharp, and thin in carving, they could be Late Gothic, and especially French or Catalan; or they could be related to the more classicizing windows of, say, the Cancelleria in Rome. They do not at all belong to the kind of facade suggested by the Palazzo Como's masonry style, which would call for large, round-arched embrasures, or an overall grid of pilasters, or both.

The Florentine building to which the Palazzo Como bears the closest resemblance is the Palazzo dello Strozzino (Fig. 15).[48] Giuliano da Maiano had worked on this as a young man, which suggests that his influence and possibly his advice (he was in Naples that year[49]) are reflected in the facade of the Neapolitan building. The smooth-faced masonry, on the other hand, could by 1489 also have been derived from other Neapolitan houses such as the Palazzo Carafa. In any case, the actual hand of Giuliano can be ruled out: as a surface the Palazzo Como facade quite lacks the vivid compressions, the lift, we see in Giuliano's work. The curious placement of the windows and the ambiguous split-level section argue the hand of a follower, or perhaps even of Francesco di Giorgio's assistant, Antonio Marchese.

Nonetheless, the facade of the Palazzo Como is interesting enough. Like certain Florentine palaces of the period, such as the Pazzi-Quaratesi (Fig. 16) and the Strozzino, the final ensemble adumbrates a common feature of the Cinquecento palace. This is the rusticated basement serving as pedestal for a colossal two-story upper division with smooth masonry and a giant Order (Fig. 14). Much more than in the two Florentine buildings, in fact, the ungainly height of the upper division of the Como achieves the basic horizontal layering of these later designs. It lacks only the giant pilasters that would ultimately articulate the upper division. As with the Arch of Alfonso I, therefore, we find in Naples an anticipation, albeit oblique, of the High Renaissance. In both cases, moreover, it is an anticipation evolved not from purism and theory but through the empirical juxtaposition of what might be called antinomial architectural ideas.

46. It became royal property after the revolt: cf. R. Filangieri, *Cronaca figurata*, p. 63.

47. Luigi Catalani, *I Palazzi di Napoli* (Naples, 1845), pp. 14-16, esp. p. 15, note, and Pane, *Architettura*, pp. 113-18, with bibliography.

48. It is now thought that the lower floor of the Strozzino was built beginning in 1458 (by Michelozzo) and the upper by Giuliano da Maiano, 1462-65 (T. C. I., *Firenze e dintorni*, Milan, 1964, s.v.).

49. Leostello, *Effemeridi delle cose fatte per il duca di Calabria (1484-1491)*, in G. Filangieri, *Documenti*, 1 (Naples, 1883), 240 [July 16, 1489].

SCULPTURE   Neapolitan sculpture was most often a mixture of sharp characterization and physical grace derived from Florence, and a more traditional, generalized, rigid mode. The latter is a sort of Neoclassicism, in fact, slow and heavy, expressed in large details and sharp ridges. It creates a solemn world, ornate, full of ceremony and repetition, and peopled with fierce military guardians and caryatids who lift their burdens resolutely aloft. Such Quattrocento "Neoclassicism" also existed in Venice, in parts of Dalmatia, and in Rome.

One might call the Neapolitan version of this sculpture the Aragonese court style. We recognize it in the Arch of Alfonso I, and in the work of Jacopo della Pila and Tommaso and Giantommaso Malvito.[50] In Naples it had a particular historic depth, for a long taproot led back through earlier artists who had utilized it to Tino da Camaino, and even to Frederick II Hohenstaufen's Porta Romana at Capua. In fostering it, therefore, Alfonso I and Ferrante had been preserving a local classicism often assumed or paraphrased by artists of varied backgrounds working in the south. Another characteristic example is the tomb of Malizia Carafa (c. 1470) by unknown artists, possibly in Pietro da Milano's shop, in San Domenico Maggiore (Figs. 17, 18).[51] It is a medley of two sources: it combines the sarcophagus superstructure, angels, and curtains of the tomb of Ladislas (1414?–28) in San Giovanni a Carbonara, with the pavilion of the tomb of Rinaldo Brancacci by Donatello and Michelozzo (1427–28) in Sant'Angelo a Nilo.[52] The sarcophagus itself is meanwhile Gothic in style and date. The tender open axial twist of its waist-length relief figures contrasts with the thrusting statues in the rest of the tomb. As in the Brancacci monument, the effigy, rigid in armor, is being borne through the arch rather than lying within it. But the caryatids have the static, presentational psychology of the Ladislas figures.

There are elements in this tomb however that derive neither from Neapolitan tradition nor from the monuments to Rinaldo Brancacci and Ladislas. These are the broad, smooth fascias, simple plane surfaces, thick columns, and other effects of massive support. The sarcophagus group is sharply compressed by the arch, and the enormous entablature almost reads as a lintel. In the tomb of Ferdinando Carafa (d. 1470), also in San Domenico Maggiore, these effects are even more marked, and figures are relentlessly imprisoned by the

50. Raffaello Causa, "Contributi alla conoscenza della scultura del '400 a Napoli," in Bruno Molajoli, ed., *Sculture lignee nella Campania* (Naples, 1950), pp. 105–21, with earlier bibliography; Oreste Ferrari, "Per la conoscenza della scultura del primo Quattrocento a Napoli," *Bollettino d'Arte, 39* (1954), 11–24; John Pope-Hennessy, *Italian Renaissance Sculpture* (London, 1958), pp. 80–82, 330–31; and Charles Seymour, Jr., *Sculpture in Italy: 1400–1500* (Harmondsworth, Mddx., England, 1966), pp. 134–38.

51. Cf. M. d'Ayala, "Intorno alle Sculture nella chiesa di San Domenico ed in espezialità sulle tombe di Malizia Carafa e dei D'Aquino," *Annali civili del regno delle due Sicilie, 41* (1846), fasc. 82, 99–105 (which follows the unreliable De Domenici). Cf. also Raffaello Maria Valle, *Descrizione storica artistica letteraria della*

chiesa e convento di San Domenico Maggiore, continued by B. Minichini (Naples, 1853–54); Causa, "Contributi," p. 119; and R. Filangieri, "La scultura in Napoli nei primi albori del rinascimento," *NN,* ser. 2, *1* (1920), 95.

52. For the use of the Rinaldo Brancacci tomb as a model, cf. the commission by Tommaso Brancacci's widow Giulia for a tomb for her husband. It is dated March 20, 1492, and mentions an "inbassiamentum inferiorem adornatum prout est in cantaro domini Cardinalis brancatii posito intus ecclesiam sancti Angeli ad Nidum" (G. Filangieri, *Documenti, 3,* 19). The Tommaso Brancacci tomb still exists in the Cappella San Jacopo, San Domenico Maggiore, and the artist, again, is Jacopo della Pila.

powerful rectilinear structure of the pavilion. The earlier formula with its angels, curtains, caryatids, and so on, has been sacrificed to a more architectonic scheme in which the structural forces have drunk up the life of the figure sculpture. This is to my mind a further example of Alberti's influence.

There were two other elements—personalities rather than currents of influence—on the sculptural scene in the 1470s and early 1480s, Francesco Laurana and Domenico Gagini. Laurana's sculpture is unquestionably the finest produced for Naples during these years.[53] Aside from this, it is important because it links the more medieval tastes of the first two Aragonese rulers with those of Alfonso of Calabria. It has almost nothing to do with the "Neoclassical" currents I have described, despite Laurana's Dalmatian birth,[54] nor is it particularly Florentine.

Laurana's style is difficult to define. On the surface it seems all Renaissance, below that surface all Gothic. The sweetness of Laurana's heads somewhat recalls Luca della Robbia, and his figures have a limp inner core with shell-like surfaces that is Botticellian. But unlike Botticelli Laurana never felt the human figure as a substantive thing. His figures rise through a turbid flux of drapery that almost accidentally reveals beautiful forms, like severed heads and arms emerging from a cloud. This can be seen in the marble Madonna and Child (c. 1474) in the Church of Materdomini in Naples (Figs. 19, 20).[55] The figure at first glance is a gentle bow whose garments bind it elastically to the earth. The stance is that of a softened Late Gothic statue, an armature without much vertical force. Yet there is a surprisingly stiff thrust to the gesture with which the Virgin helps her son to hold the orb, a stiffness only partly caused by the spatulate, undifferentiated fingers and wrist. Fundamental insecurities and rigidities are also revealed in the child, with his stiff-backed, upward gaze. On the other hand the flowing shell-like planes of the Virgin's face, meeting in almost invisible ripples, and the eyebrows curving outward in soft arcs, would delight the most demanding patron.

Such Madonnas are a welcome contrast to the remote, sphynx-like figures of the Aragonese court style. But they are only halfway on the road to a new sort of physical presence in sculpture, as we see when we contrast the later more compact and sedate Laurana (Fig. 21), the seated figure in Sant'Agostino della Zecca (c. 1487),[56] with the figure of Charity (Fig. 115) made by Benedetto da Maiano for the San Bartolo altar in Sant'Agostino, San Gimignano (1492–94). Aside from the immobile body, the viscous drapery, and the lack of force in the silhouette, there is indubitably, in the generalized, radiant gaze of Laurana's Madonna, a less immediate quality. By contrast Benedetto's work is a personal confrontation.

53. For Laurana cf. Wilhelm Rolfs, *Franz Laurana* (Berlin, 1907); Fritz Burger, *Francesco Laurana: Eine Studie zur italienischen Quattrocentoskulptur* (Strassburg, 1907); and Causa, "Contributi." Other bibliography for the portrait busts is given in Chapter 3.

54. For this question see especially the review of Rolfs, *Laurana*, by Adolfo Venturi in *L'Arte, 10* (1907), 472–74.

55. The attribution was made by Longhi in 1916, and the statue published by R. Causa in "Sagrera, Laurana e l'Arco di Castel Nuovo," *Paragone, 5* (July 1954), 3–23, esp. 18. Cf. also Salvatore Loschiaro, "Una Scultura ignorata di Francesco Laurana a Napoli," *Il Rievocatore*, 1953, p. 3.

56. Causa, "Contributi," pp. 143–48.

The Charity has solid hands and a resolved, three-dimensional structure. The child is not merely seated in his mother's lap, he is locked into dramatic ovals whose edges flash around the pair. Benedetto's statue also makes Laurana's seem curiously Roman-revivalistic, e.g. in the Trajanic countenance of the Child and in the Madonna's Julia Domna-like head. The comparison brings out well the kind of classical and medieval juxtapositions of which Laurana's art, like so much other art in Naples then, consisted.

Another highly individual sculptor, who links the taste of Ferrante to that of his son, was Domenico Gagini.[57] In a Madonna made (c. 1458?) for the tabernacle in the Chapel of Santa Barbara (Figs. 22, 23), Gagini showed that he could create harder, more jubilant surfaces that almost suggest shiny metal, heads with flowing eyes sunk into the continuous surfaces of the face, and a far more logical play of draperies than Laurana. Gagini's strength, and the effervescence of his style, broadened Laurana's impact, and Gagini was probably employed at least once to make a marble bust of Ferrante (Figs. 29, 30).

PAINTING   The role of painting in Alfonso's program was minor and, as far as we can now judge, the programs were more important than their artistic quality.[58] Alfonso introduced into Naples the monumental fresco cycle, a secular version of a type that was simultaneously being represented on the walls of the Sistine Chapel, and slightly later in Pinturicchio's Piccolomini Library in Siena and in the St. Benedict cycle at Monteoliveto Maggiore by Signorelli and Sodoma. The effect of such cycles was to transform an interior into a raised pavilion or arbor at the center of radiating wedges of panoramic distance. Hence we see once again that juxtaposition of interior rectangular space with exterior curved distances that we noted in the urbanism of Urbino and Pienza. But despite this architectural scale and function, such scenes could have the gaiety of the miniature, manifested in their shapely edges, hallucinatory brightness, and deep, erratic recessions.

Naples was the perfect place for painting in this mood, for in contrast to their more austere taste in sculpture and architecture, both Alfonso I and Ferrante loved the International Style in painting.[59] Thus the art of Colantonio, the most important International Style painter who worked extensively in Naples, has something of the typical Neapolitan expressive antinomy between medievalizing and classicizing modes.[60] As might be expected, the latter aspects of

57. See G. di Marzo, and E. Mauceri, "L'Opera di Domenico Gagini in Sicilia," *L'Arte*, 6 (1903), 147–58; Stefano Bottari, "Per Domenico Gaggini," *Rivista d'arte*, 17 (1935), 77–85; W. R. Valentiner, "The Early Development of Domenico Gagini," *Burlington Magazine*, 76 (Jan./June 1940), 76–87; idem, "A Madonna Statuette of Domenico Gagini," *Art in America*, 25 (1937), 104–17.

58. Cf. Wilhelm Rolfs, *Geschichte der Malerei Neapels* (Leipzig, 1910), pp. 78–174; Raffaello Causa, *Pittura napoletana dal XV al XIX Secolo* (Bergamo, 1957), pp. 7–26; and Liana Castelfranchi Vegas, "I

Rapporti Italia-Fiandra," *Paragone*, n.s. no. 15 (May 1966), 9–24, n.s. no. 21 (Nov. 1966), 42–69.

59. Pietro Summonte, in Fausto Nicolini, *L'Arte napoletana del rinascimento* (Naples, 1925), p. 159.

60. R. Filangieri, "Les Origines de la peinture flamande à Naples," in *Actes du XII° Congrès International d'histoire de l'art* (Brussels, 1930), pp. 560–76; Roberto Longhi, "Una 'Crocifissione' di Colantonio," *Paragone*, 63 (1935), 3–10; and F. Bologna, "Il Politico di San Severino apostolo del Norico," *Paragone*, n.s., 6 (1955), 3–17, esp. 11–12.

Colantonio's work are normally active, exploratory, and peripheral, and the Gothic aspects passive, secure, and central.

The hard charm of Colantonio's pictures apparently appealed to Alfonso of Calabria, and something of their character reappears, on a larger scale, in the fresco cycles Alfonso commissioned for his villas and churches (Figs. 123, 124). The well-known triptych by Jean Bourdichon of the Madonna and saints, painted for Ferrante and now in Capodimonte, can be likened to Pietro Donzello's Annunciation (1497–98) in Santo Spirito, Florence (Fig. 85), and to other Neapolitan paintings of the age (Fig. 24).[61] All are distinguished by melting pneumatic forms and a conscious archaism. One can imagine these same qualities, more convincingly present, in Laurana's sculptured madonnas and princesses beneath their original coatings of gilt and color (Fig. 20).

61. The painting by Bourdichon had been given to the Certosa of San Martino by Ferrante, which also possessed a Book of Hours by the artist. Cf. J. Dupont, "Un Triptyque de Jean Bourdichon au musée de Naples," *Fondation Eugène Piot. Monuments et Mémoires. Aca-* *démie d'inscriptions et belles-lettres, 35* (1935–36), 179–88; K. Perls, "Le Maître de Charles VIII," *L'Amour de l'art, 16* (1935), 95–99; and L. Dimier, "Les Primitifs français," *Gazette des Beaux-arts,* ser. 6, 20 (1938), 208–12.

Chapter 2: LITERARY REFLECTIONS OF THE RENEWAL

**P**ONTANO'S *LEPIDINA* Alfonso's renewal was designed to help Ferrante achieve stable alliances and the recognition of his legitimacy: thus far it was political. But its literary imagery was created in the Duke of Calabria's humanist court, which was one of the most splendid in Europe.[1] Alfonso boasted an important library under the supervision of Giovanni Albino.[2] Besides the frequent and elaborate triumphs and visitations, there were banquets, parties, joustings, and theatrical entertainments at the Castel Capuano, the Duke's official residence. All these events helped shape the renewal, as did the personality of Ippolita Sforza, Duchess of Calabria, who was a queenly figure in this life, a perhaps more than worthy consort for Alfonso.[3] Everyone paid tribute to her beauty and first-rate mind.[4]

The mind behind the renewal, however, was Pontano's.[5] An Umbrian by birth, Pontano had been at the court of Alfonso I. As noted, he was the younger Alfonso's tutor and later his minister and ambassador to Rome. He also campaigned beside his master, and is said to have negotiated the Peace of Bagnolo and settled the Barons' Revolt. It was he, also, who arranged the marriage between Giangaleazzo Sforza and Isabella of Aragon. In 1486, like Platina in Melozzo's fresco, Pontano was crowned with laurel by the Pope, and the Neapolitan Academy still bears his name.

Pontano's vision of the renewal was derived from the myths of the city's foundation,[6] which had it that a band of Greeks originally settled at Cuma, where the immigrants were welcomed by the sight of a nude pregnant woman asleep under a tree.[7] This vision gave the

1. Pietro Giannone, *Istoria civile del regno di Napoli*, 3 (Palmyra, 1762), 471–78; Julia Cartwright, *Beatrice d'Este, Duchess of Milan* (London, 1903), pp. 6–7; E. Gothein, *Il Rinascimento*, pp. 188–309; T. Persico, *Gli Scrittori politici napoletani del 1400 al 1700* (Naples, 1912), pp. 44–94; Lina Montalto, "Vesti e gale alla corte aragonese," *NN*, ser. 2, 1 (1920), 25–29, 41–44, 70–73, 127–30, 142–47; Casimir von Chtedowski, *Neapolitanische Kulturbilder XIV–XVIII Jahrhundert* (2nd ed., Berlin, 1920), pp. 186–97; Antonio Altamura, *L'Umanesimo nel mezzogiorno d'Italia* (Florence, 1941); and Adelaide Cirillo Mastrocinque, "Personaggi e costumi della Napoli aragonese," *Partenope*, 1 (1960), 17–32.

2. Tammaro De Marinis, *La Biblioteca napoletana dei re d'Aragona*, 1 (Milan, 1947–52), 97–115.

3. Montalto, "La Corte aragonese," pp. 142–47.

4. Cf. A. Baccelli, "Ippolita Sforza Duchessa di Calabria," *Rassegna nazionale*, ser. 3, 52 (1930), 21; Nicola Ratti, *Della Famiglia Sforza*, 2 (Rome, 1794), 11–19; and Masuccio Salernitano, *Il Novellino*, ed. Alfredo Mauro (Bari, 1940), p. 3.

5. For Pontano see C. M. Tallarigo, *Giovanni Pontano e i suoi Tempi* (Naples, 1874); Erasmo Pèrcopo, "La Vita di Giovanni Pontano," *ASPN*, 61 (1937), 116–250; and idem, "Gli Scritti di Giovanni Pontano," ibid., 62 (1937), 57–234.

6. Pèrcopo, "Gli Scritti," esp. pp. 111–16.

7. Cf. J. Beloch, *Campanien* (Berlin, 1879), pp. 62–70; E. Gàbrici, "Contributo archeologico alla topografia di Napoli della Campania," *Monumenti antichi*, 41 (1951), cols. 553–674; G. P. Caratelli, "Napoli antica," *La Parola del passato*, 7 (1952), 243–68; Mario Napoli, "Realtà storica di Partenope," ibid., pp. 269–85; idem, *Napoli greco-romana* (Naples, 1959), esp. pp. 68–73; Ettore Gàbrici, *Problemi di numismatica greca della Sicilia e Magna Grecia* (Naples, 1959), pp. 90–97; Giuseppe Russo, "La Città di Napoli dalle origini al 1860," in M. Napoli, ed., *Contributi allo studio della città* (Naples, 1960), pp. 43–52; idem, *Napoli come Città* (Naples, 1966), pp. 3–23.

town its name (from ἐγκύμων, pregnant) and therefore its poetic meaning.[8] What is now Naples was an offshoot of Cuma. It, too, was originally named after a woman, Parthenope. Indeed, there were two Parthenopes: one was of course the siren who with her sisters sang to Ulysses, and whose tomb was built in what is now Naples. Parthenope the siren was beautiful but unchaste and fatal, and she symbolized Naples' charm which is only a cloak for its wretchedness.[9] The other Parthenope had been queen of the island of Chalcitis in the Sea of Marmora. She had brought her subjects to the Campanian shore and there, like Dido or Semiramis, founded a city over which she ruled.[10] Later on the inhabitants abandoned their city, but a plague broke out in their new quarters. They were told that it would go away only if they returned to the old site. This they did, rebuilding their old city and renaming it Neapolis.[11]

The Cumean idea of a recumbent woman, nude, pregnant, and in a sense the namesake of a city, is close to the governing image of Pontano's poem *Lepidina*. Even more, the Parthenope stories help account for the woman-centeredness of Alfonso's renewal. Indeed the very name, Naples, mythologically signifies the cleaning, restoring, and decorating of an ancient city.

Pèrcopo tells us that *Lepidina* was composed about 1496 (though planned earlier),[12] i.e. when King Federigo was continuing the work his brother had begun. The poem is divided into seven "pomps" or processions, in which the nymphs and other creatures who represent the seggi and suburbs of Naples describe the gifts they are bringing to Parthenope's wedding. The bridegroom is the Sebeto River, which rises a few miles northwest of the city. At the end, Antiniana, the nymph of Pontano's villa, sings an epithalamium.[13]

Several recurrent images are woven into this joyful poem. One has to do with bathing and shining cleanliness. At the beginning the interlocutors, Lepidina and her husband Macron, reminisce about an earlier meeting when Lepidina revealed her white breasts. But Lepidina's whiteness is nothing compared to that of Parthenope, who has just bathed in the fountain of Doliolum (ll. 28–34). Parthenope's brightness shines in every part of the countryside.

8. G. A. Summonte, *Historia della città e regno di Napoli, 1* (Naples, 1748), 4–6.

9. Pontano's interest in the Parthenope legends is reflected in *Lepidina* (discussed later), a group of poems called *Parthenopaeus* (1455–58?), esp. Book 2, ll. 51–52, and the essay *De aspiratione* (Naples, 1481). Cf. Percopo, "Gli scritti," p. 61. A copy of Statius' *Sylvae*, the most important classical poems dealing with these stories, was in Alfonso I's library (De Marinis, *La Biblioteca napoletana*, 2, 194).

10. Summonte, loc. cit. Cf. also Nicola Toppi, *De origine omnium tribunalium* (Naples, 1655), pp. 24–25. It is Summonte who makes the comparison with Dido and Semiramis.

11. For other tales, cf. Vittorio Spinazzola, "Il nome di Napoli," *NN, 1* (1892), 33–35, 49–51.

12. Pèrcopo, "Gli scritti," pp. 111–16. On p. 68 he says the poem had been planned in 1457–58. Cf. also Pontano's *Carmina, 2,* Soldati, ed., Parthenopaeus II,

"Ad musam, de conversione Sebethi in Fluvium," ll. 65ff.; and Tallarigo, *Pontano*, pp. 619–24; Enrico Carrara, *La Poesia pastorale* (Milan, 1909?), pp. 276–78; Vittorio Rossi, "Il Quattrocento," in idem, ed., *Storia letteraria d'Italia*, 5th ed., rev. Aldo Vallone (Milan, 1950); and W. L. Grant, "An Eclogue of Giovanni Pontano," *Philological Quarterly, 36* (1957), 76–83. Grant suggests that *Lepidina* may have been performed dramatically.

13. Thomas M. Greene, in "Spenser and the Epithalamic Convention," *Comparative Literature, 9* (1952), 215–28, describes the Renaissance character of this form and mentions the two epithalamiums Pontano wrote for his daughters. He says that normally these poems were written about real people and referred to a specific day (pp. 216, 219). While in *Lepidina* Parthenope and the Sebeto are not real personages their marriage was real enough, as we shall see below, and may have been consummated on a specific day.

Resina's newly washed breasts are like crystal, they shine so (II, 53–56), while Hercli's "candens papilla" contrasts with her black brows (II, 66–67). Only distant Vesuvius still has dark breasts, covered with violets and veined with milky streams; but even so her ancient disasters and evil outpourings are forgotten on this happy day (V, 1–3).

Then there is a contrasting imagery of black caves, tunnels, and rivers. Posillipo's cavern is a black mole on her white breast (II, 9), and the black shanks of Capri are covered with prickly bushes that hide her grottoes (II, 85–86). Above all Parthenope's black eyes (I, 9) are magnets that pull the fish from the sea and deer from the forest, and young men and old to their death (42–47). "Alas," says Macron, "lest she should turn that look on me and I be torn from these arms" (48–49). Pontano's Parthenope is both siren and queen, a source of death and life.

It is Sebethus, not Macron, who is pulled by the siren's black gaze. He is dressed in wedding garments and the trumpet salutes him:

> New bridegroom . . . put on the garments that the dell nymphs of Acerra have spun for you from golden moss, and which Pomelia has embroidered so that the lowest hem is leafed with open branches of savory [V, 96–99].

Other waters besides the Sebeto come to the feast. In the fifth pomp Planuris is accompanied by a ringing tumult of water gods, her "hymenaeos comites," who plunge down from the surrounding hills and lakes:

> They descend, O sister [Lepidina], grove and deep river tumble to the marriage couch; a thousand caves pour forth their deities, and from the high mountains the native fauns push onward and tumble at the gates. Their path does not follow the flow of underground waters which the throats of Lake Acherusia, new deities, discharge, and which the marshes of Bolla, and that rich sacrifice Lake Avernus, and the river-lake of the Adytum Araxi, all emit.[14]

The bride is meanwhile decked in gifts from the sea. The tempest-quieting tritons, the rock-bearing sons of Neptune, carry garlands with berries of gold and branches of coral, Indian pearls, frankincense, amber, and hundreds of new drinking cups made of gold and covered with gems (III, 1–18): "To thee, Parthenope, a thousand snow-white virgins bear a garland entwined with gold and coral branches."[15]

A final group of images has to do with pregnancy and birth. Lepidina herself is pregnant and, throughout the seven pomps, there is constant talk of motherhood. In the end it is the

---

14. Descendunt, soror, et nemora, et cava flumina currunt / Ad thalamos, mille antra deos vomuere, et ab altis / Montibus indigenae Fauni proteruntque ruuntque / Ad portas; iter ingentes non explicat Orcos, / Quos acherusiacae fauces, nova numina, mittunt, / Stagnaque Baulorum, quos hostia pinguis Averni / Emisere adytis lacus et fluitantis Araxi (V, 12–18). The "adytum Araxi" was a well between Pozzuoli and Naples (Pliny, *H. Nat.*, 18, 29, 114). Lake Acherusia, near Cuma, is now called Fusaro.

15. "En tibi mille ferunt niveae sua serta puellae, / Serta auro intertexta et ramiferis corallis" (III, 8–9).

bride's offspring of heroes and poets, as much as her wedding, that Antiniana sings of in the epithalamium.

Lepidina is a difficult poem, offering several problems of language and imagery. But one point is clear, if so far unnoticed by students: it is an allegory of the renewal. It describes the restoration of the Bolla water system, which in antiquity had carried the waters of the Sebeto and other streams into Naples. Parthenope's bath is the cleansing and restoration of the city by these waters. The new fountains are the nymphs' white breasts, as are also the new drinking cups brought by the tritons. The caves and tunnels, and above all Parthenope's black gaze which pulls Sebethus to her, are the new conduits Alfonso excavated beneath the city. The "hymenaeos comites," the waters of Acherusia, Bolla, Avernus, and the Adytum Araxi, are all involved in the system. The new walls of red piperno, white marble, and yellow tufa are the wedding garlands of coral, pearl, and gold. The bridegroom's costume is the mossy stone aqueduct, the Acqua della Bolla, which Alfonso built.[16] Even the marriage bed, Doliolum, is a real place, where Alfonso's water system came together in a sequence of cisterns and canals (Fig. 1). Doliolum was also the site of Alfonso's villa, Poggioreale, which thus became a metaphor for the consummation of the marriage. The ostensible time of the wedding, during the rule of Queen Parthenope, is therefore merged by Pontano with the time of the poem's composition—and, one is tempted to say, the occasion of the work as well —when Alfonso's conduits, aqueduct, fountains, and villa were all being erected.[17]

PROSE DOCUMENTS   A second aspect of the renewal's literary sources has to do with its moral quality. We can see this in Pontano's *De bello neapolitano,* in my opinion written about 1489.[18] Here Alfonso himself appears as the high priest of the renewal, as successor to the long line of Neapolitan kings who stem from Parthenope, and as rebuilder of her city:

16. And when the acqueduct enters the city it goes underground, i.e., "Ingeminant plausus, et vox sonat: 'Exue, nupta, / Exue gausapinas et nudo corpore ramum / Excipe, puniceo praefert quem cortice coniux. / Exue gausapinas, coniux, ramoque valenti / Sterne aciem, clausis uxorisque ingrue portis / Comminus arma ciens, telumque in sanguine tinge' " (V, 151–56).

17. Statius makes Parthenope a mother with the line "et pulchra tumeat Sebethos alumna" (*Sylvae,* I, 2, 263). Her son is the poet Stella, to whom Statius' poem is addressed; Statius too is also a child of Parthenope (ibid., ll. 260ff.). The date of *Lepidina,* by the way, is not as certain as Pèrcopo makes it. Gabriele Altilio, a pupil of Pontano's, wrote an epithalamium for Isabella of Aragon (discussed below) which is clearly an imitation of *Lepidina,* including references to the marriage celebrated in that poem, to the nymphs of the suburbs, to the jaws of the Sebeto, and to Parthenope's daughters who sing in honor of the marriage. Isabella was married in 1488–89, which would disestablish Percopo's date for *Lepidina* of 1496 ("Scritti," p. 68), at least for pre-

liminary versions (for Altilio see Tallarigo, *Giovanni Pontano,* pp. 137–40). A second poem dedicated at least partly to the building of a hydraulic system is attributed to Ariosto: "Epicedio de morte illustrissimae Lionorae Estensis de Aragonia, ducissae Ferrariae." This praises Biagio Rossetti's works for Ercole d'Este and Eleonora (cf. Riccardo Bacchelli, *La Congiura di Don Giulio d'Este, 1,* Milan, 1931, 90–96). The joining of Parthenope and the Sebeto was again celebrated in viceregal times, G. A. Summonte tells us. A triumphal arch was erected near the Porta Capuana for the entry of Charles V in 1535, and was decorated with colossal statues of the two personages (*Historia,* 5, 191–92).

18. On the last page Pontano refers to Ferrante's having ruled "more than 30 years" but makes no reference to the French invasion (Gravier, *Raccolta,* 5, 148). Remembering that Ferrante came to the throne in 1458 but did not take control of Naples until 1465, this suggests the period 1488–94 for the composition of the book. For a later date see Percopo, "Gli Scritti," p. 206, who cites a letter of 1499 indicating that Pontano was

In our own time Alfonso, son of Ferdinand, having extended the walls toward the east and north, strengthened and beautified that part of the city with thick walls of piperno. But these things were only the beginning of what I know he had it in mind to do. Another sign of this one-time magnificence, besides the walls, is the river that was brought into the city by stone pipes. The ancient city was built over these, and these pipes and open conduits were placed under the main streets and brought to the individual squares into which the whole city was once divided. Then wells were erected which drew water for each quarter. From these conduits the water went to the further parts of the city, not only to wells in the houses of the nobles, but also to the fountains in the quarters bordering on the sea. The conduits and tunnels were wide and hollow, and their course was not at all straight. This caused the water to splash frequently, and made it healthier. The water rumbled like a rocky river, a work of great antiquity, and an outstanding testimony to the original glory of Naples.[19]

This much is a sort of prose echo of *Lepidina.* Then, however, Pontano goes on to describe the other vestiges of antiquity in Naples. He tells how the Roman emperors competed with one another in enlarging and beautifying the city, and of the "most constant loyalty" the citizens gave in return. He emphasizes the continuity of this tradition, the repetition in it of events and personages. The citizens had always honored the State of Rome, no matter what battered form it took; and their loyalty had especially been given to Roman rulers who ornamented Naples. Even in the Middle Ages these continuities were maintained. Great medieval kings like Conrad and Robert had restored temples, tombs, palaces, and castles built long before by the Romans or the Greeks. The implication is that this must continue; and we learn that although Alfonso had revived the process with his reconstructed water system and walls, that which he was intending to do (*quod nos ipsi scimus animo illum destinasse*) was even greater.

Pontano identifies and discusses this princely duty more abstractly in his essay, "De magnificentia" (c. 1494).[20] The patron of great architectural and artistic works, the proponent of

---

then still at work on it. But this could have been a subsequent polishing. Pontano seems to have spent his later years revising all his earlier works for publication during the early sixteenth century.

19. "Nostra vero aetate Alphonsus Ferdinandi filius, prolato ad solis ortum, atque ad septentrionem pomaerio, et munivit eam partem urbis, et illustravit, erectis ingentis crassitudinis muris piperino e lapide, quamquam inchoasse videri solum potest id, quod nos ipsi scimus animo illum destinasse. Priscae quoque urbis magnificentiae propter ipsa moenia maximo est indicio fluvius intra urbem inductus excavato saxo, in quo vetus urbs tota inerat fundata, eaque cuniculatio, atque effossae specus, deductae subter maxime celebres urbis vias, atque ad singula quadrivia, in quae urbs quondam omnis distributa erat, excisi putei, e quibus vicinia hauriat. Ab

hac autem ipsa cuniculatione deducuntur ad alia urbis loca, aedesque nobilium aquae tum ad puteorum usum, tum etiam fontium in urbis iis partibus, quae vergunt ad mare. Ipsa vero cuniculata effossio, ductilesque aquarum cavae et latae sunt admodum, et decursu minime recto, quo dum ad angulos saepius aqua refringitur, reddatur salubrior. Quocirca et decurrit, et strepit sonorum in saxosi modum fluminis, antiquum sane opus, ac priscae cuiusdam magnificentiae praeclarum testimonium." *De bello neapolitano*, in Gravier, *Raccolta, 5*, pp. 146–47.

20. Pèrcopo, "Gli Scritti," p. 174. For the concept of magnificentia, see Morisani, *Letteratura*, pp. 25–26. I quote from the Venice, 1518 [Aldine] edition of Pontano's prose essays; but cf. also Pontano, *Trattati delle virtù sociali*, ed. and trans. by Francesco Tateo (Rome, 1965).

magnificentia, is a hero. Building is the ruler's moral duty to his heritage, his subjects, and the future.[21] Monuments possess and proclaim magnificentia because they teach posterity of the power and goodness of those who erected them. Pontano implies that, as gifts of the prince to his people, works of art and urbanism are simultaneously the expression and cause of virtue in a ruler.

Two other writers, Galateo and the Duke's delightful "governatore de li paggi," Joampiero Leostello, amplify the concept in a more practical way. Leostello, writing at about the same time as Pontano, says of his master:

> He greatly delighted in building, which he did in numerous lovely spots, so that he made many poor men rich, and many builders who had four or five daughters to marry off, though they had formerly been poor, were now very easily able to find husbands for these daughters . . . because of the money coming into these builders' hands from the constant construction of palaces and fine houses, such as Poggioreale, two miles from Naples, or La Duchesca, as well as many gardens and farms. Oh, where did he not build? In Calabria, in Apulia, in Gaeta, in Casal di Principe. On both sides [of the city] he dedicated himself to this work. And since in another of our works we describe his life more amply, I say no more about it here, in order not to bore the reader, and still further break up and warp the matter of these daily narratives.[22]

Antonio Galateo, in an epitaph composed after Alfonso II's death, also mentions the enormous outlays for achitecture and artistic patronage. Indeed, the Duke's expenditures between 1485 and 1495 really must have benefited the building industry. Cava dei Tirreni, the masons' town just north of Salerno, would have been among the most blooming nymphs of the Campanian countryside.

But the real burden of Galateo's epitaph is of course sorrow for what might have been. Once again, as in *Lepidina,* choruses of nymphs appear, but now they people the lonely shore, where the poet builds an imaginery tomb. The dead king's projects for rebuilding Naples were famous:

> Everyone knew how great you were, Alfonso, in building fortifications, in restoring churches, in ornamenting houses, and in every sort of royal ceremony. You called in

21. "Quae autem opera magnificorum sint propria, distinctius dicenda sunt, quorum alia publica sunt, alia privata, publica ut porticus, templa, moles in mare iactae, viae stratae, theatra, pontes et eiusmodi alia, privata ut aedes magnificae, ut villae sumptuosae, turres, sepulchra." *Opera omnia* (Venice, 1518), 128r.

22. "In frabiche molto se delectava et in più lochi ameni facea fabricare: ita et taliter che a facto molto poveri homini richi, et molto fabricatori che teneano quactro et cinque figliole da maritare et poverissimi in quello tempo le maritoro molto facilmente per li danari veniano in loro mano fabricando da continuo palazi et

case molto amene come a lo Poggio reale vicino a Napoli a due miglia: come la Duchesca et molti jardini et massarie. O dove non fabricava? In Calabria, in Puglia, in Gayeta, a Casa di Principe. Utrobique ad id operam dabat. Et perché in altre opere nostre tractamo la sua vita amplamente non me distendo più in ciò per non tediare li lectori ne ancora violare et contaminare la materia di queste giornate." Leostello, *Effemeridi delle cose fatte per il Duca di Calabria,* in Filangieri, *Documenti, 1,* 323. The work on Alfonso's building activity that Leostello refers to does not seem to have survived.

the most noble sculptors, painters, architects, and craftsmen from all over Italy, nay from the whole world, with great employments and fees.[23]

PIETRO SUMMONTE'S LETTER   We have seen Alfonso's renewal mirrored in an eclogue, an imitation of Caesar, a philosophical essay, a diary, and an epitaph. Let us look at it finally in the famous epistle of Pietro Summonte to Marcantonio Michiel, the Venetian chronicler of art. Dated March 20, 1524, this document has been thoroughly studied for information about art in Naples.[24] So far as I know, however, its original function has not been pointed out: this was to put Alfonso's abortive plan into its historical setting. In this manner Pietro Summonte would have assured the renewal a place in history—specifically in the history of Italian art Michiel was then writing and for which he had solicited Summonte's letter.

Summonte sets the scene by describing the Neapolitan work of Giotto, for him the founder and hero of Italian painting. After Giotto's sojourn there is a marked degeneration. Alfonso I and Ferrante, for example, possessed essentially frivolous, even corrupt, taste. They so greatly preferred "things of Flanders" that Ferrante actually demolished Giotto's frescoes in the Cappella Santa Barbara. But Summonte's description of painting after 1475 or so is more favorable. He mentions Costanzo Lombardo, who seems to have worked for the Duke of Calabria, and Paolo de Agostini, a disciple of Giovanni Bellini, as two harbingers of a better style, if not themselves better artists. In his discussion of sculpture, Summonte identifies Donatello as its modern founder and mentions the Arch of Alfonso I. He says it is not bad for its era and attributes it to Laurana.[25] But after this brief revival, sculpture too lapses into barbarism: "They made nothing but flat things, German, French, and barbaric things."[26] A turn for the better only comes with the portal of the Palazzo Sanseverino and other works of the 1470s.

As Giotto is the hero of painting and Donatello of sculpture, Alberti is the hero of architecture.[27] Summonte is enthusiastic about his buildings, but complains that Alberti has been completely without influence in Naples. To deny Alberti's influence (which was actually quite noticeable as we have seen) may have reflected Summonte's real beliefs; or it may merely have been a dramatic preparation for the climax of the letter:

23. Antonio Galateo, "In Alphonsum regem epitaphium," in Domenico Giordano, ed., *Delectus scriptorum . . . .* (Naples, 1735), col. 643: "Qualis eras in extruendis arcibus, qualis in instaurandis templis, qualis in ornandis domibus, qualis in omni regio apparatu, omnes noverunt. Omnes nobiles sculptores, pictores, architectos, omnes denique artifices ex tota Italia, imo ex toto orbe, in regnum tuum magnis, et muneribus, et sumptibus contraxisti."

24. Cf. Fausto Nicolini, *L'Arte napoletana,* pp. 157–76 (the best text); N. Mancinelli, *Pietro Summonte Umanista napoletano* (Rome, 1923), and Morisani, *Letteratura,* pp. 50–61. Other information in C. von

Fabriczy, "Summontes Brief an Marcantonio Michiel," *Repertorium für Kunstwissenschaft,* 30 (1907), 143–68.

25. Nicolini, *L'Arte napoletana,* p. 166. Neither Nicolini nor Morisani comments on Pietro Summonte's strange omission of Donatello's Brancacci tomb. But this suggests there may still be lacunae in the text. Summonte also mentions a seated portrait of Alfonso I by Laurana, now thought to be that in the collection of Tammaro De Marinis in Florence.

26. Ibid., p. 167.

27. Ibid., p. 170.

In our own day King Alfonso II of happiest memory was so devoted to building and desirous of doing great things that had not evil fortune removed him from his throne so quickly, without doubt he would have ornamented the city in a most distinguished manner. He had it in mind to bring a distant river into the city by means of great aqueducts; and when the great walls of the city were finished, a good part of which had already been built when he came to the throne, he wanted to extend all the main streets in straight lines from wall to wall, removing all porticoes, corners, and protrusions, and then to lay out transversely, also in straight lines, the cross-streets from one end of the city to the other. In this way, both through the straightness of the streets and alleys, and through the natural slope of the site from north to south, the city would have been, quite apart from the beauty of its regularity, the cleanest and neatest in Europe, to say nothing of other parts of the world. At every little rainstorm it would have been cleaner than a polished silver piaster. Besides this, the private houses having been provided with fountains, public fountains and drinking troughs were to be constructed at the crossroads and at convenient places. From these one could have sprayed water through the streets, so that as they were swept, in summer, the ground would have been kept free from dust and very clean. Alfonso also wanted to build a most sumptuous church and place in it the bones of all the descendants of the Aragonese lords who had died here; and a great palace near the Castel Nuovo, in the Piazza dell'Incoronata, where the various law courts would have been located in different rooms. In this way the men of affairs would not have to go to different places to transact their business, but could here take care of whatever they had to do without suffering rain or sun, or fatiguing themselves too much [by hurrying] hither and thither. Nor was His Majesty of a nature not to execute the projects mentioned above, when he had planned them, nor afraid of spending money. Those projects pleased him most which involved the greatest expense.

All these noble and holy ideas were interrupted and completely extinguished by the sudden barbaric invasion of Charles VIII, King of France, who brought about the destruction of the Aragonese dynasty in this kingdom.[28]

28. "Ad tempi nostri lo signor re Alfonso secondo di felicissima memoria fo tanto dedito alla fabrica e cupido di far cose grandi, che, se la iniqua fortuna non lo avesse deturbato così presto dal suo solio, senza dubbio averia sommamente ornata questa città. Erat illi in animo fluvium e longinquo per magnos aquaeductus in urbem ducere; e, finite le gran mura della città, in buona parte già facte, extendere ad linea recte tucte le strade maestre, da muro a muro, della città, tolti via portichi, cantonî e gibbi ineguali, e così per traverso extendere pure ad directura, tucti li vichi da capo ad capo della città, per modo che, sì per la directura delle strade e delli vichi, sì anco per la naturale dependenzia del sito da septentrione ad mezzodì, questa città seria stata, oltre la bellezza della equalità, la più necta e polita città (aliarum pace dixerim) di tutta Europa, la quale ad ogni minima pioggia serìa più expurgata che una piastra di forbito argento. Oltra questo, date le fontane per le case particulari, si aveano ad construire le fontane e abbreveratorii publici per li quatrivi e lochi idonei, dalli quali si possea spargere l'acqua per le strade, poi che quelle erano scopate, la estate, per tenere la terra senza polvere e politissima. Oltre a ciò, volea ancora edificare un templo sumptuosissimo e ivi ponere le ossa di tutta la progenia Aragonia delli signori ch'erano morti qua, e un palazzo grande vicino al Castello Novo nella piazza della Coronata, nella quale volea per diverse stanzie collocare tutti li tribunali, ad tal che non bisognasse alli negozianti andare in diversi lochi, ma che qua potessero expedire qualsivoglia loro negozio, senza patire pioggia o

The result of this tragedy, according to Summonte, was an artistic lethargy from which Naples has not yet recovered. The one good architect of Summonte's era, truly capable of "the total imitation of antique things," was Giovanni Donadio, called Mormando, but he has been given no worthy opportunity.[29] This was perhaps less true of the sculptor Giovanni da Nola. But on the whole, Charles' victory halted the momentum of Neapolitan art in the midst of the crucial renewal; this is the real theme of Pietro Summonte's letter.

Unfortunately, Alfonso was destined to be thwarted not only in the accomplishment of his intentions but even in the recording of them. Michiel's history was not published in his own time. Part of it survived as the *Anonimo morelliano,* but the letter was not included.[30]

In his letter Summonte re-expresses many of the ideas introduced earlier by Pontano and his contemporaries. When he mentions the Aragonese pantheon and palace of justice, furthermore, he gives us an idea of what Pontano meant in *De bello neapolitano* by the unnamed things Alfonso had it in mind to do. In fact, he conveniently lists all the specific projects around which the renewal was planned: the new walls, the hydraulic system, Poggioreale (in the passage cited at the end of n. 28), the palace of justice, and the royal pantheon.

---

sole e senza faticare troppo lo corpo in qua e in là. Né era la Maestà Sua di natura che non exequesse le cose dicto citius poi che le avea deliberate, nè che si spaventasse del spendere. Alla quale quelli disegni piacevano più, dove andava maior dispesa."

"Tucti questi nobili e sancti pensieri li interroppe ed extinse in tutto la sùbita barbarica invasione di Carlo ottavo, re di Franza, lo qual fo causa di exterminare la Aragonia famiglia da questo Regno." Summonte then goes on: "Questo infelice signore, prima che arrivasse al sceptro regale, essendo duca di Calabria, cominciò ad exequir sue magnanime imprese nella fabrica; e, per fabricare lo Poggio Regale, conduxe in questa terra alcun di quelli architecti che più allora erano stimati: Iulian da Maiano fiorentino, Francesco da Siena, maestro Antonio fiorentino, benchè costui fusse più per cose belliche e machinamenti di fortezze; e sopra tutti ebbe qua il bono e singulare fra' Iucundo da verona." Quoted in Nicolini, *L'Arte napoletana,* pp. 171–72. Per Hamberg suggests that Fra Giocondo was in charge of widening the streets, and that the project may be linked to a drawing he publishes (Uffizi A4142v), attributed to Fra Giocondo, which certainly may depict the Greek plan of Naples. Cf. Hamberg, "Vitruvius, Fra Giocondo and the City Plan of Naples," *Acta archaeologica, 36* (1965), 105–25.

29. Nicolini, p. 173. For Mormando see below, Chapter 7, n. 38.

30. See n. 24 above, and Emmanuele A. Cicogna, "Intorno la Vita e le opere di Marc Antonio Michiel," *Atti del r. istituto veneto di scienze lettere ed arti, 9* (1860), 359–425; and Theodor Frimmel, ed., "Der Anonimo Morelliano," in *Quellenschriften für Kunstgeschichte und Kunsttechnik,* n.s. *1* (Vienna, 1888).

Chapter 3: THE PORTRAIT SCULPTURE

ERRANTE AND ALFONSO Much of the portrait sculpture made during the renewal still exists. Though the individual works are well known, many problems remain to be solved, such as identifying correctly the portraits of Alfonso and his father. For this, the inscribed contemporary portraits on coins and medals will be my starting place,[1] for in contrast to the coin issues of their predecessors, even those of Alfonso I, the portraits on Ferrante's and Alfonso's ducats, coronati, and carlini are detailed and naturalistic.[2] Most of them are the work of Girolamo Liparolo, the royal die and seal engraver during the first twenty years of Ferrante's reign. Liparolo was also responsible for a larger medallion portraying his master (Fig. 25; Hill 324);[3] quite probably all his portraits are from the life.

Liparolo's portraits of Ferrante show a great head set forward on a slender neck and dominated by an enormous nose flowing continuously down from the forehead between large-lidded eyes (Figs. 25, 27). A dense planar helmet of hair fits over the skull, bordering the eyebrows. The upper lip is set back, and lifted, within the flat volumes of the cheeks, and the chin is big and strongly shaped, flowing down into the neck around the massive skull. These features are consistently preserved in even the smallest coin portraits (Fig. 26).[4] In the Ferraiolo manuscript are other inscribed portraits of Ferrante in his old age. These too are consistent. Figure 28 shows one that commemorates Ferrante's 1486 triumph after the Barons' Revolt.

A handsome uninscribed portrait, usually identified as Ferrante, is a marble life-size bust,

---

1. For possible painted portraits of Ferrante, see R. Filangieri, "Les Origines de la peinture flamande à Naples," *Actes du XIIᵉ Congrès international d'histoire de l'art* (Brussels, 1930), p. 575 (an Adoration of the Magi formerly in the Castel Nuovo and now in Capodimonte); and Tammaro De Marinis, *La Biblioteca napoletana dei re d'Aragona*, *1* (Milan, 1952), 39–40. Vasari, *2*, 516–17, mentions a portrait by Fra Angelico in the Chapel of the Sacrament (now destroyed) in the Vatican. Among the miniatures of Ferrante there is a Latin manuscript of Aristotle's *Ethics* (Paris, Bib. Nat. Lat. 6309, fol. 4) wherein Ferrante appears at the age of about 16. In a magnificent Livy manuscript now in the University Library, Valencia (Bib. Univ. cod. lat. 762, sec. XV), we have a portrait frontispiece to the third decade showing him at the age of 26. There is also an initial portrait in the *Obiurgatio in platonis calumniatorum* by Andrea Contrario (Paris, Bib. Nat. Lat. 12947, fol. 4) which may have been painted by Cola di Rapicano, as well as an equestrian portrait, possibly by the same artist, on fol. 4r.

2. *Corpus nummorum italicorum*, *19* (Rome, 1940), passim. Here the earliest Neapolitan coin to contain what may be called a royal likeness, as opposed to a symbol or effigy, is in pl. iv. fig. 14. It represents Alfonso I. But even this is rough; much better likenesses come only with Ferrante.

3. For Liparolo (fl. 1462–97) see Hill, *1*, 81, with earlier bibliography including especially A. Sambon "I 'Carlini' e la medaglia trionfale di Ferdinando I d'Aragona Re di Napoli," *Rivista italiana di numismatica*, *4* (1891), 481–88; *6* (1893), 75–78; and idem, "Incisori dei conii della moneta napoletana," loc. cit., *6* (1893), 69–82.

4. They also agree with G. A. Summonte's verbal description, *Historia*, *4*, 625: "Fu il re Ferrante di mediocre statura, con testa grande, con bella, e lunga Zazzera di color castagno, buono di faccia, e pieno, di bel fronte, di proporzionata vita, fu assai robusto." Sanudo confirms that Ferrante was short and strong ("La Spedizione di Carlo VIII in Italia," *Archivio veneto*, *2*, 1873, Supplement, 35).

formerly painted, now in the Louvre (Figs. 29, 30). To judge from Ferrante's age, it was probably done about 1465–70.[5] Here in this earlier likeness we see the same features. The head juts forward from a thinnish neck and the chest is tautly held. There is a stiffness in the posture, which is sensed also in Liparolo's medal and even in another more dubious piece, a reconstituted medal possibly after an original by Pietro da Milano (Hill 326). In contrast to these pedestrian works, however, the Louvre bust is decorative and heroic. The hair turbulently frames the face. The profile has been tightened and stylized and follows a sequence of buoyant curves. The eyes arch architecturally, like volutes, up to the bridge of the nose, pulling the cheeks with them. In all this the work is characteristic of Domenico Gagini, as in the way the volume of the face tends to form a cylindrical plane (cf. Fig. 23); Gagini was, as a matter of fact, in Naples and Sicily during these years.[6]

Alfonso's appearance was quite different from his father's. Where the latter was big-boned in old age, gaunt, and long-haired, Alfonso was rotund, short, and fattish to the end of his life, and small-boned, except for the great skull he inherited from his father. He had emphatic, jerky features: "severe in mien and short in body," said Camillo Porzio.[7] Two inscribed medals, one by Andrea Guacialoti[8] and one by Francesco di Giorgio, portray the son's physiognomy. The Francesco di Giorgio medal (Fig. 33; Hill 311) shows the Duke's round head with its continuous cap of surfaces in which the small, bunched features have been centered. He has swelling jowls, a pointed, receding little chin with other chins under it, and sharp little coarse-lidded eyes. The nose leaps abruptly outward in a compound curve, the lips are compressed, the mouth and nostrils squarish. The lower part of the face recedes. The execution of the eyes and eye sockets here as in other portraits of Alfonso is insecure, resulting no doubt from trying to play down the sitter's squint.

The medal by Guacialoti, a three-quarter view of about 1481 celebrating the victory at

5. I have found no document for it, though Sanudo mentions a *bronze* "ymagine" of Ferrante in one of the rooms at Castel Capuano. "La Spedizione," pp. 36–40.

6. For this bust see Martin Weinberger, "Bildnisbüsten von Guido Mazzoni," *Pantheon, 5* (1930), 191–94, which attributes the work to the influence of Mazzoni. Another bust that should be mentioned here is the marble portrait formerly in the T. F. Ryan collection, New York, and now in another private collection. Valentiner attributes this to Pietro da Milano, dates it c. 1472, and says it represents Alfonso (Valentiner, "Andrea dell' Aquila, Painter and Sculptor," *Art Bulletin, 19,* 1937, 503–36, esp. 509). However the portrait is really more like the young Ferrante than Alfonso. Formerly on the entrance to the Camera degli Angeli in the Gran Sala of Castel Nuovo was a relief panel with the head of a young boy, executed before 1457. Riccardo Filangieri, "Rassegna critica delle fonti per la storia di Castel Nuovo," *ASPN, 62* (1937), 327, says it probably represented Alfonso. It was destroyed in the fire of 1919.

7. Camillo Porzio, *La Congiura dei baroni* in Gravier, *Raccolta, 5,* 47. For miniatures of Alfonso cf. the manuscript of Seneca, now in the University Library at Valencia (Cod. lat. 827, sec. XV) on the first page of whose *De Quaestionibus naturalibus* is a floral border, executed, thinks Marinis, by Attavante. The portrait in the lower left-hand corner of this border is clearly the young Alfonso, and is probably based on Guacialoti's medallion. Cf. Marinis, *Biblioteca napoletana, 1,* 101, 145–49, and 2, 150. For a portrait of Alfonso as a young boy in Colantonio's painting in San Pietro Martire, cf. Nicolini *L'Arte napoletana,* pp. 217–20. A full-sized painted portrait of him may also appear in the Adoration of the Magi by Marco Cardisco (fl. 1486–1546) now in San Martino. This contains an obvious likeness of the future Charles V as one of the Magi, on the right, while the two figures on the left seem to be Federigo (far left; compare Hill 312) and, kneeling, Alfonso II. They are of an age, and the features of Alfonso seem to have been taken from the Capodimonte bust discussed below. Cf. also R. Filangieri, *Castel Nuovo* (Naples, 1964), p. 220, which says this was formerly the altarpiece of the Cappella Santa Barbara, Castel Nuovo.

8. Hill, *1,* 191–95.

Otranto (Fig. 32; Hill 745) again displays these features. One gets the same impression in another late portrait, Ferraiolo's drawing of Alfonso's coronation in 1494 (Fig. 34). Here Alfonso's puffed-out chest is held stubbornly erect, the head in line with the back of the body, and puddles of flesh now appear around the nose and chin. The same is true of the coin portraits of his actual reign (Fig. 31).

On this basis I would like to identify as Alfonso another uninscribed portrait of the 1490s. This is the famous life-size bronze bust in Capodimonte usually attributed to Guido Mazzoni (Figs. 35, 36). While always presumed to be a portrait of Ferrante, we can now see that it clearly depicts the son.[9] Documentary support for this identification is provided by Scipione Mazzella, who informs us that the bust was originally in Alfonso's chapel in Monteoliveto.[10]

Then there is the unfinished coronation portrait by Benedetto da Maiano in the Bargello, whose purpose will be discussed in Chapter 7 (Figs. 110, 111, 112). This may have been partly based on one of the medals, although, as we shall see, Benedetto was in Naples in 1492. The Bargello portrait is a vaguer likeness than the others, mainly because of its unfinished state and the damage it has sustained from the weather, and perhaps because of the artist's unfamiliarity with the sitter. It possesses, however, the same articulation of the surface into weighted patches that we see in the other portraits, and one even perceives in it something of the heaviness and pain of the King's career as it was unfolding in 1490–95.

Finally there is the terra-cotta portrait by Mazzoni, which belongs to the Lamentation group in Alfonso's chapel in Monteoliveto (Figs. 172, 173). This fearful naturalistic vision will be discussed later. Here it is enough to say that the new photograph (Fig. 172) unquestionably relates Mazzoni's work both to the Capodimonte bronze and to the Bargello fragment.

These portraits, ranging from the confident, rather cocky youth of 1479 to the defeated, prematurely aged man of the 1490s, tally with the events of Alfonso's life. The medals show us the hero, in Galateo's words "skillful, restless, indefatigable, active, headstrong, and most willing to bear heat, cold, vigils, and labors of all kinds."[11] In the Capodimonte bronze the Duke is in his middle forties, older-looking, with his troubles and pleasures now making their mark on him. In the Monteoliveto portrait we have a glimpse of the furies that came with his abdication and death.[12]

9. Cf. my "Alfonso II Benedetto e Giuliano da Maiano e la Porta Reale," *NN*, ser. 3, 4 (1964), 84–86. Another artist often proposed for this is Adriano Fiorentino, a bronze-caster who was in Naples at this time. Cf. Erasmo Pèrcopo, "Guido Mazzoni e le sue Opere in Napoli," *NN*, 3 (1894), 41–43 with note, pp. 43–45, by Benedetto Croce; C. von Fabriczy, "Adriano Fiorentino," *Jahrbuch der preussischen Kunstsammlungen*, 24 (1903), 71–98, esp. 78–82; and "Don Ferrante" [B. Croce], notes in *NN*, 12 (1903), 79–80, and 13 (1904), 48.

10. Scipione Mazzella, *Le Vite dei re di Napoli* (Naples, 1594), p. 397. See also Giuseppe Maria Fusco, *Intorno all'Ordine dell'armellino* (Naples, 1844); and

idem, *I Capitoli dell'ordine dell'armellino* (Naples, 1845). The fact that the sitter wears the chain, pendant, and cap pin of this order does not interfere with my identification, since Alfonso was a member and became head of the order on his father's death.

11. Antonio Galateo, "In Alphonsum regem epitaphium," in Domenico Giordano, ed., *Delectus scriptorum rerum neapolitanarum* (Naples, 1735), col. 643.

12. Another marble bust, formerly over the portal of the palace of Giulio Scorziatis on the Vicolo dei Cinque Santi, and now destroyed, revealed something of the jovial companion of Poggioreale. This is a smiling portrait, and a grotesque one, and thus related in spirit to the marble bust of Ferrante formerly in the collection

We can round out the gallery with some other faces in the court. Pontano appears in a forceful medal by Adriano Fiorentino (Hill 340), which shows the cavernous bow of his brows, his high forehead frowning with fierce intelligence, and his delicate mouth. Here Pontano has something of the primitivism of a bronze fourth-century Roman emperor. The same characteristics appear in an austere life-size bust, probably also by Adriano, now in the Museo del Palazzo Bianco, Genoa (Fig. 39). This work is comparable to the Louvre Ferrante, but it is simpler—as hollow as a gong.[13] The chin is deep and sharp, and the brows and lips are two self-consciously sculptural bows.[14] Francesco di Giorgio depicted the gentle, tentative face of Federigo with its heavy nose and deep-set eyes (Fig. 28; Hill 312), making him very little the man of action. Ferrandino, on the contrary, was an excellent fighter, and his portrait comes down to us as suitably belligerent (Fig. 37; Hill 335). Adriano portrays him with a short, upturned nose, long, powerful jaw, and scowling brows (see also Hill 336, 337).

THE LAURANA BUSTS   The most famous works of portrait sculpture produced for the renewal are a group of life-size marble busts made by Francesco Laurana. Up to now we have been absolutely sure of the identity of only one of them, a portrait of Alfonso's sister Beatrice. However there is general agreement that the other sitters include Alfonso's wife Ippolita Sforza and their daughter Isabella.[15] I will suggest that we can add a bust of Ferrandino as a young boy.

of T. F. Ryan mentioned above in note 6. The Scorziatis portrait is clearly of Alfonso, although before the Second World War it stood on a pedestal inscribed REX INCLYTUS FERDINANDUS. But this inscription was not original, for in the 1640s Celano (Notizie, 3, 208–09), records a different one: SI BENE PRO MERITIS, CUIQUE SUA MUNERA DANTUR? HAEC SUNT[,] REX VICTOR, PREMIA IURE TUA. Giulio Scorziatis as we have seen was the Duke's secretary. The Duke was also godfather to Scorziatis' son Giovanni Antonio, later Bishop of Aversa. The bust, with its inscription to Alfonso as king, may have been set up at the time of the coronation, and be the recipient's courteous thanks for royal privileges. For earlier ideas on it see A. Maresca, "Battenti e decorazione marmorea di antiche porte esistenti in Napoli," NN, 9 (1900), 51–58, esp. 55–56, and G. Castaldi, "Il Palazzo di Giulio de Scorciatis," NN, 12 (1903), 180–83. The bust is illustrated in Ernesto Pontieri, Per la storia del regno di Ferrante I d'Aragona (Naples, 1946), opp. p. 128. Cf. also Valentiner, "Laurana's Portrait Busts of Women," Art Quarterly, 5 (1942), 273–98, where it is attributed to Laurana. Four other documented sculptural portraits of Alfonso, now lost, are (1) the cornelian for which Andrea di Mesagne was paid 3 ducats on December 24, 1487 (Barone, "Cedole," ASPN, 9 [1884], 626–27); (2) a life-sized silver head made for the shrine at Loreto in 1489 by Gabriele de Pontill (Barone, "Cedole," ASPN,

10 [1885], 6); (3) the "immagine" by a certain Francesco [Laurana?] made for Santa Maria la Nova in 1489 (Barone, "Cedole," loc. cit.); and (4) the kneeling full-length sculpture in the oratory at la Duchesca (Sanudo, "La Spedizione," p. 240).

13. Cf. P. Schubring, Die Plastik Sienas im Quattrocento (Berlin, 1907), p. 194; L. Volpicella, "Le Porte di Castel Nuovo e il bottino di Carlo VIII," NN, ser. 2, 1 (1920), 153–60, esp. p. 160; and Marinis, La Biblioteca napoletana, 1, 113, n. 4. It is said that Alfonso had a bronze "statue" of Pontano made for La Duchesca. Conceivably it is this (Volpicella, "Le porte," p. 160). A later portrait may be the terra-cotta bust, now or formerly in a private collection in America, and published in Luigi Pompili, Dai Carmi di Giovano Pontano (Spoleto, 1928), frontispiece and pp. 138–39, where it is convincingly attributed to Benedetto da Maiano.

14. For Sannazaro's portrait see Hill, 343. Michiel refers to a portrait of Sannazaro in the House of Pietro Bembo in Padua, "di mano di Sebastiano Venitiano ritratto di un altro ritratto," possibly based on this one (Theodor Frimmel, ed., Der Anonimo Morelliano, Vienna, 1888, p. 20).

15. The fundamental article on these portraits is W. R. Valentiner, "Laurana's Portrait Busts of Women," Art Quarterly, 5 (1942), 273–98. For earlier literature see Louis Courajod, "Observations sur deux bustes du musée de sculpture de la renaissance au

The dates of the portraits can be partly deduced from the three occasions when Laurana was in Naples or available for Neapolitan commissions, i.e. before 1458, in 1465–75, and perhaps more intermittently between 1483 and 1498. On the first occasion Laurana worked for Alfonso I, on the second for Ferrante, and on the third for Alfonso of Calabria. He was, therefore, more than any other artist a family sculptor. This, and his style which partook so interestingly both of International Gothic and Early Renaissance, made him something of a constant within the changing taste of the dynasty. And yet as noted his style does change, and these changes can be measured by comparing the Materdomini Madonna of about 1474 (Figs. 19, 20), and the Sant'Agostino Madonna of about 1487 (Fig. 21); the differences between these will help us with the differences between the portraits.

Another device for dating the busts will be provided by the occasions for which they would most likely have been needed. It has been suggested by Valentiner that some were made for royal marriages. Ferrante had had trouble with marriage negotiations—those involving Matthias Corvinus apparently on the grounds of the prospective fiancée's looks[16]—and it is possible that the portraits were intended to convince on this point. This in fact will provide new dates: thus Valentiner, and others, put the portraits of Ippolita in 1472–74, that of Beatrice in 1473, and the three of Isabella in 1487–88. While the early date for the Beatrice is unquestionable, I will show that it is more logical to group the portraits of Ippolita and Isabella all together in 1487–89.[17]

The first important matrimonial occasion would have been the protracted negotiations of Beatrice's marriage. As noted, Ferrante had offered her to the future Charles VIII and to the future Duke of Savoy, Filiberto, as well as to Matthias Corvinus. Any of these offers might have involved portrait busts. The one inscribed Laurana portrait of an Aragonese princess,

Louvre," *Gazette des beaux-arts,* ser. 2, 28 (1883), 24–28, another fundamental article and the first to connect the portraits with the well-known death masks in Provence and elsewhere. See also Wilhelm von Bode, "Desiderio da Settignano und Francesco Laurana: Zwei italienische Frauenbüsten des Quattrocento im Berliner Museum," *Jahrbuch der Preussischen Kunstsammlungen,* 9 (1888), 209–27; Maxe-Werly, "Francesco da Laurana Fondeur—ciseleur à la cour de Lorraine," *Réunion des Sociétés des Beaux-Arts des Départements* (Paris, 1899), 276–85; André Michel et al., "La Question Laurana," *Les Arts, 1* (May 1902), 37–44; Antonino Salinas (Dec. 1902), 29–30; George Ferrier, "De Francesco Laurana," *Les Arts, 4* (June 1905), p. 41; Wilhelm Rolfs, *Franz Laurana* (Berlin, 1907), pp. 331–65; Fritz Burger, *Francesco Laurana: Eine Studie zur italienischen Quattrocentoskulptur* (Strassburg, 1907), pp. 126–38; W. R. Valentiner, "A Portrait Bust of King Alfonso I of Naples," *Art Quarterly, 1* (1938), 61–88; O. Brendel, "Laurana's Bust of Ippolita Sforza," ibid., 7 (1944); 59–62; R. Causa, "Contributi alla conoscenza della scultura del '400 a Napoli," in B. Molajoli, ed., *Sculture lignee nella Campania* (Naples, 1950), pp. 143–48; ibid., "Sagrera, Laurana, e l'arco di

Castel Nuovo," *Paragone,* n.s. no. 5 (1954), 3–23; Michele D'Elia, "Ipotesi intorno a un bassorilievo di Santeramo," *Commentari, 10* (1959), 108–14; R. W. Kennedy, *Four Portrait Busts by Francesco Laurana* (n.p., 1962); John Pope-Hennessy, *Italian Renaissance Sculpture* (New York, 1958), p. 330; and Charles Seymour, Jr., *Sculpture in Italy: 1400–1500* (Harmondsworth, Mddx., England, 1966), pp. 164–66.

16. A. Brezeviczy, "Rapporti storici fra Napoli e l'Ungheria nell'epoca degli aragonesi (1442–1501)," *Atti della Accademia Pontaniana, 58* (1928), 180–202.

17. For the marriage connection see Valentiner, "Portrait Busts," pp. 283–84. Causa ("Sagrera, Laurana," p. 20), agrees with Valentiner's date of 1487 for the busts of Isabella and for that in Vienna, as do Pope-Hennessy, loc. cit., and Seymour, *Italian Sculpture,* p. 165. I do not see the greater abstraction Seymour mentions in the portraits of Isabella as opposed to those of Ippolita: nor do I see why the rough surfaces of Isabella's gown, and the greater reliance on paint that this suggests, should necessarily as Valentiner says be an indication of a later date: the different surfaces may simply represent a different fabric.

TABLE I. LAURANA PORTRAIT BUSTS OF THE ARAGONESE

Sitter	Date	Provenance	Identification	Present Location
Beatrice	c. 1474	Dreyfus Coll., Paris (6)	Inscribed	Rockefeller Coll., New York
Battista Sforza	c. 1474	Urbino Palace of Federigo da Montefeltro	Inscribed	Bargello, Florence
Ippolita (?)	c. 1482	Vienna (with Bianca Maria Visconti?) (5), then Ambraser Coll., Vienna (3).	Miniatures in MS Servius, Biblioteca Universitaria, Valencia, Cod. Lat. 780	Kunsthistorisches Museum, Vienna
Ferrandino (?)	1487–89	From Mazzara del Vallo (my speculation)	Hill, *Corpus*, 335, 336, 337	Galleria Nazionale dell'Arte della Sicilia, Palermo
Isabella	1487–89	Mazzara del Vallo, Santa Maria del Bosco, then Sciacca (both Sicily) (4)	Inscribed pencil drawing by Bernardino da Conti, c. 1489, Uffizi, Florence; Hill *Corpus*, 223, 652, 652b	Galleria Nazionale dell'Arte della Sicilia, Palermo
Isabella	1487–89	Naples; Ecouen (before 1793) (2) or alternatively, Amboise 1495 (1).	Same	Louvre, Paris
Isabella	1487–89	Naples; then Bardini Collection, Florence (3).	Same	Musée Jacquemart-André, Paris
Ippolita	1488–89	1877 Strozzi Coll., Florence (3)	Miniatures in Servius MS, see above	Staatliche Museen, Berlin
Ippolita	1488–89	Naples; Alessandro Castellani Coll., Rome, sold to Duveen, 1933 (3) then T. F. Ryan Coll., New York (6)		Washington, National Gallery
Ippolita	1489–90	Marseilles before 1747, then Coll. Mme. de Narbonne; then Paris, c. 1747–95 (6, 7)	(Uninscribed drawing of bust by Fauris de Saint-Vincens, Académie, Marseilles)	Frick Collection, New York

(1) Lud. Lalanne, "Transport d'oeuvres d'art de Naples au Château d'Amboise en 1495," *Archives de l'art français*, 3 (1852–53), 305.

(2) Louis Courajod, "Observations sur deux bustes du musée de sculpture de la renaissance au Louvre," *Gazette des Beaux-Arts*, ser. 2, 28 (1883), 24–42.

(3) Wilhelm von Bode, *Italienische Bildhauer der Renaissance* (Berlin, 1887), pp. 225–28.

(4) A. Venturi, *Storia dell'arte italiana*, 6 (Milan, 1908), 1032.

(5) W. R. Valentiner, "Laurana's Portrait Busts of Women," *Art Quarterly*, 5 (1942), 273–98.

(6) [Duveen Brothers] *Duveen Sculpture in Public Collections of America* (New York, 1944), nos. 75–77 (Washington bust) and 78–79 (Frick bust).

(7) Otto Brendel, "Laurana's Bust of Ippolita Sforza: a letter to the editor," *Art Quarterly*, 7 (1944), 59–62.

which is now in the Rockefeller Collection, New York, is in fact of Beatrice (Figs. 40, 41). The words DIVA BEATRIX ARAGONIA on the cartouche mean that it was made before her coronation and marriage of 1476, and therefore during Laurana's second stay in Naples. Like the others it is life-size, though diminutive in scale; it was once at least partly polychromed, and it shows the girl sumptuously clad in a low-necked outer vestito worn over a gamurra edged with litterated borders, formerly gilded.

Beatrice possesses the large head, the short, abrupt features, and the rounded chin and cheeks of her elder brother (Fig. 34). That in later life she filled out to resemble him even more is disclosed by the relief portrait—now in the Museum of Fine Arts, Budapest—made after her reign as Queen of Hungary (Fig. 42).[18]

The Rockefeller portrait is fully in Laurana's style of the mid-1470s. Beatrice shares with the contemporaneous Materdomini Madonna (Fig. 20) and that in the Castel Nuovo their characteristic diminutive smoothness of feature. The eyes float softly upward at the outer ends and rise from contoured planes flowing from nose to cheek to brow and forehead. One sees some of these characteristics, but with a bonier profile emerging from an ampler fullness, in Laurana's bust of Battista Sforza in the Bargello. This dates from the same period and could have been made in Urbino or even in Naples.[19]

Another Laurana portrait bust, in the Galleria Nazionale della Sicilia, Palermo, represents a boy of 10 or so (Fig. 50). It is life-size and carved from a cloudy gray marble not unlike that used for the Materdomini Madonna. Conceivably it was taken to Sicily by Alfonso along with the portrait of Isabella in the same collection. I think it represents Alfonso's other child, Ferrandino, who would have been the right age when Laurana was making his portrait of Beatrice about 1475 (cf. Figs. 40, 41).[20]

A third Laurana portrait, in the Kunsthistorisches Museum, Vienna (Fig. 49), is usually identified as Ippolita's daughter Isabella, but the head is heavy and big-cheeked, with a carefully adjusted, faceted bow-like mouth. There is a relatively short, round curve to the forehead, a broadly projecting nose cocked forward, and a pronounced oblique plane across the top of the nostrils. The face of this bust is too knotted and particularized to suit Laurana's conception of Isabella. But with its brownish hair, crimson lips, and headgear (a gilded net over crimson cloth), we get an idea of the original appearance of the other portraits. The tight vestito is horizontally striped in brown. Actually the piece is not really a bust at all,

18. For Beatrice see Giuseppe Cosenza, "La Chiesa e il convento di S. Pietro Martire III," *NN*, 9 (1900), 104–09; A. Berzeviczy, "Rapporti storici fra Napoli e l'Ungheria nell'epoca degli aragonesi (1442–1501)," *Atti della Accademia Pontaniana*, 58 (1928), 180–202; and idem, "Les Fiançailles successives de Béatrice d'Aragon," *Revue de Hongrie*, 2 (1909), 146–65. For the Budapest portrait see Ladislas Gerevich, "Le Maître des reliefs en marbre du roi Mathias et de sa femme Béatrice," *Bulletin du Musée hongrois des Beaux-Arts*, no. 27 (1965), 15–32.

19. It is also the one known female portrait by Laurana which certainly does not portray an Aragonese lady, though Battista was Ippolita Sforza's first cousin. Cf. Valentiner, "Portrait Busts," p. 280, where he dates it 1475–76, i.e. after Battista's death in 1472.

20. A portrait similar to the Palermo carving, but of a different child, is now in a private collection in New York. The Palermo bust has no inscription; the one in New York is inscribed FOELIX AETAS / DIVI AUG. I would attribute the latter to one of the Malvito.

for it includes the sitter's waist and is therefore what was known as a "half statue," like the portrait of Alfonso owned by Giulio Scorziatis.

It is thus possible that the sitter is Ippolita Sforza (cf. esp. Figs. 48, 49, 51), though more certain likenesses show her with a daintier physiognomy. Ippolita would have been 29 in 1474—a suitable age for the Vienna portrait. Valentiner has suggested that it could have reached Vienna through Bianca Maria Sforza, daughter of Galeazzo Maria, when in 1494 she became the wife of the Emperor Maximilian.[21] On the other hand, its clearly marked, more ridged features, the greater decision with which they work through the volumes of the head—these things make the portrait more compatible with Laurana's work of the 1480s. I would tentatively assign it to the early part of this decade. There is no specific occasion I can think of for its having been commissioned.

The marriage in 1477 between Ferrante and Giovanna of Aragon does not seem to have resulted in a Laurana portrait, but presumably the negotiations over the next ten years for the disposal of Alfonso's daughter Isabella resulted in the three magnificent busts of her: one in Palermo in the Galleria Nazionale (Fig. 44), another in the Louvre (Fig. 45), and the third in the Musée Jacquemart-André (Fig. 46). A possibly comparable portrait, a drawing with a subjoined inscription identifying it as Isabella and the artist as Bernardino da Conti, is by no means strikingly similar (Fig. 43), but is acceptable.[22] The Louvre bust could have been brought to France along with the works of art that Charles VIII took north with him in 1495, and the one in Palermo, as noted, could have been taken there by Alfonso on his abdication. The Jacquemart-André portrait remained in Naples.[23]

21. Valentiner, "Portrait busts," p. 292.

22. This drawing is reproduced without discussion by Valentiner, loc. cit., and is mentioned by F. Malaguzzi Valeri, *La corte di Lodovico il Moro*, 1 (Milan, 1913), 38. See also Robert de la Sizeranne, *Béatrice d'Este et sa cour* (Paris, 1920), pp. 87–115, who lists other portraits of Isabella on pp. 88–89, n. 1. Most of these are pretty dubious.

23. Mme André bought the bust in 1885 from Bardini in Florence. It had been discovered in Naples in 1883. The Palermo portrait was identified as Eleonora because of a confusion between two ladies with this name. One is Alfonso's sister, born in 1450, who married Ercole I d'Este, and who had no resemblance to any of these Laurana portraits. The other Eleonora came from the Sicilian branch of the family and died in 1404. She is buried in the Olivetan monastery of Santa Maria del Bosco, Sciacca, Sicily, which she had founded. Adolfo Venturi, *Storia dell'arte italiana*, 6, 1032–35, implies that the Palermo bust is a portrait of this lady on the grounds that it came to the Galleria Nazionale della Sicilia from this monastery. But according to Venturi's own interpretation the bust was carved by Laurana when he was in Sciacca in 1468—i.e. when the Sicilian Eleonora had been dead more than 60 years. At the same time there is no reason to connect Alfonso's sister

with this monastery or with Sicily at all. What is likely is that Alfonso took the Palermo bust, a portrait of his daughter, to the Olivetan monastery at Mazara del Vallo when he abdicated. The portrait would then have been transferred some time after his death to the order's neighboring house in Sciacca. There, being the portrait of a royal Aragonese lady, it could quite easily have been identified with the foundress of the house, and even as some reports indicate have been placed on her tomb which still exists in the small chamber between the cloister and the church. Thence it would have gone to Palermo as Eleonora. See, besides Venturi, Rolfs, *Laurana*, pp. 331–65, and Causa, *Sculture lignee*, p. 148. As to the provenance of the Louvre portrait, Courajod ("Observations," p. 36) suggests this might have been at Ecouen before 1793, where a former governor of Naples, the Connétable de Montmorency, lived. But it is also possible that this, the only one of Laurana's busts to have entered a French royal collection so far as I know, was one of the marbles brought from Naples by Charles VIII and kept at Amboise. See the document published in Lud. Lalanne, "Transport d'oeuvres d'art de Naples au Château d'Amboise en 1495," *Archives de l'art français*, 3 (1852–53), 305. We must finally allow for the possibility that one or more of these duplicate portraits was a copy by Laurana's co-worker, Tommaso

These three portraits possess magical profiles, almost archaic Greek in their abstraction and slight, Apollonian smiles. Compared to the portrait of Beatrice, the lips and the flat cones of the eyes are smoothed more deeply into the globe of the head. In the Jacquemart-André portrait the head is held high, swinging slightly to the right, and the shoulders seem wider than in the others. The Louvre bust is more perfectly preserved, though the nose and other parts have been repaired. The Palermo bust is, I think, the most beautiful of the three (Fig. 44), with its long straight nose and oriental eyes with rather strangely crude, leathery lids. In all three portraits the sitter is shown in a pleated cuffietta and simple coiffure (as also in an inscribed medallion by Giancristoforo Romano; Hill 223).

These three portraits of Isabella display Laurana's measurable advance over the earlier busts. The head in each swells roundly beyond the features, and the eyes slide deeply upward. As in the Sant'Agostino Madonna, there is now an immensely skillful simplification and an ability to let curved planes meet in soft edges. The Madonna also shows, though more mechanically, a similar new classicizing rigor.

The portraits of Isabella and Beatrice may be called epithalamiums in marble. They celebrate youth and expectancy. At the same time, the ladies' colored gowns and headdresses were perhaps an expression of their dowries (which indeed often took the form of jeweled dresses). Except for the eyes and lips their smooth marble faces were left without color. This helped to identify them as Parthenope's daughters, embodiments of the marble beauty that was emerging throughout the renewal. The epithalamium written by Gabriele Altilio for Isabella's wedding confirms that Isabella was seen as a child of Parthenope and of the Sebeto, i.e. as a talisman of the renewal. The poet could even have been referring to a sculptured portrait when he said of the bride: "The dear image will remain with us forever when thou leavest."[24]

LAURANA'S BUSTS OF IPPOLITA   The last three portraits in Laurana's Aragonese group are usually identified as Ippolita Sforza, though hitherto on purely circumstantial

---

Malvito. We know he made similar portraits on his own (see n. 24), and he is documented in Naples in 1484, 1489, and 1491 (Filangieri, *Documenti, 6,* 474). The logical candidate for Malvito's hand would be the Washington bust.

24. "Cara, tui sic nos memores abitura reliquis / Aeternum . . . imago:" from Gabriele Altilio, *Epithalamium in nuptias Joannis Galeatii Sfortiae, Ducis Mediolanensis, et Isabellae Aragoniae, Alfonsi II Regis Neapolitani filiae* (Pavia, 1718), p. 7, ll. 174–75. The Parthenopean imagery here is also worth quoting: "Quas inter mediae magna cingente corona / Bis senae superant forma praestante Sorores, / Aurea Sebethi soboles, quas caerula mater / Parthenope una sciens Musarum, et docta canendi / Parthenope primis teneras formavit ab annis, / Imbuerat cantusque novo nume-

risque modisque" (ibid., 40–45). See also G. A. Summonte, *Historia, 1,* 278, and Achille Dina, "Isabella d'Aragona," *Archivio storico Lombardo, 48* (1921), 283–86. As to the practice of making portrait sculptures to complement poems about ladies, I know of at least one such made at this time and place. It was the work of Tommaso Malvito, Laurana's former companion, and it depicted a certain Beatrice dei Notari of Nola. Her literary praises were composed at the same time by various poets, one of whom was probably Sannazaro. Cf. E. Percopo, "Una Statua di Tommaso Malvico ed alcuni sonetti del Tebaldeo," *NN, 2* (1893), 10–13; Antonio Muñoz, "Studii sulla scultura napoletana del rinascimento," *Bollettino d'arte,* ser. 1, 3 (1909), 55–73, 83–98, esp. 72–73.

grounds. One is in the Staatliche Museen, Berlin (almost completely ruined; Figs. 51, 53); one is in the National Gallery of Art, Washington, D.C. (Fig. 54); the third is in the Frick Collection, New York (Figs. 55, 56, 57).[25]

Valentiner has stated that there are no known portraits of Alfonso's wife, and this has weakened his identification of these sculptures. However, since Valentiner's articles appeared, De Marinis has published two inscribed, dated miniatures of her, though he does not apply them to the question of the Laurana portraits.[26] They are in a manuscript of Servius' commentaries on Virgil, a wedding gift to Ippolita from her father, presented on June 10, 1465. The book is now in the Biblioteca Universitaria, Valencia (cod. lat. XVs., 780). In the finest of the two miniatures Ippolita is shown in a rich green gown with crimson sleeves, her delicate profile contrasting with the heavy form of the letter (Fig. 47). She has a certain girlish plumpness lacking in Laurana's portraits. Nevertheless, the sharp narrow thrust of the chin and its subtle bowed contour as it joins the neck, the gentle curve of the forehead, and the nose cocked very delicately forward (all effects which reappear in the second miniature; Fig. 48), match the Laurana portraits and make Valentiner's identification fairly certain.

Laurana's portraits of Ippolita are an interesting contrast to those of Beatrice and Isabella. Ippolita is shown as a matron rather than as a bride. She is wearing a popular and fortunately datable coiffure which prevailed throughout Italy in the last fifteen years of the Quattrocento. This consisted of parting the hair in the middle and letting it fall in curves over the temples while "serpentinelli riccioli ladri" escaped in front of the ears. The filletted snake of hair draped around the back is probably a hairpiece. One sees the same feature in two paintings by Domenico Ghirlandaio, one of a young woman in the National Gallery, London, and the other, dated 1488, in the Van Thyssen Collection, Lugano. There is nothing particularly Milanese about this coiffure, pace Valentiner, and it would not have been worn at the very earliest before about 1480.[27] Ippolita's dress is also different from those worn by

25. The provenances of these portraits are promising. Cf. T. Leman Hare, "Sculptured Marble Bust Presumed Portrait of Princess Beatrice of Aragon," *Apollo*, *19* (Jan. 1934), 57; and Rudolph Wittkower, "Sculpture in the Mellon Collection," *Apollo*, *26* (Aug. 1937), 79–94. [Duveen Brothers], *Duveen Sculpture in Public Collections of America* (New York, 1944), nos. 75–79, gives more bibliography, mostly sale notices. These reveal that the Washington bust was discovered in Naples before 1883. Brendel, "Laurana's Bust," publishes a drawing by Fauris de Saint-Vincens, now in the Library of the Académie, Marseilles. The bust itself had been in Marseilles before 1747, which means it could easily have come from Naples, either with the artist in 1500 or with one of the Neapolitan refugees of 1501–03. The Berlin bust was acquired in 1877 from the Palazzo Strozzi. Cf. Wilhelm von Bode, *Italienische Bildhauer der Renaissance* [Berlin, 1887],

pp. 225–28, and Frida Schottmüller, *Die italienischen und spanischen Bildwerke der Renaissance und des Barocks* [Königliche Museen zu Berlin] (Berlin, 1913), no. 339, pp. 138–39. The Strozzi as we have seen had been bankers in Naples and the portrait of Ippolita could well have been pawned along with other Aragonese artistic possessions that ended up in their collection, e.g. the Tavola Strozzi.

26. Valentiner, "Laurana's Portrait Busts," p. 288. De Marinis, *La Biblioteca napoletana, 2*, s.v. Servius.

27. Valentiner, "Laurana's Portrait Busts," pp. 288–89. The source for my information about Ippolita's coiffure is Rosita Levi Pisetzky, *Storia del costume in Italia, 2* (Milan, 1964), 227–311, esp. 288–92. The tight sleeves of the vestito are also peculiarly southern as is the general severity of the gowns of Ippolita, Beatrice, Isabella. The vestito, by the way, is another end-of-the-century fashion (ibid., p. 238).

Isabella and Beatrice. It is not the tight, maidenly gonella or vestito, but a heavy brocade gown, perhaps like the "gamorra de brocato bianco" she was buried in.[28] The pedestals of the busts, with their strongly framed panels and active rounded reliefs, are a third obvious innovation. The shift of scale gives the portraits a monumentality the others lack. And yet the actual faces, within this richer setting, are handled like the others. There is even the same abstraction, the same exploitation of smoothly curved planes in floating contact, and the same curiously Greek quality (Fig. 52).

One reason for the elaborate bases may be that the portraits of Ippolita had a different function from the others. The imagery of these bases, adapted from antique sarcophagi, refers to marriage retrospectively, as from the end of a happy wedded life. The jolly naiads and erotes on the Berlin base (Fig. 53) have an obvious hymeneal-cum-funeral meaning. The same is true of the Washington base, which depicts wedding sacrifices—two centaurs fleeing with Lapiths' wives, dashing toward each other on either side of a central cartouche (Fig. 54).

The choice of such imagery for the portrait of a departed wife is consistent with classical funeral practice,[29] but it is especially appropriate in Ippolita's case, since negotiations and ceremonies for her daughter's wedding were in course at the time of her death.[30] The occasion also paralleled that of her own wedding of 1465, which had occurred within a few months of the death of her mother-in-law.

In this situation, and because she was marrying a Sforza, Isabella was thought of as her mother's literal continuator, almost in the sense of a reincarnation. Altilio even anticipated the idea in his epithalamium, written before Ippolita's death on August 18, 1488. Bernardo Bellincioni, the Milanese court versifier, writing afterward, carried the theme farther.[31] When at the end of 1488 Hermes Sforza arrived in Naples for the double purpose of attending Ippolita's funeral and acting for his brother in the proxy wedding, the notion of an unbroken continuum between mother and daughter, and of a funeral–wedding, was again present. At this time Isabella was already named in Neapolitan documents as Duchess of Milan, and part of her dowry of 100,000 ducats had been paid.[32] Again, both for the proxy wedding in Naples and for the real one in Milan, the splendors of matrimonial costume were reserved for the actual ceremonies; at other times mourning for Ippolita was worn. Everything about the situation helped create a funeral–matrimonial background, with Isabella as the new Ippolita.

All of this suggests that the three portraits of Ippolita were made after her death. It is true

28. Notar Giacomo, *Cronaca di Napoli* (Naples, 1845), p. 167.

29. There is also a drawing in the Codex Vallardi (2397; cf. G. F. Hill, *Dessins de Pisanello,* Paris, 1929, pl. 1 and p. 27.) taken from an Orestes sarcophagus, and which may be the model for the far left-hand male figure on the base of the Frick bust (Fig. 58).

30. Achille Dina, "Isabella d'Aragona, Duchessa di Milano e di Bari," *Archivio storico lombardo, 48* (1921), 269–98.

31. Gabriele Altilio, *Epithalamion,* ll. 147ff.; Dina, "Isabella," pp. 272, 310; and Bernardo Bellincioni, *Rime,* ed. Pietro Fanfani, 1 (Bologna, 1876), pp. 60–61, sonnet xxxii.

32. Barone, "Cedole," ASPN, 9 (1884), 636 [Dec. 8, 1488].

that by this time she was a middle-aged lady of 43. But an idealized likeness literally recalling her youth would be almost mandatory in the circumstances, i.e. to portray a personality which had metaphorically coalesced with that of a bride. Such a rejuvenation would also echo the sentiments of Pontano's epitaph in which Ippolita is said to have become a third goddess along with Venus and Pallas.[33]

There is more evidence on the date and meaning of these portraits, at least for the Frick specimen. Stylistically, the rubicund figures on its plinth have the same activity seen in the other friezes. But unlike the others, the Frick scenes are narrative episodes. Otto Brendel, using Hyginus' *Fabulae* as a source, has given a promising interpretation of them. My own reading is based on his.[34]

Brendel identifies the far left-hand event (Fig. 58) as Alcestis killing herself, presumably in the presence of her son Eumelus and her husband Admetus. Alcestis, who nobly volunteered to die in Admetus' place, is mentioned by Hyginus as a type of wifely loyalty (li, ccli, cclvi). The next scene, which shows two women on either side of a large semicircular vessel, Brendel interprets as the daughters of Pelias cooking their dismembered father, having been tricked by Medea into thinking this would rejuvenate him (xxiv). On the opposite side of the base (Fig. 59), Brendel sees, first, King Athamas sacrificing his son Phrixus (ii) and then Pentheus about to be cut to pieces by his mother, the Maenad Agave (ccxxxix). Brendel gives the themes as female passions and virtues, human sacrifice, the uncommon or hideous deeds of sisters, and Alcestis as the prototype for Ippolita. (One might mention also the presence of Eumelus, Parthenope's father.)

On the other hand, none of the ladies Brendel names makes a flattering prototype for Ippolita Sforza. All of them are murderesses, even Alcestis, for Hyginus emphasizes that she helped cook her father even though she said the rejuvenation process would not work (xxiv). And yet it is essential to Brendel's interpretation that Alcestis refuse to take part in the murder so as to contrast her virtue with her sisters' folly. Secondly, Alcestis did not die by the sword; rather, so far as I know, she is always shown expiring on a couch. Above all, there is nothing in any of these stories that links them with Ippolita Sforza's placid life.

In my opinion, the series depicts the events Hyginus tells of in the first five chapters of his book, the story of Athamas, the Thessalian king whom Brendel has already identified in the third episode. It will be remembered that Athamas had three rival wives, each of whom bore him two children. These children were all successively killed except for one son, Phrixus, who thus became the heir to his father's kingdom. One wife was Themisto, who tried to murder all four of her rivals' offspring but was tricked into killing her own children. As a result she committed suicide. I think the far left-hand scene shows her doing this, in the approved manner for those who have disgraced themselves. She is in her husband's presence, from whom she turns in shame, while he almost seems to urge her on, this being the only

---

33. Pontano, *Carmina,* "De tumulis," II, 6.   34. Brendel, "Laurana's Bust."

course open after such infamy. The child would be Phrixus, who leaps to stop her even though she had tried to murder him. He is now safely past the first of several attempts on his life.

Another attempt to kill Phrixus came when Ino, a second wife of Athamas, decided to get rid of both Phrixus and his sister Helle. Ino took more elaborate measures than Themisto: with the help of her maternal relatives, she parched the seed that was to be planted for the city's crops, thus assuring that when eaten they would spread disease. The second scene would show Ino and one of her sisters doing this. (While the fire has disappeared in restoration, its flames are preserved in a drawing of the bust by Fauris de Saint-Vincens, now in the library of the Académie, Marseilles.)

During the resulting illness and starvation, Athamas sent to Apollo for advice. Ino, however, intercepted the messenger and told him to tell the king that his country's afflictions would not cease until Athamas had sacrificed Phrixus to Jove. The boy was brought to the altar and the ceremony began. As Brendel suggests, the third scene shows it—Athamas bracing himself for the hideous task, his knife raised, his son bound on the altar. In another version of the story (*Fasti*, iii, 863–64), Ovid has both Phrixus and Helle come forward to be sacrificed, and she may be the figure on the right imploring Athamas to stop. But it is more likely to be Ino, assisting at the triumph of her trickery. At any rate, just at this point the corrupted messenger from Apollo relents and tells all. Liber (i.e. Dionysius), who was Ino's supporter, intervenes and prevents her punishment, but she and her son Melicertes later die at sea while, in a fit of insanity sent by Jove, Ino's other son is killed by Athamas himself.

Liber's wrath would have finished off Athamas' last two remaining offspring, Phrixus and Helle, had not their mother, Nebula or Nephele, given them a magical ram with a golden fleece. On this they escaped, though in the process Helle fell into the sea (hence the name of the Hellespont). Nebula, in a final meeting with Phrixus, warned him that to save himself he must sacrifice the ram to Jove and afterward take its golden fleece to the temple of Mars in Colchis. This would be the event pictured in Laurana's last scene: the mother wild with haste as she overcomes the objections of the flaccid youth.

Unfortunately, no copy of Hyginus' *Fabulae* is known to have been in the Aragonese library.[35] Ippolita's own copy of Servius, of course, would refer to the tale (*Aen.* V, 241),

35. The trouble with Hyginus as sole literary source is not only this, but the fact that only one text is known to have survived at all. It is a manuscript dating from the ninth or tenth century and was not rediscovered until 1535. Cf. Hyginus, *Fabulae*, ed. H. J. Rose (Leyden, n.d.) p. xvi, and ibid., ed. and trans. Mary Grant (Lawrence, Kansas, 1960), p. 1. However a number of Hyginus fragments existed in Renaissance collections of classical fables. Some of the ambiguous untraced entries in the Neapolitan library inventories may even refer to such compilations. One entry, "Libellus Apolonii, in papiro, grecus," cited in De Marinis, *La Biblioteca napoletana*, 2, 187–92, probably means Philostratus' life of Apollonius of Tyana. This in turn would probably have included all or parts of Philostratus the Younger's *Imagines*, as well as the *Callistrati descriptiones*, which normally appear together. The latter tell the story of Phrixus. So do other Hyginian manuscripts such as those published in G. H. Bode, *Scriptores rerum mythicarum latini tres* (Zella, Hanover, 1834), one of which is partly fifteenth century, and all of which were in the Vatican Library. The story also appears in Boccaccio's

but without the incidents I have narrated. However, Ovid does describe them (*Fasti,* iii, 853–75); and the *Fasti,* of course, would have been available in numerous copies. Statius, also, refers to Phrixus frequently in the *Sylvae.* And though, so far as I know, the death of Themisto is found only in Hyginus, it is safe to assume that scholars at Alfonso's and Ferrante's courts would have been familiar enough with these and other Greek and Roman fabulists to account for all four episodes in the story as Laurana presents them.

THE IMAGERY OF THE FRICK BUST The contemporary application of Laurana's pedestal reliefs must be approached more cautiously. Here I shall offer a hypothesis that reflects the delicate relationship between Naples and Milan in 1489 and early 1490.

Ferrante's policy vis-à-vis Milan was threefold: first, the sickly and ineffectual Giangaleazzo, Duke of Milan, had to obtain actual power from his regent Lodovico il Moro; second, there had to be a new heir to assure the succession; third, this reinforced succession had to be poised against the pretensions of Charles VIII who, though still a minor, was from 1487 Angevin heir to the throne of Naples. Unfortunately, none of these conditions showed any promise of being fulfilled as the months after the wedding rolled by. Lodovico continued to rule, keeping his nephew and niece on a straitened budget. He flirted with Charles VIII. Worse still, Giangaleazzo turned out to be sexually impotent with his wife.

Though there is little doubt that Lodovico wanted to become duke himself, and would therefore not genuinely have welcomed Giangaleazzo's heir, he nevertheless bullied his nephew about his impotence. Quite possibly to Il Moro's satisfaction, this seemed to make poor Giangaleazzo all the less able. It was even rumored that Lodovico was poisoning his nephew to achieve this end. Also, the young man was an alcoholic, and to this weakness his others were attributed.[36] Nonetheless, Isabella remained loyal, though she called herself "the worst-married woman in the world," and she stood up to her husband's Svengali as the vigilant guardian of Giangaleazzo's rights.[37]

Lodovico's exhortations on Giangaleazzo's impotence—"lectiones," he called them—took place in front of the court, with Giangaleazzo, we are told, shuffling and hanging his head or trying to smile as if it was meant to be funny. Meanwhile the Archbishop of Milan threat-

---

De genealogia deorum (xiii, xiv) [new edition printed in Vicenza, 1487]. And it is represented in art: in classical times Phrixus and Helle on the ram seems to have been a favorite event (e.g. the fifth-century terra-cotta reliefs from Melos in the National Museum, Athens, and in the Metropolitan Museum, New York), while Christine de Pisan's *Cent Histoires de Troye,* which appears in a number of illustrated manuscripts as well as in printed editions, tells of Ino's parching the grain, Phrixus and Helle on the ram, and Phrixus' sacrifice of that animal. The same events were illustrated in editions of *Ovide moralisée* (e.g. Paris, Bibliothèque de l'Arsenal, Cod. Fr. XIV C. 5069). Another scene, Ino chasing Phrixus from his father's kingdom, brandishing a knife, is on an amphora in the Museo Nazionale, Naples (Roscher, *Lexikon,* s.v. Phrixos). Cf. also Minervini, "Il mito di Frisso ed Elle, in un vaso dipinto," *Bullettino archaeologico napoletano,* n.s., No. 155, anno 7 (1858), 33–42. But I do not claim that Laurana's scenes were influenced by earlier graphic representations of the story.

36. Dina, "Isabella," pp. 302–04. For contemporary rumors see Bernardino Corio, *L'Historia di Milano* [c. 1500] (Padua, 1646), p. 879, and Paolo Giovio, *Delle Istorie del suo tempo,* trans. Lodovico Domenich (Venice, 1608), pp. 10–14.

37. Dina, "Isabella," p. 299.

ened Giangaleazzo with eternal hellfire if the match was not consummated forthwith.[38] In these circumstances the nuptial splendors, especially Bellincioni's wedding masque (with decorations by Leonardo), in which Giangaleazzo appeared as Jove, was an ironic joke.

The situation was taken very seriously in Naples. Ferrante's ambassador to Milan called the Duke's frigidity a national scandal. Lodovico had earlier insulted the Neapolitans by accusing them of giving short weight in the dowry payments. And yet he had been greatly honored by Ferrante, having been made Duke of Bari and in 1487 Prince of Rossano, so that Ferrante was literally his liege lord; or, one might say that Il Moro was, for the Neapolitan king, yet another rebellious baron.[39]

Lodovico therefore had every reason to fear that Ferrante would demand redress. There were rumors that Ferrante intended to take back his daughter and stop further dowry payments. Lodovico even suspected that Alfonso would march north and try to seize power in Milan. The Duke of Calabria was much more intractable than his father toward Il Moro; and, as a matter of fact, years ago Filippo Maria Visconti had actually promised Alfonso I the Milanese succession. On Filippo's death, indeed, one faction in Milan had proclaimed Alfonso I their duke. A case was therefore to be made that the Aragonese and not the Sforzas were the legitimate rulers in Lombardy.[40]

However, what Ferrante actually did was to attempt a peaceful settlement, utilizing a combination of science and rhetoric. In December 1489 he sent north two different embassies. The first, including matrons and gentlemen, was to make a medical inspection of the bride and groom. The other embassy was to persuade Lodovico that a usurping course would lead to disaster. The head of this delegation was Camillo De Scorziatis, brother of Giulio, Alfonso's secretary and intimate counselor.[41] In my opinion, the Frick portrait could have been made as a gift for Lodovico Sforza from Ferrante, to be presented on this occasion.

Laurana's portrait would have suited Ferrante's purposes well. Superficially it was a simple memorial bust like the other two, a sculptural expression of the intimate links between the two countries. But on deeper acquaintance the Frick bust had a puzzling tale to tell, a tale that was in fact a rebuke against trickery, poisoning, and the prevention of an heir's accession. Phrixus, though protected by Jove, is cheated of his kingdom, undone by Dionysius: this was precisely Giangaleazzo's position if we accept Lodovico as Jove and Dionysius (Liber) as Giangaleazzo's penchant for drink. In some versions of the fable (e.g. Boccaccio, *De genealogia deorum*, xiii, 67–70; xiv), Phrixus is a weakling like Giangaleazzo and, also like Giangaleazzo, he becomes the frightened husband of his cousin. Even the word phrixus, both in Greek and Latin, bespeaks the young Duke's problems: frigus and φρῖκάλέος or φρικτός.

38. Ibid., p. 306.

39. Ibid., and R. de la Sizeranne, *Béatrice d'Este*, p. 92. For Lodovico's Neapolitan titles see Ludovico Pepe, *Storia della successione degli Sforzeschi negli stati di Puglia e Calabria* (Bari, 1900).

40. Giovanni Simonetta, *Rerum gestarum francisci sfortiae commentari*, RIS, 21, 2, 180; H. F. Delaborde,

L'Expédition de Charles VIII (Paris, 1888), pp. 217–18; and Alan F. C. Ryder, "La Politica italiana di Alfonso d'Aragona (1442–1458)," *ASPN*, 77 (1959), 43–106.

41. Dina, "Isabella," p. 311. According to Notar Giacomo, *Cronica*, p. 169, it was these medical missionaries who ultimately cleared up the problem.

Indeed, in Greek φρίξος is the personification of comic horror; related words mean to rise up or stand out.[42] The very name of this early antihero, therefore, expresses the plight of a man who has to be frightened into sexual adequacy.

Such a tale would be appropriate for a portrait of Ippolita Sforza. A Greek and Latin pun would suit this lady who was famous for her mastery of these tongues.[43] Ippolita's very name, that of the Amazon queen, expresses the antithesis of Phrixus, the manly woman as opposed to the womanly man. And as Giangaleazzo's mother-in-law, Ippolita would at once be admonishing her son and stressing the strength of her daughter-successor, the high-mettled loyal girl who, because of the Duke's weakness, was forced to play the man.

The climax to the story of Phrixus, however, is left untold by Laurana. This of course comes when Phrixus dedicates the golden fleece to Mars, making it the talisman of one of the greatest military and naval expeditions in all legend. But surely, once the events in Laurana's story are explained, the famous sequel needs no stating. Anyone, after hearing the obscure, harmless, and comic story of Phrixus, would immediately think of its terrible aftermath in which Jason banded together with his allies to remove the usurper Pelias from his throne.

There are correspondences between this unstated sequel and the situation between Milan and Naples. Lodovico, as a potential usurper (and of course ultimately a real one), was a Pelias; indeed Pelias means "the Black." Similarly, Ferrante was an Argonaut, for he was a Knight of the Order of the Golden Fleece. As such he could call on the help of powerful allies: Philip, Duke of Burgundy, and Maximilian, King of the Romans and future Emperor, who was to become the Grand Master of the Order—Jason himself. These knights were pledged to unite against anyone who offered an insult to one of their number.[44] It was this very order, moreover, that was now seeking to form a coalition against France and her allies.[45] Under this interpretation the portrait of Ippolita Sforza is not only a rebuke to evil protectors and a weakling prince but also the veiled threat of an expedition to reestablish Isabella's honor and perhaps even to "restore" the duchy to the heirs of Alfonso I: the very fears we know Lodovico was prey to.

Suddenly, however, just before Camillo De Scorziatis' arrival with this presumed gift from Ferrante and Alfonso the situation changed. On the night of April 25, 1490, in Vigevano, the Duke of Milan overcame his impotence. According to the papal nuncio, Enrico Gherardi,

42. Roscher, *Lexikon,* s.v. Phrixos.

43. Nicola Ratti, *Della famiglia Sforza, 2* (Rome, 1795), 11–19.

44. Henri Desbordes (?) *La Mausolée de la toison d'or ou les tombeaux des chefs et des chevaliers du noble ordre de la toison d'or* (Amsterdam, 1689), esp. pp. 54–55; G. A. L. Cibrario, *Descrizione storica degli ordini cavallereschi, 1* (Turin, 1846), 86–92; and F. A. F. T. de Reiffenberg, *Histoire de l'ordre de la toison d'or* (Brussels, 1830), esp. *1,* 175–77, which

describes the order's meetings in July 1490, at which its enmity to France was fully manifested. The order had been founded in 1429/30 by Philip the Good of Burgundy. Other members were, or had been, Ferrante's father, Alfonso I, and his uncle, Juan of Aragon. Alfonso wears the official collar in the bust by Domenico da Montemignaio in the Kunsthistorisches Museum, Vienna.

45. Cibrario, *Descrizione storica,* pp. 86–92, and de Reiffenberg, *Histoire,* loc. cit. and *1,* 21–22.

Isabella herself informed the court the next morning. The Cardinal congratulated the pair in the name of Innocent VIII. In due course a son, the young "duchetto," Francesco, appeared. One of the Aragonese purposes was achieved in Milan, and Laurana's sculptural "lectio" became unnecessary.

But unhappily the other two Neapolitan aims, power for Giangaleazzo and an alliance with Milan against the French, were not secured. Now that Giangaleazzo had an heir, Il Moro's strategy changed, and an old plan to marry Beatrice d'Este was reactivated. The ceremony took place in January 1491, just two years after Isabella's wedding and only eight months after the consummation of her marriage. At the same time, the tortuous Lodovico managed to dissuade Maximilian from any future alliance with Naples against France. In 1493 the Emperor invested Lodovico with the Duchy of Milan, and Giangaleazzo was deposed. As noted, he died the following year, the same year Lodovico's sister Bianca Maria married the Emperor. And thus did Pelias form an unlikely alliance with Jason.

Chapter 4: THE EASTERN WALLS AND THE PORTA CAPUANA

THE WALLS   In the fifteenth century, only the substance but not the general form of ancient Naples was obscured by later building.[1] Indeed, the forthright quadrilateral grid of streets dating from classical times is still visible (Fig. 1), and the three decumani running east and west are still the major streets: on the south the one that begins at Piazza Nilo and becomes the via San Biagio dei Librai; in the middle the via Tribunali; and on the north the succession of streets of which via Anticaglia is the middle part. Many of the narrow transverse cardines are also still in existence, and parts of the old Greek walls (fragments of which have now been re-excavated) were known to Alfonso.[2] The forum is presumed to have occupied the space in front of the Church of San Paolo Maggiore on via Tribunali. Columns from the portico of the Augustan temple of the Dioscuri still stand on the podium of that church. In the fifteenth century more of this portico remained, and parts of the adjacent theater were visible as well. The rotundity of the latter's cavea can still be seen in the street pattern given by the via San Paolo, the via Anticaglia, and the vico Gigante, and two of the theater's brick arches form part of a wall on the last street.[3] Thus Alfonso's widened, straightened streets would have been a restoration of antiquity; and the new walls, both actually as well as poetically, constituted Pontano's garland of gold and coral for Parthenope's Greek form.

The earliest of these new walls was erected on the eastern side of the city.[4] In July 1484, according to G. A. Summonte, Ferrante himself set out in procession from the Carmine, at the southeastern corner of Naples, and dedicated the first stone.[5] Already in the previous

1. For modern reconstructions of Greco-Roman Naples, cf. Bartolommeo Capasso, *Monumenta ad neapolitani ducatus historiam pertinentia* (Naples, 1868); idem, "Pianta della città di Napoli nel secolo XI," *ASPN,* 16 (1891), 832–62; Michelangelo Schipa, "Napoli greco-romana," *NN, 14* (1905), 97–101; and M. Napoli, *Napoli greco-romana* (Naples, 1959), esp. pp. 68–107. Cf. also Chapter 2, n. 7.

2. These walls were said to be immensely thick and to have turned back Hannibal's siege (Pontano, "De magnificentia" in *Opera omnia,* Venice, 1518, 128r). Parts of them near the Porta Nolana were still visible in the fifteenth century (idem, *De bello neapolitano,* Gravier, *Raccolta, 5,* 144). Cf. also Giulio De Petra, "Nuovi Avanzi delle antiche mura di Napoli," *NN, 14* (1905), 113–14; and G. A. Summonte, *Historia, 1,* 41–43, which says the sea came in as far as San Giovanni Maggiore. Following Pontano he gives the original form of the city as circular.

3. Gino Doria, *Storia di una capitale* (3rd ed. rev., Naples, 1958), pp. 1–18, 249–53.

4. Bartolommeo Capasso, *Sulla Circoscrizione civile ed ecclesiastica,* etc. (Naples, 1882), p. 23, n. 3, and p. 29; idem, "Le Denominazioni delle torri di Napoli nella murazione aragonese e viceregale," *NN, 2* (1893), 30–31; L. De la Ville sur-Yllon, "Le mura e le porte di Napoli," *NN, 12* (1903), 49–56; Giovanni Sepe, *La Murazione aragonese di Napoli. Studio di restituzione* (Naples, 1942); and Morisani, *Letteratura,* pp. 32–37.

5. Notar Giacomo, *Cronica di Napoli* (Naples, 1845), p. 151, gives July 15 as the date, and Giulio Passero, *Giornali* (Naples, 1785), p. 43, June 15. G. A. Summonte, *Historia, 4,* 589, says it was on July 3. That Summonte, the later historian, was correct and the two contemporaries wrong, was proven when the dedication stone was unearthed in 1906.

year a tax had been levied to pay for the walls,[6] but actual construction did not begin until the following November.[7] The work was supervised by a certain Antonio Spinello.[8] No documents suggest that any substantial amount of the construction was finished at this time, and there is reason to believe that work was temporarily abandoned. The hiatus would have been more than justified by the turmoil of the Barons' Revolt, which broke out in 1485 and consumed the energies and finances of the crown during most of this and the following year.

Construction seems to have been resumed in 1487. The first specific document is dated July 12. On this day piperno for the new walls was sold to Spinello's replacement, Antonio Latro.[9] Another sale took place on the following September 28 when 20,000 palmi of piperno were bought.[10] On December 11, 1487, Latro bought 20,000 palmi of tufa from Monte di Soccavo,[11] and on February 11, 1488, 20,000 more palmi of piperno were purchased.[12] I have found no further notices until January 20, 1490, when Latro bought 50,000 palmi of the same material.[13] On the following June 16, Leonetto di Sanseverino sold, again to Latro, all the stone necessary for "two sections" of the city walls.[14] Then, after another hiatus, Leostello reports that by August 14, 1490, the walls had been carried as far as San Giovanni a Carbonara. This means they were nearly finished.[15]

Originally, Spinello was the designer as well as the supervisor of the work, and he is thus immortalized on the cornerstone. However, he disappears from the documents after November 1485. Certainly the walls were not designed by Giuliano da Maiano, as some have claimed, for he did not arrive on the scene until April 1485, or shortly before.[16] The Duke of Calabria himself is called the designer by Leostello, but neither was he in the city during the summer of 1484 when presumably the general character of the walls was set; Alfonso is not even mentioned in the inscription on the cornerstone.[17]

6. N. Barone, "Notizie storiche raccolte dai registri curiae della Cancelleria aragonese," *ASPN*, *14* (1889), 9 [June 11, 1484] and Morisani, *Letteratura*, p. 33.

7. Leostello, *Effermeridi*, in G. Filangieri, *Documenti per la storia le arti . . .*, *1* (Naples, 1883), 48.

8. "Don Fastidio" [B. Croce], "La Torre Spinella," *NN*, *15* (1906), 57–58; and Barone, "Notizie," loc. cit.

9. G. Filangieri, *Documenti*, 5, 187; 6, 444.

10. Ibid. The price was 15 tarì per 100 palmi. A Neapolitan palmo equaled 0.264 meters; 8 or 10 palmi, depending, equaled 1 canna (ell, rod), i.e. either 2.645 or 2.109 meters. The canna quadrata was 100 palmi quadrati, or 6.9986 square meters. Such a phrase as "20,000 palmi of piperno" was of course an expression of some cubic quantity, but I don't know what. The Neapolitan ducat was divided into 5 tarì, 100 carlini, or 100 grani; 30 tarì weighed 1 ounce. The ducat could be gold, and the tarì, under the Aragonese at any rate, was silver. For information on prices and the value of money, see N. F. Faraglia, *Storia dei prezzi in Napoli dal 1131 al 1860* (Naples, 1878), pp. 65–106.

11. Filangieri, *Documenti, 6*, 132–33.

12. Ibid., 5, 143.

13. Ibid., 5, 201.

14. Ibid., 6, 417.

15. Leostello, *Effemeridi*, p. 359. In L. Salazar, ed., "Racconti di storia napoletana," *ASPN, 33* (1908), 507–08, under the date 15 June, 1484, we read that gold sirene, worth 6 ducats, were placed under the new walls, and that though Spinello was in charge of the work, there was also "soprastante l'ingeniere capo Maestro Francesco da Siena." This probably refers to Francesco di Giorgio, but I think the anonymous writer is confusing Francesco's documented work on the western walls (1491ff.) with these earlier eastern structures.

16. Giuliano may have arrived in 1484, says Morisani (*Letteratura*, p. 34, n. 2), but he gives no documentation.

17. As Captain-General of the "Santissima e Serenissima Liga" Alfonso was leaving Cremona to fight the Venetians that July (Leostello, *Effemeridi*, pp. 45–49). He returned to Naples however by November 3, specifically to work on the walls, says Leostello (p. 48).

On the other hand, after the revolt and Alfonso's return to Naples, there are numerous suggestions that he did supervise the new defense system. The earliest one that I have found is not actually conclusive: Leostello says that on October 12, 1488 the Duke "measured out certain walls and towers, and looked over certain of his gardens, and certain models [modolj] and also looked over and measured the Torre del Molo [the beacon on the Castel Nuovo's breakwater]."[18] I conclude that because of the Barons' Revolt, work on the eastern walls was stopped after the first campaign, which lasted from November 1484 to November 1485; that most of the new system was actually built from July 1487 to November 1488 with a different supervisor, Antonio Latro, and probably under the advice of Alfonso of Calabria;[19] and that after a second, shorter hiatus, the work was finished between January and August 1490.[20]

As a result of all this, many new houses and streets were built. On March 4, 1494, for example, Giovanni Ricca was working on his houses at Porta Capuana, in the area formed by the new walls,[21] and in the following April similar work was undertaken in the nearby Piazza Formello.[22] The monasteries or churches of San Giovanni a Carbonara, San Martino, San Benedetto, and San Pietro ad Aram were all brought inside the new circuit, as was the future site of La Duchesca and the Piazza Orto del Conte.[23] Piazza Forcella was moved south and became the Piazza Nolana, adjacent to the new gate (Fig. 2). The new Piazza del Carmine contained a new fountain, the headquarters of the Seggio di Portanova,[24] and an arcaded portico.

The course of the new walls was as follows (Fig. 60). They began on the south, at the harbor edge, and incorporated the two seaward towers of the old Forte dello Sperone, now the Castel del Carmine, on which Ferrante had already done some rebuilding in 1468.[25] They then turned at right angles to the shore and ran north in a fairly straight stretch that included the Porta del Carmine and the Porta Nolana. According to a reconstruction by Giovanni Sepe they jogged inward at a point southeast of the Porta Capuana and began zigzagging northwest.[26] This section included the new Porta Capuana and, on the north end at

18. Leostello, *Effemeridi*, p. 165.

19. Morisani, *Letteratura*, p. 35; Leostello, *Effemeridi*, pp. 285, 287; and cf. ibid., p. 187 [Dec. 26, 1488] where Alfonso supervises the wall construction.

20. G. A. Summonte says only that the new eastern walls were completed before Ferrante's death, i.e. before January 25, 1494 (*Historia, 4*, 589).

21. G. Filangieri, *Documenti, 6*, 133.

22. Ibid., p. 42.

23. Here I follow Pietro Giannone, *Istoria, 3*, 444.

24. G. A. Summonte, *Historia, 1*, 245, and Camillo Tutini, *Origine de' seggi*, passim. For the appearance of these meeting places cf. Michelangelo Schipa, "Alcuni Opinioni intorno ai seggi o sedili di Napoli nel Medioevo," *NN, 15* (1906), 97–99, 113–15; and Benedetto Croce, "I Seggi di Napoli," *NN*, ser. 2, *1* (1920), 17–

19, where the author describes some of them as being four-sided porticoes with iron railings and with a closed room on one side; and R. di Stefano, "La Chiesa di Sant' Angelo a Nilo e il Seggio di Nido," *NN*, ser. 3, *4* (1964), 12–21.

25. Morisani, *Letteratura*, p. 31.

26. However older views of the city, which Sepe ignores, show this line as fairly straight (e.g. Lafrery, 1566 [Fig. 60], and Stoopendael, 1705 [Fig. 82]). For Lafrery see M. Schipa, "Una Pianta topografica di Napoli del 1566," *NN, 4* (1895), 161–66. Other early views of the city are less dependable, e.g. in the *Cosmographei* of Sebastian Münster, or that in Giulio Ballino, *Disegni delle più illustri città et fortezze del mondo*, etc., pt. I (Venice, 1549), pp. 14–15.

an unknown location, the Porta Santa Sofia (thereafter sometimes also known as the Porta San Giovanni).[27] The new walls then turned more directly west, near the Monastery of San Giovanni, where they joined the existing northern walls in this quarter. In all there were four new gates and twenty-one or twenty-two new towers.[28] (Not all of these are shown in Fig. 60, which includes Don Pietro di Toledo's modifications of the 1530s.)

The walls were between 5 and 7 meters thick, vertical in section, and made of a tufa core sheathed with 50-cm. slabs or lastre, of dark gray Vesuvian stone.[29] They were thus not composed of massive rectangular blocks like those in the original Greek defenses, which Pontano praised.[30] The towers, except for those flanking the gates, were solid. All seem to have been semicircular in plan with the exception of one or possibly two square ones at the shore.

Except for the Porta Capuana the gates were utilitarian (Figs. 61, 62).[31] They consisted of arched openings in curtain walls, with wide filleted marble archivolts and no imposts. Behind the curtain was a tunnel-vaulted entrance, 3 or 4 meters deep, and made of the same materials as the walls. Guardrooms[32] were located at the bases of the gate towers, and long straight staircases led within the adjacent wall sections to the ramparts. All the new gates, except possibly the Porta Santa Sofia, were set between pairs of towers.[33] The old bridges and moats were removed.[34] The backs of the towers were flat and undefended, probably so

27. G. A. Summonte, *Historia, 4,* 590, and De la Ville sur-Yllon, "Le Mura," p. 54. According to the latter, Don Pietro of Toledo moved the Porta San Gennaro forward and built new walls as far as the corner of Sant'Aniello, at which point he also built a new gate, the Porta di Costantinopoli.

28. Sepe, *Murazione,* pp. 10–11. De la Ville, "Le Mura," p. 53, says there were 27 towers and only 3 gates. Even more confusingly Bartolommeo Capasso in "La Vicaria Vecchia," *ASPN, 15* (1890), 423, says the new walls were carried all the way to the Porta Reale, near what is now the Gesù, but he does not say this happened during the 1484–90 campaigns. I know of no documents or sources corroborating the suggestion that new walls were built on the north at this time.

29. Sepe, *Murazione,* p. 16. In the *Journal* of Philippe de Vigneulles, who saw and described Naples and the Castel Nuovo in 1487, the walls were "tant espais que le plus gros chair c'on poult trouver eust bien allé pardessus et ung home de chacun couste tout a leur aixe; et les tours tout massices, fors des archières pour traire et estoient de xl pas en xl pas loing l'une de l'aultre, et tout de pierre de taille par dehors." From Philippe de Vigneulles, *Journal,* ed. H. Michelant, in *Bibliothek des Litterarischen Vereins in Stuttgart, 24* (1852), 22–23. L. Volpicella, in "Le Artiglierie di Castel Nuovo nell' anno 1500," *ASPN, 35* (1910), pp. 308–48, mistakenly attributes this description to 1499 and thinks it applies to the new western walls of those years (p. 310).

30. De la Ville sur-Yllon implies that such blocks

were used ("Le Mura," p. 53) but I follow Sepe who seems to have made a careful physical survey of the fabric, whatever his lack of literary documentation. Vigneulles' expression "pierre de taille par dehors" obviously means revetments. This type of construction can still be seen on the stretch of wall just north of the Porta Capuana.

31. Sepe's reconstruction of the gates is partly based on four drawings, at least one of them done in the nineteenth century, in the Archivio Storico del Commune di Napoli. He does not give dates for these (except for the one dated April 12, 1865). All are of the Porta del Carmine (Sepe, *Murazione,* pp. 6–7). Sepe also used plans in the Museo San Martino, but he gives no date for these either (ibid., p. 10). I have assumed that the other minor gates were like the one that still stands, the Porta Nolana, and that Sepe's own drawings are accurate.

32. These may have been later additions: G. Filangieri, *Documenti, 5,* 74, cites a contract of September 3, 1495, in which Alfonso and Fiorentino Cafaro are to make nine guardrooms in the towers of the walls of the city; which walls, he does not say. But this would have been just after Ferrandino retook Naples in May 1495, and before the French had been driven from the Castel Nuovo the following December, so it is likely that the guardrooms belonged to the eastern gates.

33. Sepe, *Murazione,* p. 14. The Porta Santa Sofia may have had only a single tower.

34. Cf. Giannone, *Historia, 3,* 444–45.

that the enemy, if he captured one, could not then attack the inhabitants from it (Cf. Alberti, *De re aed.*, IV, 4).

From the military or urbanistic viewpoint, there was little that was extraordinary in these arrangements. The walls were innocent of those deep ravelins, high scarps, and vaulted casemates in the design of which Alfonso's later architects were to be innovators. Nor do the layouts of the squares, the arcades, the fountains, and other amenities seem to have been particularly striking; indeed, the new wall system as depicted in a sixteenth-century relief by Giovanni da Nola (Fig. 74) is very much like that built thirty or forty years earlier by Alfonso I, and shown in the Strozzi panel (Fig. 4). Alfonso's first essay in urbanism and military architecture must be classified as traditional.

THE GATE SCULPTURE   The new eastern defense system made significant reference to the Barons' Revolt. On many of the new gates, perhaps on all, over the arch, were small, sculptured rectangular panels of white marble depicting profile equestrian figures. Smaller panels of the same material, carved with the arms of Aragon, were set below them on either side.[35] The Porta Nolana is the only surviving gate that still displays its equestrian panel (Fig. 67), but a second such plaque with its two subsidiaries[36] was removed from the Porta del Carmine in 1862 when that gate was demolished.[37] These are now in the Museo San Martino (Fig. 68).

The two designs are not identical. The Porta Nolana figure rides to the right (north), while the San Martino rider heads in the opposite direction. The latter's silhouette is more disciplined, and the horseman rides more stiffly, holding his sword ceremoniously upright as if in procession. He wears a crown, tournament armor, and a surcoat. The Porta Nolana figure is uncrowned and carries his sword diagonally, in a more threatening fashion, and both horse and rider turn outward toward the observer as the rider bends slightly forward. Both panels are probably from the workshop of Jacopo della Pila, though by different hands; the Museo San Martino relief indeed may be by Jacopo himself. The other carving is reminiscent of the hand that carved the two saints, Agnello (on the left) and Gennaro in the attic of the Porta Capuana, and perhaps also the putti carrying the shield in the central merlon of this gate.

While the face of the rider on the Porta del Carmine seems to be that of Alfonso of Calabria, it is inscribed FERDINANDUS REX NOBILISSIME PATRIAE, and the figure wears a crown. The explanation is that the inscription and crown are later. One can see, even in the photo-

35. Lorenzo Salazar, "Marmi di Porta Medina e di Porta Capuana," *NN, 10* (1901), 40–42.

36. They entered the Museum in 1873. Salazar was under the curious impression that they came from the Porta Capuana, and identifies the king on iconographic grounds as one of the Durazzo monarchs. For the controversy over all this see also Vittorio Spinazzola, "Due Marmi figurati nel Museo Nazionale di San Martino,"

NN, 10 (1901), 97–101, in which the author maintains for stylistic reasons that the San Martino sculpture must be Quattrocento and claims that the other similar relief on the Porta Nolana is of an older man. See letters, *NN, 10* (1901), 128, 143–44; and V. Spinazzola, "Porta Nolana," *NN, 15* (1906), 111.

37. De la Ville sur-Yllon, "Le Mura," p. 53.

graph, that the lettering has been carved in an area roughly chipped out below the ground of the rest of the relief. The change, from DUX ALPHONSUS CALABRIAE, or whatever, might have been made in honor of King Ferrandino's entry into the capital on July 7, 1495, when he had captured it from the French. Passero and Ferraiolo both confirm that the new king— his official name was of course Ferdinand—entered through this very gate, the Porta del Carmine.[38] The panel on the Porta Nolana, which also seems to be a portrait of Alfonso, has a similar chipped recession but no new inscription.

Since Alfonso was apparently advising on the construction of these new walls, his portrait was an appropriate ornament for their gates. Nor is there any reason why, later on, Ferrandino would have minded attaching his own name to his father's portrait. He had done the same with his new coin issues, as, indeed, had Alfonso before him, with coins bearing a portrait of Ferrante.[39]

These portraits belong to a tradition of equestrian symbolism that goes back to Conrad IV in the thirteenth century. According to this tradition, the horse represents the people of Naples while the bridle stands for royal power.[40] The two seggi located along the via Tribunali, Nido on the west and Capuana on the east, displayed two versions of this animal on their arms (Figs. 64, 65), and Summonte confirms that these images refer to kingly vs. baronial rule, i.e. rule by the seggi.[41] It is my opinion that the equestrian statue of Ladislas on his tomb is another development of this idea (Fig. 66). Here once again is Conrad's horse, symbolizing the people, but now the king has not only harnessed the animal, he has mounted it. At the same time the rider appears in tournament armor with his sword upraised: thus the image of a courtly champion is also present. Scipione Mazzella tells us that in this pose Ladislas is the defender of Christianity.[42] In other words (according to my interpretation) in this statue Ladislas the king-knight rides forth in the cause of the Faith, carried by a charger symbolizing his obedient subjects.

The compound significance of this image was carried on by the Aragonese rulers. Alfonso I had desired an equestrian statue of himself in the upper arch of Castel Nuovo. Crowned equestrian figures garbed for ceremonial combat also appear on the larger coins, the ducatoni or alfonsini d'oro of Alfonso I.[43] At the same time, a lesser coin, the cavallo, displays an unreined, riderless horse presumably signifying lesser, nonroyal power. Cavalli were issued by Ferrante (Fig. 63), though I know of no corresponding larger equestrian coins from his or

38. Passero, *Giornali*, pp. 76–77. The Castel Capuano surrendered that same morning. Cf. also R. Filangieri, *Cronaca figurata*, pl. LII, where Ferrandino is shown at the Porta del Carmine. (Sanudo, in "La Spedizione," pp. 501–02, incorrectly says Ferrandino entered through the Porta del Formello, near the Castel Capuano, and that this occurred on July 13.)

39. *Corpus nummorum italicorum* (Rome, 1940), *19*, pl. 9, fig. 4, and pl. 10, figs. 9, 10.

40. G. A. Summonte, *Historia*, *1*, 354. Carlo Celano, *Notizie del bello dell'antico e del curioso della* *città di Napoli*, ed. G. B. Chiarini, 2 (Naples, 1856), 311–14; Gaetano Filangieri, "La Testa di cavallo in bronzo già di casa Maddaloni," *ASPN*, 7 (1882), 407–20; and Antonio Filangieri, "La colossale Testa di cavallo in bronzo del Museo Nazionale di Napoli," *Arte e Storia* (Oct. 15, 1901).

41. G. A. Summonte, *Historia*, 2, 354. Cf. also Scipione Mazzella, *Descrittione del regno di Napoli* (Naples, 1586), p. 482, and B. Croce, "I Seggi," p. 17.

42. Mazella, *Descrittione*, p. 344.

43. *Corpus nummorum italicorum*, 19, pl. 4, fig. 6.

his son's reigns. Nonetheless, such coins would have been in circulation in the 1480s and 1490s, and their inscriptions, which refer to God's aid to the king against the throne's enemies, would have been a common interpretation for this type of portrait.[44]

Ferrante and Alfonso II carried on the Conradian tradition in a different way. In 1484, during the excavations for the new walls, a second antique horse was found. This one was of marble, without head or legs. Like Conrad before him, Ferrante converted the find into a symbol of the crown—we are unfortunately not told exactly how—and set it up over the entrance to the Castel dell'Ovo.[45] Thus the original tradition was now confirmed by a second find, which had actually occurred in the context of the new defense program. Not only was this second horse associated specifically with the new walls, it also became part of a fortified gate. We might note in passing that one of the functions of the ruling committees of each seggio was to guard its gate; they sometimes actually lived in the towers.[46]

All this would have reinforced the emanations of royal power implicit in the equestrian figure, and these would have been especially marked just after the settlement of the revolt. When the Porta del Carmine and the Porta Nolana were erected with their equestrian portraits, they were not merely general expressions of royal supremacy but specific reminders of the recent refounding of the Conradian tradition. They proclaimed that it was by permission of the figure they portrayed, Alfonso of Calabria, heir to the throne, builder of these defenses, and hero of the recent war, that access to the seggi was now provided.[47]

GIULIANO DA MAIANO AND THE PORTA CAPUANA   In the spring of 1485, five years before the new walls were finished, Giuliano da Maiano arrived in Naples. He brought with him a reputation as a far-ranging artistic administrator and as the architectural half of an important partnership in Florence, where his brother Benedetto was chargé d'af-

44. Ibid. Pontano in one of the *Lyra,* "Laudes Alphonsi Ducis Calabriae de victoria hydruntina" (VII, 33ff.), points out many of these same aspects of the hero of Otranto as he returns in triumph and begins the reconstruction of his capital: "Ensis ille est, quo totiens Ameti / Terga verterunt trepidae cohortes; / Hasta et illa est, qua cecidere pulsae / In mare turmae; / Ille equus, quo fulmineo sequente / Persicum in fossas violenter agmen / Est datum praeceps: age, 'io triumphe' / Dicite vulgus. . . . / Hiccine Alphonsus patriae receptor, / Hostium victor, pepulit qui ab oris / Italis classem argolicam et furentes / Contudit ictus? Ite dis nostris meritos honores / Solvite; ornentur fora, templa, et aedes, / Atria argento niteant, fluatque / Molle falernum." A comparable relief of about the same size and date as that in the Museo San Martino is now in the Louvre. It is from the tomb of Roberto Malatesta (1484) and was formerly in St. Peter's.

45. G. A. Summonte, *Historia, 2,* 354.

46. G. Toffanin, Jr., "I Seggi di Napoli," *Il Fuidoro*

3 (1956), 16–27, esp. 16–17.

47. Access to the gates was not merely symbolic. Capaccio, in *Il Forastiero* (Naples, 1634), p. 809, says the Aragonese decreed that every gate had to have two keys, one to be held by the nobili and the other by the popoli or tradesmen. Meanwhile the symbolism of the reined horse was pursued in Charles V's triumph in 1535: two nobili guided the Emperor's horse as he toured the city, the guides being changed as he entered each new seggio (G. A. Summonte, *Historia, 5,* 192). This association of the equestrian image with power over the seggi appeared even in the nineteenth century. Thus Vincenzo Florio, in his *Memorie storiche,* a manuscript in the Biblioteca Società di Storia Patria, Naples (XXVI.D.14 pt. 6, fol. 31), records that in 1801, after Ferdinand I had suppressed them, the meeting places of the seggi were destroyed or converted to other purposes. The structure belonging to the Seggio al Porto however was preserved, either to house or support an equestrian statue of the king.

faires and sculptor.[48] Giuliano's work in the 1460s for the Pazzi family and on the Palazzo dello Strozzino (1462) had established him as one of Brunelleschi's and Michelozzo's more gifted followers (Figs. 15, 16). His first important extra-Florentine commission, for widening the nave and choir and building a new sacristy for the Collegiata in San Gimignano, is recorded in a contract of July 16, 1466. This was followed in 1468 and 1475 by the Santa Fina Chapel in the same church, on which he collaborated with his brother, and by work in Siena and Arezzo.[49] On April 2, 1477, Giuliano reached a high level in the Florentine architectural bureaucracy when he was appointed capomaestro of the Opera del Duomo. In this capacity, however, he accomplished little, and he held the post intermittently.[50] His collaboration with Benedetto continued, mainly for export purposes, though in Florence the two brothers had helped decorate interiors in the Palazzo Vecchio after 1473. In 1478–80 they executed the tabernacle in the Church of the Madonna dell'Ulivo in Prato (now in the cathedral); and it was presumably as early as the next year that Giuliano's advice was needed for new work at the Basilica of the Santa Casa in Loreto.[51] We know he visited that city in 1481, on his way probably stopping at Urbino.[52]

There is a spirit of revivalism in Giuliano's architecture. Though his palaces at first seem seriously severe, even fortress-like, on prolonged examination they begin to take on a mock-Gothic quality, or at least a certain self-consciousness. Unlike those of Michelozzo, which they otherwise resemble, Giuliano's palaces screen the street corridor rather than immuring it. The facade seems at once to float upward and apart, its components restrained only by the resolute geometry of the silhouette. Thus in the Strozzino, for example, the visual weight moves downward in Michelozzo's lower floor; but it moves upward, to climax with the cornice, in Giuliano's upper floors. The courtyard of another palace attributed to Giuliano, the Pazzi-Quaratesi (1458–69?) in Florence (Fig. 16), is equally self-conscious and economical, and also a stern throwback to Brunelleschi, to whom it was long attributed.

Giuliano's administrative bent and his experience outside Florence helped make him potentially a useful collaborator for the Duke of Calabria. But he had his shortcomings. He

48. The main relevant items are C. von Fabriczy, "Giuliano da Maiano in Siena," *Jahrbuch der preussischen Kunstsammlungen,* 24 (1903), 137–76, 320–37; and Rolfs, *Laurana,* where on pp. 238–41 he corrects Vasari's account of Giuliano's work in Naples.

49. Fabriczy, "Giuliano in Siena," p. 140.

50. Paatz, *Die Kirchen von Florenz* (Frankfurt, 1952), 3, 334–35.

51. Fabriczy, "Toscanische und oberitalienische Künstler im Diensten der Aragonesen zu Neapel," *Repertorium für Kunstwissenschaft,* 20 (1897), 87, Doc. 1. Cf. also Luitpold Dussler, *Benedetto da Maiano* (Munich, 1924), p. 38. Benedetto also worked at Loreto, executing the lavabo and Evangelist tondi in the shrine church in 1484–87.

52. L. Venturi, "Studii sul Palazzo Ducale di Urbino," *L'Arte,* 17 (1914), 456–59, where some of the intarsias are attributed to Giuliano. Cf. also Johann Gaye, *Carteggio inedito d'artisti dei secoli XIV, XV, XVI,* 1 (Florence, 1839), 224, which shows that Lorenzo de Medici received a drawing by Giuliano of the ducal palace at Urbino on June 18, 1481. For the Palazzo Pazzi-Quaratesi, Florence, discussed below, see Arnoldo Moscato, *Il Palazzo Pazzi a Firenze* (Rome, 1963), which makes the attribution to Giuliano, and Howard Saalman, "The Authorship of the Pazzi Palace," *Art Bulletin,* 46 (1964), 388–94, which tentatively claims Giuliano da Sangallo as designer, and gives the building a date toward the end of the century.

had no particular reputation as a scholar of antiquity, nor could he boast important achievements as an urban planner or hydraulic engineer.[53] He was the perfect architect for the villas, but with the other municipal works he was entering relatively unknown territory.

Giuliano's traveling expenses from Florence to Naples were paid by the Duke on March 2, 1485.[54] The architect arrived some time before the following April 27, when he received a bay mule and 96 ducats for designs and models of an unspecified joint project for the Duke and Ferrante.[55] The joint nature of the transaction probably excludes the two villas and suggests some public project; the payment is accordingly regarded as having been for the main gate in the new eastern walls, the Porta Capuana.[56]

The Roman Porta Capuana had been the principal eastern entrance to Naples and had stood across the city's central decumanus, the via Tribunali (Fig. 1).[57] A medieval replacement had been erected somewhat to the east, and this served as the entrance to the eastern citadel, the Castel Capuano, which stood partly inside and partly outside the walls.[58] The third Porta Capuana was built even farther east (Fig. 60) so that the walls on either side of it brought the citadel entirely inside the city. The new gate also had other functions: it stopped the axis of the new avenue leading to Poggioreale, and it maintained at least the memory of its earlier relationships with the Castel Capuano and the via SS Apostoli. This was apparently what led Giuliano to set it at an angle to the southern walls so that, instead of being a climax in a flat continuum like the Porta Nolana, it marked a change of direction.

Not until two years after Giuliano presented his designs did work begin. In August 1487 the architect returned to Naples after a stay in Florence,[59] and on September 10 Giulio Marinis de Cava contracted to build the two flanking towers and complete the surrounding wall.[60] Seven months later, on April 15, 1488, "Maestro Jacopo della Pila da Milano" sup-

53. Cf. Vasari, 2, 468: "sebbene andò unpezzo Giuliano alla scuola di grammatica, non vi ebbe mai il capo, e per conseguenza non vi fece frutto nessuno." On the other hand Vasari (2, 470) does give Giuliano credit for the waterworks at Poggioreale, and the architect is said to have created fortifications at Montepoggiolo (according to Lorenzo Cèndali, Giuliano e Benedetto da Maiano, Florence, 1926, p. 172).

54. Fabriczy, "Toscanische und oberitalienische," p. 87.

55. Ibid., and N. Barone, "Le Cedole di tesoreria dell' archivio di stato di Napoli dal 1460 al 1504," ASPN, 9 (1884), 604.

56. Cf. E. Percopo, "Nuovi Documenti su gli scrittori e gli artisti dei tempi aragonesi," ASPN, 19 (1894), 560–91; Fabriczy, "Toscanische und oberitalienische," p. 87; Cèndali, Giuliano e Benedetto, p. 48, and Pane, Architettura, pp. 92–98.

57. The first version of it stood as far west as the cathedral, on what is now the Via Duomo (G. A. Summonte, Historia, 1, 52). According to De la Ville sur-Yllon, "Le Mura e le porte," p. 50, in Roman times

each of the three decumani had had terminal gates, and the Porta Cumana then stood at the eastern end of the middle decumanus. De la Ville speculates on the architectural character of these Roman gates, basing his conclusions on remains found when the finial designed by Francesco Picchiati in front of San Domenico Maggiore was erected in c. 1656. At that time fragments of the Roman gate were found. Picchiati made a drawing of them. De la Ville also says there was a Roman gate with flanking towers on the Via Tribunali near the Church of the Croce di Lucca (i.e. near the present Policlinico).

58. Marino Sanudo refers to another, adjacent gate, which he wrongly says Ferrandino used in 1495 in order to enter the city (see above, n. 38). This he calls the "Porta di Formello, a lato del Castello di Capua, quale era stata abandonata" (Sanudo, "La Spedizione," pp. 501–02).

59. Fabriczy, "Toscanische und oberitalienische," p. 88; cf. also Leostello, Effemeridi, p. 132: "Et sua I. S. comincio a dare ordine a fare fabrica et mando per messer Juliano designatore a fiorenze."

60. G. Filangieri, Documenti, 6, 120.

plied marble for the gate itself (which is in line with my idea that Jacopo also carved some of the sculpture).[61] Work probably still continued in July 1492, two years after Giuliano's death.[62] Riccardo Filangieri has recorded a visit by Benedetto da Maiano to Naples in the following August, and it is possible that this had to do with completing the gate Benedetto's late brother had designed.[63] Nothing in the extant sculpture on the Porta Capuana, however, suggests Benedetto's hand. One can only assume that if he did make a contribution it was the frieze that formerly decorated the attic and was removed in 1535. In any case the gate was probably not actually completed until May 2, 1494. On this day Goffré Borgia made his ceremonial entrance through what was only now for the first time called by Ferraiolo the "Porta nova de Capoana."[64] I conclude that although the gate may have been designed in 1485 it was not completed until some time between July 1492 and May 1494.[65]

Given its location and distinguished architect, the Porta Capuana is suitably more elaborate than the earlier eastern gates (Figs. 69, 70, 75, 77). It retains from them, however, the flanking towers, the single round-arched opening with continuous archivolt uninterrupted by imposts, and something of their look of being screen walls attached to deep, barrel-vaulted passages. In its battlements it also continues, or paraphrases, forms from the other eastern gates.

The Porta Capuana also relates to the tradition of royal gates that had been established in the Angevin tombs and then transferred to the Castel Nuovo by Alfonso I. Thus, like the earlier Aragonese arches it faced a broad irregular piazza with a boulevard leading from it, and it still functioned, in spirit at least, as the entrance to a royal residence. The cornice corresponds in almost every detail to a drawing in the Codex Vallardi (Fig. 76), a sketchbook used by Castel Nuovo artists in the 1450s. There are also formal parallels to be made with the Castel Nuovo gates—e.g. the flanking towers and the attic niches. The latter recall the niches in the upper part of the Arch of Alfonso I, and the saints within them can be likened to the allegorical figures at the summit of the earlier structure. In the spandrels of Giuliano's

61. Fabriczy, "Toscanische und oberitalienische," p. 113.

62. G. Filangieri, Documenti, 6, 307, though this is only the recognition of a debt on the part of Sele di Antonio Ponte, scalpellino, and his brother Baccino, to Giovanni Grande for sums received for work on the Porta Capuana. The work itself may have been executed earlier.

63. R. Filangieri, "Rassegna critica," ASPN, 63 (1938), 273, citing vol. 145 of the Cedole di Tesoreria, fol. 205t (now destroyed). Perhaps this is the place to mention the famous "scrittoio." Vasari, 3, 334, says Benedetto "n'ebbe il re Alfonso di Napoli un fornimento d'uno scrittoio, fatto fare per ordine di Giuliano, zio di Benedetto [sic], che serviva il detto re nelle cose d'architettura; dove esso Benedetto si transferì: ma non gli piacendo la stanza, se ne tornò a Firenze." So far as I know Vasari's statement has never been related to

Riccardo Filangieri's document from the cedole. It is perfectly possible that the 1492 visit was partly connected with this project, as well as with the Porta Capuana.

64. R. Filangieri, Cronaca figurata, pp. 87–90.

65. Pane, Architettura, pp. 97–98, shows that the trophies carved on the archivolt predate 1535, since they were reproduced by Romolo Balsimelli in the chapel of Ettore Carafa, Count of Ruvo, in San Domenico Maggiore, finished in 1511. The date of 1485–88 for the gate, which I gave in a recent article ("Alfonso II Benedetto e Giuliano da Maiano e la Porta Reale di Napoli," NN, n.s., 4, 1964, 77–95) and which has always been more or less the received one, can refer only to the design and commencement of the work. Other writers have more prudently left the matter vague.

arch, Victories rush to honor the triumphator who passes beneath (Fig. 77) as they do in the earlier monument (Fig. 78), though the figures in the Porta Capuana are scrawny and fatuous compared to the earlier ones. Finally, one should add the arrangement of figure sculpture, which is divided into zones generally corresponding to those in the earlier arches (cf. Figs. 7 and 70). Thus immediately above the arch proper is an attic with end pavilions, and there was probably once a processional frieze across the center, as on the Arch of Alfonso I. Also, above the main cornice, the heraldic carving with its two putti in the center merlon is related to the corresponding sculpture on Ferrante's arch.[66]

The Porta Capuana is nonetheless essentially different from its Neapolitan predecessors, for it expands solidly and confidently between its towers. Giuliano has achieved this effect by slightly detaching his structure from its towers with a narrow segment of wall on either side. Thus the shadows of the detailing sink back against a flat frame and do not spill onto the towers, which is what happens in the Arch of Alfonso I, and which helps spoil its resoluteness. Giuliano has added to this effect of a separate building by raking the top of the wide upper corona. The lateral consoles under the cornice are then set at angles to suggest a pent roof carried around the sides. The weight, density, and height of the attic and parapet give the sense of a lintel carried on heavy piers, which rise with vast solidity to meet its weight. At the same time symbolic battlements are carried across the top of the structure, linking themselves rhythmically to the real battlements of the towers, and forming an upper frame for the arch, a slot into which it is set. Thus does Giuliano succeed, despite his program of arched screen wall between towers, in suggesting the independent three-dimensional quality of a triumphal arch all'antica.

The internal organization of Giuliano's gate is also quite different from the earlier compositions. Where the latter, especially the Castel Nuovo Arch, are rich, layered, and repetitive, Giuliano's is vertical and differentiated, a taut wide-banded rectangular frame within which the archivolt flows in a generous curve, echoing in size and in its course the outward curves of the towers. The source of Giuliano's conception could have been the Porta Romana at Capua, then thought to be a relic of Barbarossa.[67] In the Quattrocento one also sees such archivolts in the Palazzo Pazzi-Quaratesi and in the large, deep embrasures of the Ducal Palace at Urbino. The nave of the Badia at Fiesole has similar arches, on a more portal-like

66. Another interesting link between Giuliano's arch and earlier Aragonese work is that its cornice (Fig. 75) corresponds almost exactly to one drawn in the Codex Vallardi, a dismembered Quattrocento sketchbook now in the Louvre (Fig. 76), containing work by Pisanello and others, and which is associated with Pisanello's Neapolitan sojourn in 1448–50, and with the Arch of Alfonso I. Both designs consist of a delicate anthemiated cyma recta on top, with a beaded astragal (or, in the case of the Porta Capuana, bead and reel) under it. Then come a small fillet, and a narrow, fluted corona with rosetted soffit supported on floriated consoles with

blank vertical panels between. Next there is a deep-cut egg-and-dart ovolo, another fillet, then narrow, sharp dentils separated by thin slots, and finally at the bottom a cyma reversa, unemphatic in profile and enriched with leaf-and-tongue carvings.

67. Cf. Giacomo de Nicola, "Un Disegno della Porta di Capua di Federico II," *L'Arte*, *11* (1908), 384–85. The sketch is found in MS 3528, fol. 51v, in the Osterreichisches Nationalbibliotek, Misc. XVI Jahrh., with inscriptions said to be in the hands of Fra Giocondo and another person. Cf. also the more famous Uffizi A333v, possibly by Francesco di Giorgio.

scale. Then there is the system of side chapels in San Lorenzo, Florence, where the narrow continuous archivolt is provided with a consoled keystone, as in the Porta Capuana, and suspended within a rectangular pilastered bay with tall entablature (Fig. 71). An equally possible prototype is the bay system of the Palazzo Rucellai, with its much wider, heavier membering (Fig. 72). One could almost say that the Porta Capuana combines the plasticity of Brunelleschi's bay with the bolder abstraction of Alberti's. A similar combination of the two ideas had occurred around the opening of the Chapel of the Cardinal of Portugal in San Miniato, Florence, and this monument was to have other Neapolitan repercussions as well (see Chapter 8).

The sculptural detail of the Porta Capuana supports the implications of its architecture and function: it is thoroughly military. The carved trophies filling the pulvinated frieze of the archivolt are dense and bristling, though they hang from ribbons. The source of the idea may be the Temple of Vespasian in Rome, but on that building the arms and trophies are spotted at stately intervals. In the lateral weapon frieze on the Augustan arch at Pula, Yugoslavia—drawings of which may have existed in Naples since it had formed the model for the lower part of Alfonso I's frontispiece—there is something like the density of Giuliano's frieze. There are also the so-called portals of war in the Ducal Palace in Urbino.

Giuliano's frieze, however, is unlike these others in that it curves like a wreath—or like those framing vines one often sees in Renaissance sculpture, that twine together after rising from urns. One thinks of Verrocchio's Medici tomb in San Lorenzo and of Benedetto da Maiano's Strozzi tomb in Santa Maria Novella. In making this vine of weapons, Giuliano has transformed his archivolt into a kind of trophy-garden: the seized armaments of the defeated barons form an arbor for their grave.

Stylistically, the most striking thing about the gate is its Albertianism. In this sense it is a culmination of the Neapolitan architectural tendencies discussed in the first chapter. One possible immediate source of this influence was the appearance in 1485, the year the Porta Capuana was designed, of the first printed edition of *De re aedificatoria.* Although Alberti recommends the three-arched, free-standing triumphal arch rather than the towered portal, he does suggest that a triumphal arch may be a city gate.[68] He even adds that this was its usual function in antiquity and that, since it was ornamented with the trophies of defeated foes, it was often kept as a relic after the adjacent walls had been removed. In this connection, however, an even more Albertian city gate had been begun in 1475 by Alberti's assistant Agostino di Duccio in Perugia (Fig. 73), and it may have been this rather than the book that influenced Giuliano.[69] Agostino's gate is taken directly from the lower story of the

---

68. *De re aedificatoria,* VIII, 6. There is no evidence however that Alfonso of Calabria or any of the other Aragonese kings possessed a copy of Alberti's book. For the date of its composition, and the transmission of Alberti's thought, see Cecil Grayson, "Alberti's 'Decem Libri de re aedificatoria,' " *Münchner Jahrbuch, 11* (1960), 152–61.

69. Andy Pointner, *Die Werke des florentinischen Bildhauers Agostino d'Antonio di Duccio* (Strassburg, 1909), pp. 202–05. The interior gate dates from the 1300s. The outer one was begun in 1447 by Bartolommeo Mattioli da Torgiano. Agostino's original model (c. 1475) called for flanking towers, which would have brought it even more into line with the Porta Capuana.

Tempio Malatestiano, though the columns en ressaut have here become pilasters. Again, the architrave moves clear around the opening, without emphasized impost blocks.[70]

The final point about the Porta Capuana is that its present bare attic goes back not to Giuliano's original structure but to 1535, when Charles V entered the city. On this occasion the original decoration was removed and the arms of the Hapsburgs, with balancing inscriptions, were substituted.[71] I have suggested that the original attic relief was made by Benedetto da Maiano and that it was put in position in August 1492. Unfortunately, I know of no early view that will tell us what this sculpture was like. (The view in Fig. 74 was made after Charles' visit.[72]) There have been conflicting opinions about the subject matter. All agree that it contained a likeness of Ferrante, but some say it was a coronation portrait and others an equestrian. Modern scholarship inclines to the former view,[73] which stems from a book by Camillo Tutini and which was repeated by Pietro Giannone in his famous history.

What Tutini actually says, however, is that a coronation panel was made but not put in place.[74] In any case, Tutini is unreliable; he wrote in 1641, more than a hundred years after the original panel was removed. In contrast G. A. Summonte, who wrote almost half a century earlier and who could even have been an infant witness to Charles' arrival, says that a "crowned equestrian" rather than a "coronation" portrait of Ferrante was made for the gate, and that it *was* put in place. Summonte's version is more persuasive than Tutini's, for we have already seen what good reasons there were for an equestrian portrait at the entrance to a seggio—especially for this one, whose own arms featured a riderless horse. Finally, such a soldierly figure would be an appropriate climax for a structure whose other sculpture is so unremittingly military.

I thus assume that like the other eastern gates the Porta Capuana was a monument to the settlement of the Barons' Revolt, this time depicting the King instead of the Duke of Cala-

70. I have found only two derivatives of the Porta Capuana, both rather distant. One is the portal of the Palazzo Affaitati, in Bari, and the other (less distant) the Cappella Ruvo in San Domenico Maggiore, already mentioned (cf. Pane, *Architettura*, pp. 97–98). I might here quote again from Pontano's victory poem (above, n. 44), ll. 13ff.: "Cernite avulsos clipeos lacertis, / Cernite abreptas humeris pharetras, / Medicos dextris gladios, madentis / Sanguine cristas." This clearly suggests the thick groupings of enemy spoils that decorate the archivolt of the Porta Capuana.

71. G. A. Summonte, *Historia, 4*, 589–90.

72. The tomb of Don Pietro of Toledo is in the presbytery behind the high altar of San Giacomo degli Spagnuoli. It was commissioned in 1539, but Don Pedro did not die until 1553 and the monument was not finally assembled until 1570. (T. C. I., *Napoli e dintorni*, Milan, 1960, s.v.)

73. See also Vasari, *2*, 484. Milanesi gives all the sculpture to Giovanni da Nola, dating it 1535. De la Ville sur-Yllon ("Le Mura e le porte," p. 54) simply says Benedetto did the sculpture and that a portrait of Ferrante (not otherwise described) was removed from the center of the gate in 1535. He adds that a (presumably sculptured) Coronation of Ferrante by Benedetto stood in the added upper nicchione of 1656, which he takes as a part of Giuliano's original conception. I go into all this quite fully in my "Porta Reale," p. 93, n. 15.

74. Camillo Tutini, *Dell'Origine e fundation de seggi di Napoli* (Naples, 1644), pp. 11–12 and Giannone, *Istoria, 3*, 444. Giannone then immediately contradicts himself saying that Ferrante's portrait was removed in 1537 (p. 445). Cf. G. A. Summonte, *Historia, 4*, 589–90. Summonte mentions that the two saints are more recent than the rest of the sculpture, and quotes the now-vanished dedicatory inscription to Charles V (*Historia, 5*, 190–91).

bria. Indeed by exploiting the precedent of earlier royal gates as it did, the Porta Capuana suggests that the whole city was now a kind of royal seggio.[75] In its sculpture, meanwhile, it fitted in well with the admonitory tradition of Aragonese portraiture then being established in the other gates and in Laurana's Frick portrait of Ippolita Sforza.

75. De Dominici tells an anecdote about the Porta Capuana (Bernardo De Dominici, *Vite de' pittori, scultori, ed architetti napoletani*, etc., *3*, Naples, 1744, 332–33). In the summer of 1656, he says, Mattia Preti came to Naples and got into a fight with the guards at one of the city gates when he tried to enter. The city had been closed to visitors because of a plague. The artist, later repenting in jail, offered to paint frescoes of the Immaculate Conception over each of the gates. This offer was accepted by the authorities. (Cf. also Bartolommeo Capasso, "Sull' Annedoto riguardante gli affreschi del cav. Calabrese sopra le porte di Napoli," *ASPN, 3,* 1878, 597–605.) The scene over the Porta Capuana consisted of the Immaculate Conception with Saints Gennaro and Francesco Saverio kneeling on either side of the Virgin and, standing at her left, Santa Rosalia. I know nothing of documents for erecting the upper niche that housed this scene, unless a phrase in the contract Capasso publishes, about Mattia having to provide the necessary materials for his work, refers to it. But in any case by the time the painter set to work there was such an upper arch or niche on the Porta Capuana. It was flat and subdued in detailing, almost Neoclassical. And, of course, it brought Giuliano's gate into conformity with the ruling Neapolitan formula of the two-story portal. The niche was not removed until the Porta Capuana was restored just before World War II. A large drawing for a similar scene, by Preti, is now in Capodimonte.

Chapter 5: POGGIOREALE, LA DUCHESCA, AND THE PALAZZO DEI TRIBUNALI

HE IDEA OF THE VILLAS   In many ways the most important part of the renewal consisted of Alfonso's new villa, Poggioreale (now destroyed), and the projected Palazzo dei Tribunali. These made important contributions to the history of planning, and they throw light on the Neapolitan work of Giuliano da Maiano, Francesco di Giorgio, and Giuliano da Sangallo.

Ancient writers anticipate some of the ideas that produced Poggioreale. Columella notes that the villa urbana, or manor, should have separate dining and living rooms for the different seasons, and promenades that exploit the changing airs (*De re rustica,* I, 6). This desire to orient the house as a kind of breeze or temperature trap is reflected in the Renaissance in Sannazaro's description of his own villa: "Some chambers look west, others east; these grasp the north wind, while those restrain the south."[1] The two Campanian villas belonging to Manilius Vopiscus and Pollius Felix, described in the *Sylvae,* are also relevant. Over Manilius' villa, Statius exclaims: "How beautiful beyond human art the enchanted scene! Nature has never indulged herself further" (*Sylvae,* I, iii, ll. 15ff.). Like Pontano in *Lepidina,* Statius evokes the sound of water over stones. The house bridges a river and its gardens are decorated with gilded beams, marble friezes, statues of nymphs in caves, and gold and ivory figures (ibid., 35ff.). It is a true marriage altar, a thalamus for water and marble. And Pollius' villa, near Naples, is thus described:

> Between the famous walls [of the city] named for the sirens, and the cliff burdened by the temple to the Tyrrhenian Minerva [at Sorrento], a lofty villa looks out upon Dicharcus' deeps [the Bay of Naples] [ibid., II, ii, 1ff.].

This villa was approached by the "queen of long roads," the via Appia, and had a portico "in urban style" (ibid., II, ii, 10–12). Another antique villa worth mentioning here is that of Trimalchio in the *Satyricon,* 77, which consisted of large dining rooms surrounded by cubicles: "It has four dining rooms," says its owner, "twenty bedrooms, two marble porticoes, and an upstairs room for dining."[2] One should add that two of these villas certainly, and the third quite possibly, were near Naples.[3] From these accounts we can derive a com-

1. *Elegies,* III, 3, "Deos nemorum invocat. In exstruanda domo," ll. 39ff.

2. *Saturae,* ed. F. Buechler (Berlin, 1958), p. 91: "habet quatuor cenationes, cubicula vigintii, porticus marmoratas duas, suam cenationem [or cellationem]." Cf. Theodor Mommsen, "Trimalchios Heimath und Grabschrift," *Hermes, 13* (1878), 106–21; and idem,

"Inschrift Pollius Felix," *Hermes, 18* (1883), 158–60.

3. Mommsen, "Trimalchios Heimath," thinks Petronius' villa may have been near Baia. Cf. Enrico Cocchia, "Napoli e il Satyricon di Petronio Arbitro," *ASPN, 18* (1893), 278–315; and Amedeo Maiuri, *La Cena di Trimalchione di Petronio Arbitro* (Naples, 1945).

posite classical villa just outside Naples, standing in an elaborate garden with pools and moving waters, where the house is oriented to the changing seasons and has porticoes and a triclinium surrounded by small chambers; all of these were characteristics of Poggioreale.

The pleasures afforded by such places were given a moral explanation by Pontano. He speaks of it in *De splendore:*

> We wish him [the villa owner] to have gardens in which to exercise by walking, or for banquets as the occasion demands. The gardens will have exotic plants and excellent little trees, very artfully and properly arranged. In them topiary work in myrtle, box, citrus, and rosemary is most highly to be recommended. For the raison d'être of gardens should not be the same for the splendid man as for the thrifty and gain-seeking father of a family. The gardens contribute wonderfully to the splendor of the villa, which is not rustic but a magnificent villa urbana. For a splendid man ought to shine not only in the city but in the country, lest when he abandon the cares of the former he should seem to pass from light to shadow.[4]

Pontano goes on to evoke the memories of Lucullus' famous villa on Pizzofalcone—again emphasizing the villa as a dining place—and elsewhere he echoes the more common view of it as a retreat after strife (in *De amore conjugali*).[5] Also, the *Hendecasyllabi* are full of poems and epigrams in which the courtiers picture themselves leading their villa life as rustics or satyrs.[6]

This Renaissance revival of antique traditions and attitudes can be joined to the surviving conception of the medieval pleasure garden, and specifically of the great park Robert the Wise had built at Castel Nuovo, which had been rebuilt by Alfonso I and Ferrante. This too possessed varieties of trees, shrubs, walks, and retreats, like Pontano's ideal villa, and was surrounded by walls. It contained summer houses, a "ritretto" with a gilden wooden soffit, a fountain with a gilded roof, wild animals, and cages of exotic birds. In 1474, two years after Jacopo della Pila built his fountains here,[7] a frescoed "nuova camera" was constructed.[8]

---

4. From the Venice, 1518 ed., 140r: "Quem etiam hortos habere volumus, in quibus exerceri deambulationes, et convivia fieri pro tempore possint. Erunt autem horti hi ex peregrinis, et egregiis arbusculis artificiose, decenterque dispositi. In quibus e myrto, buxo, citrio, rore marino topiarum opus potissimum commendatur, neque enim quae parco, ac lucroso patri familiae, eadem splendido homini hortorum ratio esse debet. Conferunt etiam mirum in modum ad splendorem ipsum villae, non illae quidem rusticano ex opere, sed urbano, et magnifico. Oportet enim non in urbe solum, verum etiam rure splendescere nitidi hominis supellectilem, ne siquando secedendum fuerit ab urbanis negotiis, tanquam e luce in tenebras migrasse videatur."

5. *De amore coniugali*, II, "villam salutat a militia

regressus." For the site and character of Lucullus' villa see G. A. Galante, *Memorie dell' antico cenobio lucullano di San Severino abate in Napoli* (Naples, 1869), and, more important, Giulio Pane, "La Villa Carafa e la storia urbanistica di Pizzofalcone," *NN*, ser. 3, 4 (1964), 133–48, esp. 134 and n. 7. This villa is thought to have stood on the hill of Pizzofalcone and not, as used to be believed, on the site of the Castel dell'Ovo.

6. *Hendecasyllabi*, II, 20, "Ad Antonium Galateum," and "De Alphonsi Ducis Calabriae et Albini munusculus," ll. 15ff.

7. R. Filangieri, "Rassegna critica," *ASPN*, 63 (1938), 285–86.

8. Ibid., p. 264.

THE BUILDING OF POGGIOREALE   Everyone now agrees that Poggioreale was designed by Giuliano da Maiano.[9] Although the documents for Giuliano's work in the spring of 1485 are ambiguous, and we have supposed that this work included designs for the Porta Capuana, it is also possible that drawings were then made for one or both of the villas. But if so, work on them, like work on the gate, would have been interrupted by the Barons' Revolt. The definitive construction of Poggioreale probably did not begin until February 17, 1487, when Alfonso "began to give orders to build buildings, and sent for Messer Juliano the architect at Florence."[10] On May 29 Giuliano Gondi was paid 29 ducats on account with the architect, who was still in Florence though now working for the Duke; on August 8 a further payment of 232 ducats was made;[11] on August 29 Biasino d'Antonio Castruzzo, carter, was paid for transporting "two models from Florence to Naples for the design of a palace";[12] and finally on August 30 Giuliano himself arrived.[13] I assume that these models were for Poggioreale (and possibly La Duchesca) and that they were completed in Florence by Giuliano in the summer of 1487. Thus when the architect arrived in Naples in the autumn it was to supervise the execution of the new houses as well as to build the Porta Capuana.

The site of Poggioreale, a mile or so east of the city walls, was on the road to Capua. It was well above the shore, at the top of a marshy slope leading down to the Bay (Fig. 82).

9. P. Summonte in Nicolini, L'Arte napoletana, p. 172. For the villa itself see A. Colombo, "Il Palazzo e il Giardino di Poggioreale," ASPN, 10 (1885), 186–209, 309–42; ibid., NN, 1 (1892), 117–20, 136–38, 166–68. The NN article is a digest of that in ASPN but with illustrations. Cf. also Fabriczy, "Giuliano da Maiano," Jahrbuch der preussischen Kunstsammlungen, 24 (1903), Supplement, 137–76 esp. p. 144; Henny Weber, Achsialität und Symmetrie im Grundriss des italienischen Profanbaus, etc. (Berlin, 1937), p. 33; Fritz Schreiber, Die französische Renaissance-Architektur und die Poggio-Reale Variationen des Sebastiano Serlio (Halle, 1938); Christoph Luitpold Frommel, Die Farnesina und Peruzzis Architektonisches Frühwerk (Berlin, 1961), pp. 90–97; and J. S. Ackerman, "Sources of the Renaissance Villa," Acts of the Twentieth International Congress of the History of Art, 2 (Princeton, 1963), 6–18. Bernardino Baldi, in "Descrizione del Palazzo Ducale di Urbino," published in Memorie concernanti la città di Urbino [1588] (Rome, 1724), p. 44, seems to be responsible for the rumor that Poggioreale was designed by Luciano Laurana. For this error cf. R. Filangieri, "L'Architetto della reggia aragonese di Napoli," L'Arte, 31 (1928), 32–35.

10. Leostello, Effemeridi, p. 132.

11. Fabriczy, "Toscanische und oberitalienische," p. 87.

12. Ibid. "A Biasino d'Antonio Castruzzo vetturale vinticinque duc. e sonno per vettura de duy modellj a portati de Fiorenza a Napolj per disegno de uno palazo." Regarding one of these models Fra Luca Pacioli has this to say in De divina proportione (Venice, 1509, 29r): "In Firenze trovo dicta architettura molto magnificata, maxime poi ch'el magnifico Lorenzo de' Medici se ne comenzò a delectare; quel de' modelli in epsa era prontissimo; che a me fo noto per uno che con sue mani dispose al suo grandissimo domestico Giugliano da Magliano del degno palazzo detto Dogliulo [Poggioreale] a la detta città di Napoli dove in quel tempo me trovavo con lo nostro Catano Catani dal Borgo e molti altri nostri mercadanti borghesi." Quoted in E. Barfucci, Lorenzo de' Medici e la Società artistica del suo tempo (Florence, 1945), pp. 191–92. That Lorenzo made architectural models with his own hands is also suggested by correspondence in the Ginori-Conti archives. Cf. Mario Martelli, "I Pensieri architettonici del Magnifico," Commentari, 17 (1966), 107–11. Another document published by Martelli confirms that Lorenzo made such a model for Poggioreale; and it could have been one of the two taken to Naples by Biasino d'Antonio Castruzzo. But this still does not mean that Lorenzo designed the building in the modern sense: the history of architecture is filled with such pro forma attributions. It could merely signify that Lorenzo invented the basic layout of Alfonso's villa, or else that he had the hobby of making, with his own hands, models of buildings designed by others. Nonetheless we may some day have to ascribe the Neapolitan villa, and perhaps Lorenzo's own villa at Poggio a Caiano, to Lorenzo himself.

13. Fabriczy, "Toscanische und oberitalienische," p. 88.

We have seen that this place was also called Doliolum, and was the site of Parthenope's bath in *Lepidina,* where the Bolla water system had its confluence (Fig. 1).[14] Charles II had erected a house there, and in 1457 Alfonso I had either remodeled this or built a second house.[15] Both were probably hunting lodges. Also in the 1450s a certain Fabio Incarnato had built a "casa di ricreazione" at Doliolum, which he had embellished with gardens utilizing the Bolla waters,[16] and G. A. Summonte refers to a house belonging to Elia Sorgente, part of which (like the villa of Manilius Vopiscus) included a bridge across one of the canals.[17] When Giuliano da Maiano arrived, therefore, Poggioreale's site already had a reputation as a pleasure spot for villas, ornamental gardens, and waterworks.

Our supposition that some sort of proto-villa may have been in the works before 1487 is given color by a payment of 200 ducats on November 20, 1484, to Troilo de Ricca for work at Doliolum, even then "detto il Poggio Reale."[18] Troilo de Ricca became the chief contractor for Alfonso's villa in 1487, and this payment may record preparatory work done on the site. Nine months later, on August 3, 1485, Leostello refers to the farm that the Duke had recently bought at Doliolum and adds that he dined there.[19] All of this makes it probable that a structure directly preceded Giuliano's Poggioreale; but what it looked like and what effect it had on Giuliano's conception I cannot say.

There seem to be no records of work on the new building itself until the end of March 1488, when Giuliano da Maiano is reported to have been working on the fountains and on columns for the lower garden.[20] Then on the following September 4, more than a year after Giuliano's arrival, Giovanello Sparano was given 200 ducats for work at what I assume to have been the site of the new villa.[21] By September 7 considerable progress had been made on the building. Its new owner began to show it off to various official guests, including representatives of the seggi. But work was still going forward later that month.[22]

In December 1488 Hermes Sforza, brother of Giangaleazzo, arrived for the funeral of the Duchess of Calabria.[23] Leostello describes the preparations Alfonso made for the visit and says that on the 27th he took "i signori lombardi" around and showed them all the buildings

14. The site was not far from the Campo Vecchio, where Alfonso I had built a church. Cf. Colombo, "Poggioreale," p. 188, and Gino Doria, *Le Strade di Napoli* (Naples, 1943), p. 375.

15. Colombo, "Poggioreale," *ASPN,* pp. 186–87, n. 4.

16. Celano, *Notizie,* 5, 458–59. According to this tradition he built it on land won by gambling with Ferrante when the latter was Duke of Calabria. After Fabio's death, continues Celano, the house and gardens were sold and "cominciarono i Napoletani a venirvi a diporto, ed a poco a poco, perchè in breve il vizio si ingigantisce, si cominciò a darsi in mille scialacquatissime licenze."

17. G. A. Summonte, *Historia,* 1, 284.

18. Barone, "Cedole," *ASPN,* 9 (1884), 636.

19. Leostello, *Effemeridi,* p. 64. On June 1, 1488, we have this entry: "Die primo Junij lo Signore caualco al poggio reale et ibi dormiuit illa nocte" (loc. cit., p. 150). This seems to be the first use of the name "Poggioreale" in the *Effemeridi.*

20. G. Ceci, "Nuovi Documenti su Giuliano da Maiano ed altri artisti," *ASPN, 29* (1904), 784–92.

21. Barone, "Cedole," *ASPN, 9* (1884), 635.

22. Leostello, *Effemeridi,* pp. 157, 160 [Sept. 26, 1488]. Here Leostello tells of a thunderstorm that damaged the walls at Poggioreale, and of the Duke's visit of inspection the next day. On November 3, according to Barone ("Cedole," loc. cit.), Troilo de Ricca was paid 200 ducats for work at Poggioreale, which may have been in connection with the damage.

23. R. Filangieri, *Cronaca figurata,* p. 76, n. 41.

and gardens at Poggioreale.[24] Even then the house was incomplete, and Alfonso continued to ride out to it, sometimes almost daily, often dining or spending the night there.[25] In May he transacted affairs at his new villa with Pontano and a certain Messer Julio (probably his secretary Giulio de Scorziatis).[26] By this time the new road, lined with poplars and leading to the villa from Santa Caterina a Formello, was also under construction.[27]

On June 2, 1489, a housewarming party was given. It is worth quoting Leostello's description, which gives the flavor of the moment and an idea of the villa's purpose:

> The King and the Duke left on foot with the procession as far as Santa Caterina de Formello, and afterward they went on the road to the Duke's farm, as far as Santa Maria della Pace. There, after hearing mass, the King arrived at Poggioreale. He rested here for the remainder of the day, amusing himself with instrumental music and singing, and at ten o'clock His Majesty supped with many guests, and in an orderly manner, on infinite varieties of dishes. . . . And so neatly and delicately did His Majesty eat that everyone admired it. Having eaten his dinner the King rode out, giving the Duke a chance to eat, for he had not yet done so. Instead he had served the King very circumspectly by taking care of the guests. A little after midnight His Highness [the Duke] sat down at the table, under a great canopy, outdoors in the palace square, with many noblemen, courtiers of the King's who had been invited to the feast, and who had been welcomed and well treated. Having finished dinner some returned to Naples for the night, and others remained at this place, and fine beds were prepared for them. His Highness went to bed at 2:00 A.M. at Poggioreale.[28]

On June 7 the Duke returned to the villa to get ready for another party, this time for the Queen and the ambassador from Castile. A large group, including Federigo and the little Infanta Giovanna, daughter of Ferrante by his second queen, arrived the next day. "The Infanta," says Leostello, "wanted immensely to get into a boat and row with her own hands in certain waters the Duke had very ingeniously brought in."[29] There were eighty guests in all. On the next day there was yet another party, for the King.

24. Leostello, *Effemeridi,* pp. 183–84, 188.

25. Ibid., pp. 91, 214.

26. Ibid., p. 218. Cf. also Colombo, "Poggioreale," *ASPN,* p. 196.

27. Ibid., p. 195, where a payment of 150 ducats to Antonio Derzitino for the poplars and for work on the road is recorded. Alberti (*De re aed.,* VIII, 6) recommends a tree-bordered boulevard leading into the city. Cf. also Barone, "Cedole," *ASPN,* 9 (1884), 636 [Nov. 17, 1488].

28. Leostello, *Effemeridi,* p. 223: The King and Duke "se partiro ad pede con la processione fino a sancta caterina de formello et andoro postea per la via de la massaria del prefato I. S. a sancta maria de la pace ubi audita missa venne lo prefato S. Re al poggio reale: dove riposato aliquantulum tucto quello jorno se prese piacere de soni et canti et hora xxij ceno sua maesta cum

multi Signori conuitati et con tanto ordine et de infinite manere de viuande et tam actillate et dilicatamente mangio sua maesta che tucto homo ne restaua admirato: et sumpto prandio sua maesta caualco dando licentia al prefato I. S. Duca che restasse ad cenare che anchora era dejuno: che hauea seruito a sua maesta molto attillatamente accarezando tucti li conuitati. Post paulo hora xxiiij. sua I. S. se pose in tauola socto una tenda grande a lo fresco et a lo largo del palazo cum molti jentili homini del S. Re cortesani inuitati da sua I. S. et accarezati et bene tractati. Sumpta cena alchuni se ne ritornoro in napoli a dormire: alchuni restoro loco et fureno apparecchiati loro lecti nobilissimi et sua I. S. hora ij lectulum ingressus est et dormio quella sera al poggio prefato."

29. Ibid., p. 225.

But even so construction went on. In June 1489 a large marble block was brought from Teano to Naples for the fabbriche at Poggioreale.[30] On July 8 the Duke arranged for the building of "bagni e certe stanze" (probably summer houses). Meanwhile the Venetian ambassador was shown about.[31]

In November, possibly as a result of all the feastings, the Duke began to be afflicted with stomach pains, but he continued with the celebrations. He conducted his sister Eleonora's chancellor around the villa[32] and continued his own tours, dinners, and overnight stays. These, along with references to continued building, go on through 1490. One dined not only in the house itself but in a grotto or beside a pool.[33] The stomach troubles did not let up and in the late summer of 1490 Alfonso was ill again, but no complaints were recorded when an ambassador from France was entertained on November 17, 1490.[34] The last entry in Leostello's diary referring to Poggioreale is dated November 18, 1490; it says that the Queen was to dine in the "Jardino dicto de Raymo."[35] The diary itself ends soon after this, on February 6, 1491.

I have found no documents for further work on the building or gardens. I assume that Poggioreale continued to be used, and perhaps extended, as before. However, there is no reason to suppose that Giuliano's basic architectural scheme of 1487 was altered; instead the documents suggest improvements in the gardens or temporary arrangements, some possibly scenographic, for feasts.

Poggioreale was used almost purely as a place of entertainment. Like Pontano's ideal villa it was built for the sake of its own splendor. It is thus not to be compared with more ordinary villas like those of the Medici or most of Palladio's, which were manors or farmhouses, and places for family life. Poggioreale should be grouped with pure dream settings or follies, such as the Palazzo del Tè, the Villa Rotonda, or Fonthill.[36]

A RECONSTRUCTION OF POGGIOREALE

If Poggioreale was a theater to celebrate the nuptials of Parthenope and the Sebeto, its architecture and gardens expressed this function perfectly. Two attempts at reconstructing Giuliano's original design have been made, one by Stegmann and Geymüller, the other by Frommel.[37] Frommel's is an improvement but it must be somewhat modified in the light of the documents and sources. Reconstructions of Poggioreale are chiefly based on two unscaled sketch plans of the villa made in the early sixteenth century by Baldassare Peruzzi (Figs. 79, 80).[38] The house proper was built around

30. Barone, "Cedole," *ASPN, 10* (1885), 6.

31. Leostello, *Effemeridi,* pp. 237, 240.

32. Ibid., p. 279.

33. Ibid., pp. 340, 353.

34. Ibid., pp. 347, 362, 385.

35. Ibid., p. 386. For other parties see Sanudo, "La Spedizione," p. 240.

36. At least one writer praised a villa of Alfonso's, probably Poggioreale, as a farm. Cf. Michelangelo Tanaglia, *De agricultura,* ed. Aurelio Roncaglia and Tammaro De Marinis (Bologna, 1953), pp. 3–4. For Poggioreale as a possible theater, see André Chastel, "Cortile et théâtre," in *Le Lieu théâtrale à la renaissance* [*Colloques internationaux du centre national de la recherche scientifique. Sciences humaines.*] (Paris, 1964), pp. 41–47, esp. pp. 43–44.

37. Stegmann and Geymüller, *Die Architektur der Renaissance in Toscana, 11* (Munich, 1885–1906), 16, fig. 42, and Frommel, *Die Farnesina,* fig. 16.

38. There was also probably a front courtyard, not shown in Peruzzi's sketches. See n. 28 above, and Celano, *Notizie, 5,* 463.

an arcaded courtyard, either square or slightly oblong,[39] which had a sunken center and was surrounded by four tiers of stepped seats in the manner of an amphitheater. At the corners were towers, nearly square in plan, containing room stacks and staircases. The loggia was divided into cross-vaulted bays, seven along the sides and three, wider and taller, across the ends.[40] Peruzzi's drawing (Fig. 79) also shows what I take to be grouped piers at the corners of the courtyard. The front and back walls were pierced by three openings matching the loggia arches. The side walls, at first, were without entrances.

Under this arrangement there would probably have been a strong eastward movement from the piazza in front through the amphitheater to the garden behind, and across the park to a vista that included Vesuvius. The western front was similarly aimed toward the city and the Porta Capuana (Fig. 1). The towers, set almost free of the wall planes, would have helped to stretch open this tripartite channel of space.

The villa building was set within an asymmetrical frame of flowerbeds and terraces. We learn from *Le Vergier d'honneur* that an outer park to the south had "many healthy herbs [and was] much larger than the Bois de Vincennes."[41] Inside the southern garden wall was a hippodrome. East of this lay a four-bedded garden, and then a fishpool presided over by an arcaded loggia with seats. Just north of this canals formed a cross with a central pool and fountain. By the seventeenth century, and perhaps originally, there were six fountains around the edges of the canal area. I presume the central fountain also included the pavilion that, we are told, sheltered a terra-cotta sculpture group. The latter may have depicted either Parthenope with attendant putti or an ermine with hunting dogs.[42] We know also that birds and wild animals were kept, presumably in the outer park, which extended as far south as the Bay.[43]

Other descriptions provide further details. The house was actually fortlike in shape, i.e. with the corner room-stacks forming towers. Jean Burchard, who visited the villa in 1495, said the building was two stories high.[44] Marcantonio Michiel, who visited about fourteen

39. August Schmarsow, ed., "Excerpte aus Joh. Fichard's 'Italia' von 1536," *Repertorium für kunstwissenschaft*, 14 (1891), 373–83, esp. 374, where we are told that the palace was "quadratum et oblongum." Fichard adds that there were three (rather than four) tiers of seats around the courtyard, and that the arcade was ornate.

40. Celano, *Notizie*, 5, 463.

41. Quoted by Müntz, *La Renaissance en Italie et en France à l'époque de Charles VIII* (Paris, 1885), p. 435.

42. Quoted from Capaccio's *Historia* by A. Colombo, "Poggioreale," *ASPN*, p. 201: "Ex creta etiam integrum Sirenis symbolum extat, cuius pedes alter osculantur alter admirantur aspectum,—aliud Ferdinandi symbolum, Armellinum [sic] scilicet animal quod ne coeno fedatur libenter se capiendum venatoribus tradit." This refers to Ferrante's Order of the Ermine,

founded to replace the Crescenti, the followers of Jean d'Anjou. According to Giannone, Ferrante, rather than kill one of his enemies, had a collar made for him with a small sculptured ermine hanging from it. The motto of the order was "malo mori, quam foedari," ("I'd rather die than foul myself [or rebel]"). The order was bestowed on a number of Neapolitan barons, and on Ercole I d'Este (Giannone, *Historia*, 3, 424). Instructions issued to Simonetto de Belloprato and Filippo de Gallera on October 21, 1486 (Volpicella, *Liber Instructionum*, pp. 47–49), give a detailed description of the initiation ceremony. For another description of the waterworks at Poggioreale, see G. A. Summonte, *Historia*, 1, 284–85.

43. Müntz, *La Renaissance*, p. 435.

44. Burchard, *Diarium*, 2, 174. Cf. also Leandro Alberti, *Descrittione di tutta Italia . . .* (Bologna, 1550), p. 167.

years later, mentioned an upper loggia, presumably in the courtyard. He also told Serlio that the latter was roofed over.[45] Michiel may have been thinking of a temporary roof, like the canopy Leostello says was pitched in front of the building. Though the precise size of Poggioreale is unknown, certainly the courtyard seems too large for a wooden or masonry roof without intermediate supports. In any case, the amphitheater was equipped with numerous tiny pipes in the masonry joints so that it could be flooded almost instantly: thus were the elegant dinners enlivened by surprises.[46] It may also have been possible of course to stage mock naval battles, though I have found no documents for such events. While the seats indicate that some sort of theatrical spectacles were staged, these may simply have been the dinners themselves. The pool pumps and conduits were elaborate and were housed in a vaulted basement which astonished the author of *Le Vergier d'honneur*.[47] Serlio also mentions the underground and secret chambers. Finally, we know from several sources that the whole villa was frescoed inside and out with figure paintings of events from the Barons' Revolt, the work of Ippolito and Pietro Donzello. Heroes of the House of Aragon were portrayed in sculptured roundels in the courtyard spandrels,[48] and there were antique sculptures as well, taken from the Roman Porta Nolana.[49]

Unfortunately, some later descriptions of Poggioreale, both literary and graphic, add inconsistencies to this picture. Thus in his first version of the villa, Serlio shows both towers and courtyard as perfectly square, and also, unlike Peruzzi, he divides each tower interior into an L-shaped group of three small equal-size rooms (Fig. 90). The courtyard is now five bays each way, and porticoes have been added on the exterior between the towers. While Serlio (who based his drawings on Michiel's descriptions) probably departed from the original, it is interesting that in doing so he has made the design even more schematic. Thus, by repeating the courtyard loggias on the exterior, the latter became the reflex of the interior. A detailed print by Bastiaen Stoopendael, of the later seventeenth century, shows Michiel's upper loggia (Fig. 82), paired windows in the upper parts of the towers, and doors in their bases. There are also steps leading to a central door in the side wall; I assume these also to be later. Some of the added features are confirmed by Celano, who visited the villa before

45. Serlio, III, cli. However, Celano (*Notizie*, 5, 463), and Fichard (loc. cit.) say it was uncovered.

46. Serlio, loc. cit. See Martelli, "I Pensieri architettonici del Magnifico," for Lorenzo's description of similar semi-submerged dinners.

47. Dinner spectacles are described by Sanudo ("La Spedizione," p. 39), e.g. the one at which Alfonso II and Cardinal Giovanni Borgia dined on May 14, 1494. They were the only two at table; everyone else watched. For the contemporary eye-witness description of the basement waterworks see André de la Vigne and Octavien de Saint-Gelais, *Le Vergier d'honneur*, M. L. Cimber, ed., *Archives curieuses de l'histoire de France*, ser. 1, 1 (Paris, 1834), 321–435, esp. 334–36.

48. G. A. Summonte, *Historia*, 1, 284, 4, 163; Va-

sari, 2, 470; and Pietro Summonte, in Nicolini, *L'Arte napoletana*, pp. 163, 246–49. The roundels may of course have been those delivered to the "capuana" on October 12, 1492 (Barone, "Cedole," *ASPN, 10*, 1885, 19). For Ippolito and Pietro Donzello see L. de la Ville sur-Yllon, "Di un Quadro attribuito ai fratelli del Donzello," *NN, 1* (1892), 120–22; "Notizie," *Rassegna d'arte senese, 1* (1905), 88–90; Luigi Serra, "La Pittura napoletana del rinascimento," *L'Arte, 8* (1905), 340–54; Mario Bori, "'L'Annunciazione' di Piero del Donzello in una cappella Frescobaldi nella chiesa di Santo Spirito," *Rivista d'Arte, 4* (1906), 117–23; Georg Sobotka in Thieme-Becker, s.v. [1913]; and Giuseppe Fiocco, "Jacopo Ripanda," *L'Arte, 23* (1920), 27–48.

49. Celano, *Notizie, 5*, 464.

1644.[50] Giuseppe Mormile, writing in 1617, said that the lower arcades—I assume he meant those on the east and west—were "grandissimi"; he too mentions upper loggias, which he says gave access to the second-floor tower rooms.[51] Petrini, in a guidebook of about 1700, illustrates the loggias (Fig. 81), and adds pitched roofs to the towers as Serlio had done in a variant version of the villa (Fig. 91).

Both Petrini's and Stoopendael's illustrations also show that by about 1700 the surrounding gardens had been changed, and the canals filled in and covered with outbuildings. Other views confirm the relationship shown in Stoopendael to the via Vecchia di Poggioreale of 1488, as it was now called, and to the via Nuova di Poggioreale built in 1603.[52] The latter, with its great width, flanking trees, and fountain-filled central island, no doubt transcended Alfonso's original road; but both, of course, may have been inspired by the "queen of long roads" mentioned by Statius—the via Appia—which led to Pollius' villa.

In his life of Giuliano da Maiano (1768) Francesco Milizia gives an interesting circumstantial account of Poggioreale not long before it was absorbed into later structures, to disappear entirely. It is an account that has been ignored by modern students. Milizia says:

> Poggioreale is a perfect quadrilateral; in the middle of each side is an arched portico, at the ends of which are Ionic pilasters on high pedestals. On both sides are chambers. The second floor has Corinthian pilasters between which are windows with frontispieces. The main cornices are without jogs [risalti] and interruptions. Inside is a four-sided court with loggias on both stories. In the middle of this courtyard are stairs, also square, by which one descends to a tiled pavement embellished with seats, tables, and fountains.[53]

Finally, Colombo published a drawing in his article on Poggioreale showing what he says is one of its original doorways. It had been built into the wall of a tavern. It is a lean, graceful portal (Fig. 87), not unlike that of the Palazzo Carafa (Fig. 10), and even closer to the door of the so-called Temple of Jupiter at Split. There are a bolection frieze, consoles, and a narrowish molded archivolt, the last no doubt at one time the frame for a sculptured or painted panel. I assume it was a door between the cloister and one of the chambers.

There are a few more conjectural points. It seems possible that existing Quattrocento courtyards in the neighborhood of Naples—for example the one at the Convent of Santa

50. Ibid., 5, 463.

51. Giuseppe Mormile, *Descrittione dell'amenissimo distretto della città di Napoli, et dell'antichità della città di Pozzuolo* . . . (Naples, 1617), pp. 54–58.

52. By Alfonso Pimentel, Conte di Benavente (Celano, *Notizie, 5,* 459).

53. Francesco Milizia, *Le Vite de' più celebri architetti* . . . (Rome, 1768), p. 171: Poggioreale "è un quadrato perfetto. In mezzo ad ogni lato è un portico ad archi, alle alette de' quali sono pilastri Ionici sopra un alto piedestallo. Di qua e di là sono camere. Il secondo piano è di Pilastri Corinti, trà quali son finestre con frontispizi. I cornicioni sono senza risalti ed interrompimenti. Dentro è un cortile quadrato perfetto con logge a tutti due i piani. In mezzo di esso cortile è una scalinata parimente quadrata, per cui si scende ad un piano mattonato abbellito di sedili, di mense, e di giuochi d'acqua."

Maria del Pozzo, Somma Vesuviana, or even the triple-arched west front of that church—may have been partly derived from Giuliano's courtyard at Poggioreale.[54] A further echo of Poggioreale may appear in the Annunciation attributed to Pietro Donzello and now in one of the Frescobaldi Chapels in Santo Spirito, Florence (Fig. 85). The picture dates from 1497–98, i.e. after Pietro and Ippolito had finished in Naples and returned to Florence. The courtyard in it is three bays wide and an indeterminate number deep, with a sunken square center and a large entrance in the rear leading to a balustraded terrace, an axially arranged garden, fountains, and a distant mountain resembling Vesuvius. Some such spectacle—though the volcano might not have been so neatly on axis—would have been visible on looking through the courtyard of Alfonso's villa. I must also add that Donzello's architecture is different in detail: the bays are apparently equal in size, and there are no seats but only concentric square patterns on the tile floor.[55]

Neither Stegmann and Geymüller's nor Frommel's reconstructions (Figs. 83, 84) fit the facts as we now know them. In the former the building is not properly related to the garden and has the wrong bay system. Frommel on the other hand has invented a rear terrace. But a correct reading of Peruzzi's sketches, along with the other evidence, is not difficult. Frommel is right in assuming that Peruzzi's plan (UA 363v, Fig. 80) shows the walled garden behind the house rather than beside it, as with Stegmann and Geymüller. All early sources are in agreement on this. However, early views also show the house directly beside the large square garden divided into four beds (Figs. 81, 82)—a garden Peruzzi also indicates. Frommel ignores this fact and pushes the garden into the area properly occupied by the fish-pool. Then, in the void left beside the house, he creates a new area which he gratuitously labels "giardin" (Fig. 84). While this word does appear on Peruzzi's sketch (Fig. 79) as we shall see it can refer only to the large square garden also shown in Figure 80 and not to the T-shaped area Frommel creates.

Frommel also provides us with a scale for Peruzzi's drawings, derived from the maximum normal span between the lateral courtyard arches (2 meters, he says), which, he adds, is probably their actual spacing. He makes no allowance for the different spans normally achieved with brick as opposed to stone arches, with or without tie rods, on piers as opposed to columns, for the weight of the story above or for the strength of the foundations. Nor is there any reason to suppose that a maximum span was used anyway. All of this makes it

54. Cf. Giuseppe Fiengo, "La Chiesa e il convento di Santa Maria del Pozzo a Somma Vesuviana," *NN,* ser. 3, *4* (1964), 125–32; Giulio Pane, "La Villa Carafa," p. 147, n. 81; and G. C. Alisio, "La Cappella Pontano," *NN,* ser. 3, *3* (1963), 29–35. See also Giambattista Guarini, "Un Monumento obliato. L'Abbazia di Sant' Angelo in Montescagnoso," *NN, 13* (1904), 23–27.

55. A design similar to that of Poggioreale, and dating before it, is the rectangular, towered palace in the upper right background of Francesco Laurana's relief of *Christ Carrying the Cross* (1478–81) in St. Didier, Avignon. Here a square rusticated tower is visible at one corner, there is a pair of round-arched windows in each outer face of the tower's upper story, two mezzanine floors, a machicolated cornice, and pyramidal roofs to the towers. For Pietro Donzello's picture see Bori, " 'L'Annunciazione,' " 117–23.

impossible to arrive at a precise idea of the size of Poggioreale from the present evidence. Indeed, Frommel's ad hoc scale gives the staircases treads about 3½ inches wide and gives each flight a width of only about a foot.

These errors can be avoided if we establish the proper relationship between UA 363v and UA 363r. I shall assume that the latter is a plan of the main floor of the villa, while the former is of the gardens and includes the *basement plan* of what we see in 363v. The steps in other words go down, not up, and Frommel's "terrace" is actually the storage tanks, pump rooms, and other paraphernalia beneath the main floor, an installation that the authors of *Le Vergier d'honneur* marveled at, and that would have been necessary to the amphitheater's function. On either side of the tanks are the piers supporting the amphitheater seats, and Peruzzi has also indicated some of the footings of the main-floor walls. I have added the rest in dotted lines, i.e. those that would not have been visible to Peruzzi. That 363v is indeed a basement plan is also shown by the inscription "cuc/," for cucina, which Peruzzi has written near the steps (and which Frommel omits). I might mention that all the old views of Poggioreale show such a basement, and Milizia alludes to it as well as Serlio. Correspondingly, no view or written source mentions a rear terrace. I have taken the liberty in my restored view of indicating all this (Figs. 86, 88, 89).

Concerning the architectural sources of Poggioreale, one thinks first of castles rather than palaces. Certain antique villas, however, might have been known, especially those Swoboda has called "Villen mit Eckrisaliten."[56] Ruins of Roman country houses of this type with interior loggias, corner towers, and symmetrical plans (Fig. 92) may have stood near Naples in the fifteenth century and may even have been linked in people's minds with the Neapolitan villas of Statius and Petronius. Poggioreale also resembles the square Roman "serapeum" (now thought to have been a market) at Pozzuoli (Fig. 93). Here are a stepped, flooded center surrounded by vaulted loggias and, still visible today, projecting corner bays. This building, sometimes also known as Trajan's Bath, was sketched in the fifteenth century, possibly by Francesco di Giorgio.[57] There is also the possibility of the central grouping of rectangular colonnaded courtyard, with four corner room-groups, in the marine theater at Hadrian's Villa, Tivoli.

But Poggioreale's square carcass with corner towers was also a standard medieval form. One thinks of the Castello dei Quattro Torri, near Siena, for example (Fig. 94),[58] and of

56. Karl M. Swoboda, "Palazzi antichi e medioevali," *Bollettino del Centro di Studi per la Storia dell' Architettura*, 2 (1957), 3–32, e.g. the old palace at Larisa sull'Ermo, reproduced here. Cf. also E. B. Thomas, *Römische Villen in Pannonien* (Budapest, 1964).

57. Uffizi A327r. It was also known as the Temple of Neptune (Giuseppe Mormile, *Descrittione della città di Napoli*, Naples, 1675, p. 101). Cf. also Frommel, *Die Farnesina*, pp. 92–93. Other relevant Quattrocento drawings, supposedly of classical structures, are reproduced in Venturi, *Storia dell'arte italiana, 11, 1*, figs. 391–93. Sannazaro praises the towers of his own villa at Mergellina, which he says seem to make the building fly, and its reflection in a pool (*Epigrams*, I, 2, ll. 13ff., 22). The watery quality of Poggioreale is anticipated also in Statius' *Sylvae*. We have noted that Pollius Felix's villa (l. 25) straddles a river. It is even wetted with spray (l. 22) and stands near "a smoking bath-house with two domes" (ll. 16–18).

58. Bernhard Patzak, *Die Renaissance- und Barockvilla in Italien, 3* (Leipzig, 1908–12), 132, and

the Castello di San Giorgio at Mantua, built at the end of the fourteenth century, with its frescoes of 1465–74 by Mantegna—the latter possibly not dissimilar in program to some of those at Poggioreale.[59] One can go back to more purely military structures like the Hohenstaufen forts, e.g. that at Prato (Fig. 95), which Giuliano surely knew, and where in plan there is a surprising anticipation of Poggioreale, with square corner towers and a cross-vaulted series of rooms around a square court. The vaulted bays are now closed off from the courtyard by later building, but they may have been open, or have shown that they once were open, in Giuliano's time. At another Hohenstaufen fort, in Augusta, Sicily (a town with much Aragonese building in it), we find the open arcade in addition to all the rest.[60]

There are innumerable later vernacular buildings with towered, symmetrical facades, and whose walls featured triple-arched entrances. One should also mention Howard Saalman's suggestion that there are correspondences with parts of the Badia at Fiesole. Finally, Poggioreale's symmetrical courtyard and towers recall, a little, Filarete's ecclesiastical palace in Book IX of the *Trattato*.[61]

A contemporaneous parallel for Poggioreale is the villa of Poggio a Caiano, near Florence, by Giuliano da Sangallo, built for Lorenzo de' Medici (Figs. 96, 97).[62] The Duke of Calabria was dependent on Lorenzo for artistic advice, and it is accordingly not surprising that there should be a relationship between the two buildings. Indeed, as mentioned, they may both have been laid out by Il Magnifico himself (see n. 12). It is even possible that the name, Poggioreale, is an adaptation of that of the Tuscan farm and retreat. In any case, Giuliano da Maiano would have had an excellent opportunity to look at Sangallo's model for Poggio a Caiano during his stay in Florence in 1486–87.

The most striking immediate difference is that the Medici villa possesses an arched podium, lacking in Naples, which originally had straight twin flights of steps leading down from it. Set back from the terrace is the corps de logis consisting of four corner room-blocks arranged around a Greek cross of circulation space. The intersection is marked by the famous barrel-

Schreiber, *Poggio-reale Variationen,* p. 11, note, have mentioned the relationship.

59. For other similar castles, cf. the Castello di Pendino, Milan, built by Bernabò Visconti, also at the end of the fourteenth century, on a rectangular plan with four corner towers, each three stories high, and with a central two-story block (Guido Carotti, *Ville e castelli d'Italia,* Milan, 1907, p. 425). There is also the Palazzo and Rocca of Pallavicino, dating from 1470–80, in Cortemaggiore. This is square, corner-towered, with an interior court, and is illustrated in A. Cassi Ramelli, *Dalle Caverne ai rifugi blindati* (Milan, 1964), fig. 216.

60. For possible Moslem prototypes cf. Hanno Hahn, *Hohenstaufenburgen in Süditalien* (Munich, 1961), p. 24. The Casa Ruffoli, Ravello, can also be mentioned (Patzak, *Renaissance- und Barockvilla, 2,* 65). It has a cross-vaulted loggia, three bays to a side, around the courtyard. Cf. also Schreiber, *Poggio-Reale Variationen,* p. 10, and Frommel, *Die Farnesina,* p. 92.

61. Cf. Howard Saalman's review of Frommel's *Farnesina,* in *Journal of the Society of Architectural Historians,* 22 (1963), 43. For the question of the tower-flanked portico as a villa frontispiece cf. Karl M. Swoboda, "The Problem of the Iconography of the Late Antique and Early Medieval Palaces," ibid., 20 (1961), 78–89; and J. S. Ackerman, "Sources of the Renaissance Villa," p. 12.

62. For this relationship see the literature in n. 9 above, and for the villa itself, see P. G. Hamberg, "The Villa of Lorenzo il Magnifico at Poggio a Caiano and the Origin of Palladianism," *Figura,* n.s. 1 (1959), 76–87. Philip E. Foster's recent unpublished Yale master's thesis, *The Date of Lorenzo de' Medici's Villa at Poggio a Caiano,* 1965, analyzes the documents and written sources.

vaulted salon, corresponding to the courtyard of Poggioreale. The actual room arrangement of Poggio a Caiano, however, is unlike that of Alfonso's villa, for in Florence the practical spaces have encroached far more on what I will call the presentational ones (Figs. 86, 97). This is obviously because there were so many everyday activities at Poggio a Caiano, which was a farm and a family house as well as a retreat for Lorenzo's circle. It could not afford the abstraction of the Neapolitan villa.

Poggioreale was conditioned to a great extent by the background of older theatrical and military images. With this background, and its frescoes, Giuliano's structure was a fit mate for the Porta Capuana. The villa can be seen as another trophy-hung portal between towers along the road from the city, a mock-rocca in a geometrical wilderness, almost a witty paraphrase of one of the castles Alfonso had seized from the barons. One can also see its long, multi-leveled, walled garden slot, with its theatrical and sports functions, and its villa-vestibule, as an ancestor of the Cortile del Belvedere.[63]

LA DUCHESCA   Of Alfonso's second villa, La Duchesca, little is known.[64] It was apparently a small house for Ippolita Sforza—or a monument to her memory—and situated in the Giardino Grande that surrounded the Castel Capuano.[65] Later, a memorial chapel to the

63. Noted by Frommel, *Die Farnesina*, p. 96. As a villa with frescoed exteriors Poggioreale was unusual for its date. Large-scale figure pieces with secular subject matter were rare as exterior decorations in the 1480s. (Cf. Gunther and Christel Thiem, *Toskanische Fassaden-Dekoration in Sgraffito und Fresko, 14 bis 17 Jahrhundert*, Munich, 1964). Similar decorations do not seem to appear in Tuscany until such structures as the Palazzo del Borgo, c. 1580, decorated with battle scenes probably by Bernardino Poccetti. In Naples, such military events were the subject of masques. Sannazaro's two farse, *La Presa di Granata* and *Il Triunfo de la fama*, produced in March 1492 in the Castel Capuano, were in honor of the Castilian victory over the Moors at Granada. In both, a painted set-piece stood in an open central space and the audience's seats were built on surrounding platforms. (Cf. Benedetto Croce, "I Teatri di Napoli del secolo XV–XVIII," *ASPN, 14*, 1889, 556–684, esp. 562–80.) This notion of the audience being placed on outer platforms with the action unfolding around a central set-piece echoes the dining arrangements in the courtyard at Poggioreale, with its banquets watched by audience-guests. A further development of the rectangular theatre-in-the-round—or at least in the three quarters round—is the wooden theatre built, probably by Piero di Cosimo, for the bestowal of Roman citizenship on Giuliano de' Medici, September 13, 1513. A plan of this is in the Soane Museum, London (Coner Codex, 23r), and will shortly be published by Alois M. Nagler. Cf. also T. Ashby, Jr., "Sixteenth Century Drawings of Roman Buildings attributed to Andreas

Coner," *Papers of the British School of Rome, 2* (1904), 23, and Pio Pecchiai, *Il Campidoglio nel cinquecento* (Rome, 1950), p. 15.

64. Cf. A. Colombo, "Il Palazzo e giardino della Duchesca dal 1487 al 1760," *ASPN, 9* (1884), 563–74; ibid., "Il Palazzo e il giardino della Duchesca," *NN, 1* (1892), 81–83; and Pane, *Architettura*, pp. 26–28.

65. Cf. n. 64 above and Doria, *Le Strade di Napoli*, p. 160. For the Castel Capuano, see R. Filangieri, *Il Castello di Capuana, fortezza e reggia* (Naples, n.d.). The castle had of course been freed of its most immediate defense functions by the new eastern walls, which put it completely within the city. There are numerous documents for later remodelings by the Duke. In 1477 or 1478 Antonio Buschet was paid for a new clock for the "stanze nuove" (Barone, "Cedole," *ASPN, 9*, 1884, 499), and on May 28, 1487, Maestro Novello Paparo was paid 50 ducats on account for making a bathroom called the "specieria" (ibid., p. 620). Another bathroom, or perhaps the same one, was painted by no less a person than Colantonio on July 26, 1487 (ibid., p. 623); and on December 27, 1487, Giovannello Sparano received 200 ducats on account for construction at the Castel Capuano (ibid., p. 627). On April 10, 1488, Giuliano da Maiano was plastering "la camera de la terrazza al modo fiorentino" at the Capuano, and Onorato de Zotto di Napoli, piccatore, made two windows and two "corners [pilasters?] with capitals and other stone-work" (Ceci, "Nuovi documenti," *ASPN, 29*, 1904, 789). On May 2, 1488, Francesco de Tricarico installed 27 canvas panels on the walls of the "cammara

martyrs of Otranto was also built in or next to this garden. The whole complex adjoined the public piazza behind the Porta Capuana, and through that it was linked to the via Poggioreale.

The story of La Duchesca does not begin, apparently, with the house but with its garden setting. Thus on July 16, 1487, more than a month before the arrival of Giuliano's models from Florence, Calvano da Padova and others were paid for gilding shields on the ends of loggia beams in the garden.[66] This is interesting for it shows that at least one of Giuliano's assistants—for such I take Calvano to be—was in Naples while Giuliano himself was in all probability still in Florence. On September 4, 1488, Costanzo de Moysis was paid for painting the sad story of Marino Marzano, Prince of Rossano and one of the leading rebels, at the head of the stairs in La Duchesca.[67] On August 18, 1488, Ippolita died.[68] Nonetheless, work continued on the building named after her, and by June 10, 1489, it seems to have been usable. On this day Alfonso and his father ate dinner there and afterward went to see "le mure et tucte quelle stanze nuoue de lo jardino pizollo."[69] On December 28, 1489, Leostello referred to the building as the "palatio nouamente edificato dal dicto I.S. fronte a la suo jardino grande," and added that now everything was in order and well furnished with tapestries.[70] The villa was undoubtedly pretty and luxurious. Sanudo, describing it after Charles VIII's invasion, says that it possessed a fountain, that its rooms were filled with tapestries or pictures lettered in gold and silk, and that on the ground floor was an oratory with a life-size statue of the Duke at prayer. Sanudo's description suggests that the main entrance was on an upper level, and he and others imply that the stairs were an important element.[71]

According to an inscription on the facade, the grounds contained other fountains, a bath, and a hippodrome.[72] An anonymous chronicle of about this period says these gardens were immense, with alleys 40 palmi wide. At one of their intersections was a fountain-statue of Parthenope standing on a shell. Water squirted from her nipples into the mouths of three attendant putti, who dispensed it in turn through their penes. There was also a great loggia,

---

de alta de la terracza et oratorio et studio et cappella socto la cammara de paramento del Castello de Capuana" (ibid., p. 790). Calvano de Padova, on July 11, 1488, was paid for colors for the Castel Capuano (ibid., pp. 790–91), and on September 7, 1488, Troilo de Ricca received 200 ducats for work done there (Barone, "Cedole," ASPN, 9, 1884, 635). Finally on July 14, 1489, we hear that the Duke was still (in all probability) remodeling the building (Leostello, Effemeridi, p. 239).

66. Barone, "Cedole," ASPN, 9 (1884), 623.

67. Ceci, "Nuovi Documenti," ASPN, 29 (1904), 784–92. Colombo, "Poggioreale," ASPN, p. 207, says Sannazaro quotes a sonnet for Federigo on a similar fresco in Poggioreale.

68. Leostello, Effemeridi, p. 155.

69. Ibid., pp. 226, 241.

70. Ibid., p. 289. On June 29, 1490 (p. 343), "fu

facta la collatione intorno a la acqua che correva in terra. la stauano tucti prostrati a lo frescho et passoro quello jorno in molti boni et suaui ragionamenti." Cf. also ibid., pp. 347, 353–54, 363.

71. Colombo, "La Duchesca," ASPN, pp. 567–68, quoting Sanudo: "Montati su scale si trova pozuoli da star al fresco, mirabili; poi si discende in altre camere ornate ut supra, et un Oratorio dov'era il Duca di Calabria, zoè Don Alphonso, facta naturalmente, che stava in genocchioni che pareva vivo."

72. Colombo, "La Duchesca," ASPN, p. 565, n. 2: ALPHONSO FERD. REGIS TIT. ARAGONIUS: DUX CALABR. GENIO DOMUM HANC CUM FONTE, ET BALNEO DICAVIT, HIPPODROMUM CONSTITUIT: GESTATIONES HORTIS ADIECIT, QUAS MYRTIS, CITRORUMQUE: NE MORIBUS EXORNATAS SALUTI SOSPITAE, AC VOLUPTATI PERPET. CONSECR.

says the author, with four sets of steps.[73] Al fresco banquets were given at La Duchesca during the summer of 1490 as at Poggioreale.

The martyrs' memorial chapel was planned as early as February 12, 1490. On that day ten cases of bones were brought to the Duke.[74] Alfonso decided to transform all or part of a nearby monastery church, Santa Maria Maddalena, into a shrine, and the nuns of the convent were accordingly sent elsewhere. Leostello asserts that this was done sympathetically, but others have cited the incident as an example of Alfonso's disregard for others.[75] By February 19 construction was under way: I assume that the architect was Giuliano da Maiano.[76] What the church finally looked like I do not know, since it was soon demolished along with the other ducal buildings in this part of town. However, the nearby church of Santa Caterina a Formello, rebuilt 24 years later in accordance with Alfonso's wishes, may give us some idea (Fig. 127).[77]

I have been unable to find further evidence of the appearance of La Duchesca and its surroundings.[78] In the 1530s Don Pietro of Toledo transformed the Castel Capuano into a courthouse, and shortly after this, I imagine, most traces of Alfonso's occupancy disappeared.

73. L. Salazar, ed., "Racconti di storia napoletana," *ASPN*, 33 (1908), 502–05.

74. Leostello, *Effemeridi*, pp. 304–05 [Feb. 12, 1490].

75. Leostello, *Effemeridi*, pp. 304–05, and Notar Giacomo, *Cronica*, pp. 167–68 [March 14, 1490]: "per piacere sua per fare lo palazzo della duchesca et li cellari et altre cose, che fe et fo male signo perlui." Cf. also G. Filangieri, *Documenti*, 2, 261–68.

76. On February 19, 1490, the Duke was looking at the new work (Leostello, *Effemeridi*, p. 308). This is the place to mention a few other structures erected by the Duke, or under his influence. There was first the new wooden ceiling of Sant' Eligio Maggiore al Mercato (now destroyed) for which documents exist, executed by Niccolò di Tommaso de Squillace in December 1488 (Pane, *Architettura*, p. 98). Pane thinks this may be the roof we now see in the Church of Donnaregina. Cf. also Cèndali, *Giuliano da Maiano*, p. 173. For other Aragonese villas of the period, cf. Colombo, "Poggioreale," *ASPN*, p. 315 and Pane, *Architettura*, pp. 26, 28–35. According to Doria (*Le Strade di Napoli*, p. 182), Don Garcìa, son of Don Pedro of Toledo, had a villa in the Largo Ferrandino which had once been the property of Alfonso II. It was in the area occupied by the cavalry barracks of San Pasquale and is now partly demolished. For Pontano's two villas, one near Sant' Angelo a Nilo and boasting a brick tower, see B. Capasso, "La Torre d'Arco e la casa del Pontano in Napoli," *Strenna Giannini*, 4 (1892), 97–104; E. Percopo, "La Vita di Giovanni Pontano," *ASPN, 61* (1937), 171–74; idem, "Ville ed abitazioni di poeti in Napoli. I. La villa del Pontano ad Antignano," *NN*, ser. 2, 2 (1921), 1–7; idem, "La Villa del Pontano ad Antignano," in *In onore di Giovanni Gioviano Pontano nel V Centenario della sua nascita* (Naples, 1926), pp. 141–61 (with illustrations). For Sannazaro's villa at Mergellina see B. Croce, "La chiesetta di Jacopo Sannazaro," in *Storie e leggende napoletane* (Bari, 1923), 197–217; and idem, "La Tomba di Jacobo Sannazaro e la chiesa di Santa Maria del Parto," *NN, 1* (1892), 68–76.

77. Gallo, *Diurnali*, p. 37; G. Ceci, "La Chiesa e il convento di Santa Caterina a Formello," *NN, 9* (1900), 49–51, 67–70, esp. 67; B. Capasso, "Appunti per la storia delle arti in Napoli," *ASPN, 6* (1881), 535. Work on rebuilding the church proper was undertaken in 1519 (G. Filangieri, *Documenti, 6*, 102–03). There are strong resemblances as Pane notes between Santa Caterina and Santa Maria del Calcinaio, Cortona, begun in 1485, by Francesco di Giorgio; and in 1491 and 1492 Francesco was in Naples. Later, in 1517 or 1518 Antonio Marchese made a trip north (Vasari, *4, 476*, and n. 4). In traveling between Arezzo and Montepulciano he no doubt saw the new church in Cortona by his master, Francesco di Giorgio. Immediately after Antonio's trip, on February 11, 1519, the rebuilding of Santa Caterina started (Filangieri, *Documenti, 6, 443, 445*). The supervisor was Romolo di Antonio d'Alessandro Balsimelli who has been credited with designing the church (ibid., *5, 24*). He is probably the Romolo Balsimelli whose name is linked with certain tombs and chapels in San Domenico Maggiore. Now this Romolo was from Settignano, and the son of someone named Antonio; so Antonio Marchese da Settignano may well have been his father, and the architect of Santa Caterina, working in the manner of Francesco di Giorgio.

78. Colombo, "La Duchesca," *ASPN*, pp. 569–74.

With 1490 and what I assume was the completion of the two villas, we reach the end of Giuliano da Maiano's career.[79] A considerable affection had grown up between the Duke and his architect. Giuliano had passed most of the period 1488–90 in Naples, and near the end of his life, on October 15, 1490, Leostello writes:

> And hearing news that Mastro Mariano de Vayano fiorentino, a man expert in building and drawing, was very ill, the Duke sent to him his own doctors and nurses and ordered that he be given everything he needed, as was the Duke's habit with his familiars.[80]

On October 16 Giuliano made his will, asking to be buried in SS Severino e Sossio. He died the following day at the age of 58.[81] Vasari says Alfonso provided a cortege of fifty mourners, dressed in black, and a marble tomb (now lost).[82]

Soon after Giuliano's death the Duke wrote to Lorenzo de' Medici asking for a successor. Lorenzo replied that he knew of no one in Florence "della sufficienza di Giuliano predetto" but that he could suggest Luca Fancelli, Alberti's former assistant, then working on the latter's two Mantua churches. However, Luca did not come to Naples, and in February 1491 Alfonso turned to Francesco di Giorgio.[83] According to Vasari, Francesco and the Duke had known each other as early as 1462,[84] and Roberto Papini claims that the Sienese artist had worked for Ferrante in the 1470s.[85] In 1479, we know for a certainty, Francesco had been with Alfonso at the siege of Poggio Imperiale, and at that time painted a picture for the Duke. This was sent down to Ferrante on February 2, 1479.[86] A drawing now in the Graphische Sammlung, Düsseldorf, has been tentatively identified as a study for it.[87]

In 1491 Francesco di Giorgio, at 51, was at the meridian of his career.[88] Aside from his

---

79. Giuliano had not limited himself to the work in Naples during these last years. On May 17, 1485, he had submitted designs for the Church of Santa Maria delle Carceri, Prato, actually erected from designs by Giuliano da Sangallo and completed in 1495. In September 1485 Giuliano da Maiano had returned to Florence to take up his duties as Capomaestro of the Cathedral. In the late 1480s he was involved with his brother in work at Loreto, for which he signed a contract in Naples on November 27, 1487. In 1490 he submitted, again from Naples, a design for the Santa Maria del Fiore facade competition. Cf. Fabriczy, "Toscanische und oberitalienische," pp. 88 and 90–91; P. Gianuizzi, "Documenti relativi a Baccio Pontelli," *Archivio storico dell'arte* [i.e. *L'Arte*], *1* (1888), 419 [Loreto documents]; Paatz, *Die Kirchen von Florenz* (Frankfurt, 1952), *3,* 334–35 (the Santa Maria del Fiore competition); Vasari, *4,* 304, 306; and Luigi del Moro, *La Facciata di Santa Maria del Fiore* (Florence, 1888), 20–22.

80. *Effemeridi,* p. 377.

81. G. Ceci, "Nuovi documenti," *ASPN, 29* (1904), 791–92.

82. Vasari, *2,* 473–74.

83. Giovanni Gaye, *Carteggio inedito d'artisti dei*

secoli *XIV, XV, XVI, 1* (Florence, 1839), pp. 300–03. Lorenzo's letter, dated December 1490, emphasizes how incomplete Alfonso's projects still were: "la perdita che ne resulta a tucte quelle cose, che lui haveva principiate, et che per la morte sua sono restate imperfecte. alle quali la Ex. V. volendo dare parfectione, intendo che haria charo li trovassi qualchun altro simile." Cf. also E. Percopo, "Nuovi Documenti," *ASPN, 20* (1895), 300.

84. Vasari, *3, 69.*

85. Roberto Papini, *Francesco di Giorgio Architetto* (Florence, 1946), *1, 278.*

86. E. Percopo, "Nuovi Documenti," *ASPN, 20* (1895), 302–03; A. S. Weller, *Francesco di Giorgio, 1439–1501* (Chicago, 1943), p. 11, n. 18; Barone, "Cedole," *ASPN, 9* (1884), 404; and Gaye, *Carteggio, 1, 259.*

87. Weller, *Francesco di Giorgio,* pp. 198–99. Published in Bernhard Degenhart, "Unbekannte Zeichnungen Francescos di Giorgio," *Zeitschrift für Kunstgeschichte, 8* (1939), 122. However the figure tentatively identified as Alfonso bears no resemblance to him.

88. The most relevant items for Naples are: Francesco di Giorgio Martini, *Trattati di architettura in-*

work for Federigo da Montefeltro at Urbino (1475–85), and his painting, sculpture, and engineering achievements, he had undertaken two beautiful and important churches: San Bernardino, outside Urbino (after 1482?), and Santa Maria del Calcinaio, Cortona, begun in 1485. Francesco had also in all probability built a town hall at Ancona in 1484 and remodeled another at Iesi in 1486–98. In 1490 he joined the famous group in Milan, which also included Bramante and Leonardo, and by the time he made his first visit to Naples in 1491 he also had to his credit notable achievements in military architecture. But this first stay in Alfonso's capital was probably devoted to completing Giuliano's two villas and the martyrs' church. Francesco's work pleased his patron who, on May 31, 1491, wrote back to the governing council of Siena, the Balía, to praise the architect.[89]

The demands of the Sienese artist's career, however, were too great for him to remain permanently in Naples, and the Duke was soon forced to look elsewhere for help. He chose "il bono e singulare fra' Iucundo," as Pietro Summonte called him,[90] a Franciscan monk from Verona, born about 1434. According to Vasari, Fra Giocondo was a Leonardesque figure: a student of literature, philosophy, and theology as well as architecture, hydraulics, and military engineering.[91] He was a great friend of Sannazaro's and may have designed scenery for productions of the poet's masques. Various structures have been attributed to him, including the Loggia del Consiglio in Verona, the Fondaco dei Tedeschi in Venice, two bridges across the Seine in Paris, and various châteaux, including Gaillon and Bury. There is also, of course, the famous and problematical plan for St. Peter's. Fra Giocondo probably designed as well the Cappella Pontano on the via Tribunali (Fig. 126) and, having been Sannazaro's friend, he may have had a hand in the design of that poet's villa of 1493 at Mergellina. He was living in Naples in that year.[92] Other possibilities are Pontano's two villas, one on the Vomero and the other on the via Tribunali.[93] The friar's literary works—editions of Caesar's *De bello gallico,* Frontinus' *De aqueductibus,* and Vitruvius—set a seal of scholarship on his reputation as a practical architect and antiquary.

gegneria e arte militare, ed. Corrado Maltese (Milan, 1967), which supersedes Cesare Saluzzo and Carlo Promis, eds., *Il Trattato di architettura civile e militare di Francesco di Giorgio Martini* (Turin, 1841); however Maltese's edition appeared too late for me to use it, so I quote from Saluzzo and Promis. Cf. also Giorgio Vasari, *Vite cinque,* ed. Girolamo Mancini (Florence, 1917); A. Venturi, *Architetti del XV al XVIII secolo. Francesco di Giorgio* (Rome, 1925); Weller, *Francesco di Giorgio;* Rotondi, *Il Palazzo Ducale di Urbino,* I, 263–70, 291–331; Henry Millon, "The Architectural Theory of Francesco di Giorgio," *Art Bulletin,* 40 (1958), 257–61; and Papini, op. cit.

89. Gaye, *Carteggio,* I, 307.

90. In Nicolini, *L'Arte napoletana,* p. 172.

91. Cf. Vasari, 5, 262–63, Pierre Lesueur, "Fra Giocondo en France," *Bulletin de la société de l'histoire de l'art français,* année 1931, pp. 115–44; Franz Graf

Wolff von Metternich, "Der Entwurf Fra Giocondos für Sankt Peter," *Festschrift Kurt Bauch* (Munich, 1957), pp. 155–70; Raffaello Brenzoni, *Fra Giovanni Giocondo veronese* (Florence, 1960); and Lucia Ciapponi, "Appunti per una biografia di Giovanni Giocondo da Verona," *Italia medioevale e umanistica,* 4 (1961), 131–58. A bibliography on Francesco's military architecture is below in Chapter 6, nn. 33, 35, 36.

92. For Sannazaro's famous couplet on Fra Giocondo's two bridges across the Seine see Percopo, "Nuovi Documenti," *ASPN, 19,* 379–80. For the Cappella Pontano see R. Filangieri, "Il Tempietto di Gioviano Pontano in Napoli," in *In Onore di Giovanni Gioviano Pontano nel V centenario della sua nascita* (Naples, 1926), pp. 13–49; and Giancarlo Alisio, "La Cappella Pontano," *NN,* ser. 3, 3 (1963), 29–35.

93. See n. 76 above.

Fra Giocondo's first recorded trip to Naples took place in 1489, before the death of Giuliano da Maiano. On December 19 of that year he went on an outing with Sannazaro to record antiquities at Pozzuoli.[94] Two days later he and the poet made a longer trip to Mola (i.e. Formia) and to Gaeta.[95] Two years later, on January 3, 1492, Alfonso called Fra Giocondo back to Naples to supervise work at Formia, which now may have been architectural rather than archaeological.[96] On the same day the friar became official ducal architect and took on a 14-year-old apprentice named Felice de Cava for a period of five years. Payments and benefices went to him in this new capacity throughout November, 1493.[97] Some of this work probably had to do with the frantic refortification of the city in preparation for the invasion of Charles VIII. It is usually assumed that Fra Giocondo remained in Naples until he left for France with Charles in June 1495.[98]

THE PALAZZO DEI TRIBUNALI   We are left with one final project and with yet another architect: the immense palace designed for Ferrante in 1488 by Giuliano da Sangallo (Fig. 99). The plan is recorded in the *Libro di Giuliano da San Gallo* in the Vatican Library, and it is one of a group of conceptions that display a new layout technique related to the plan of Poggioreale, but used mainly for large civic structures.[99]

In 1488, when the palace was designed, Giuliano da Sangallo was already becoming famous as a designer on the grand scale, though unfortunately most of these larger schemes

94. Fabriczy, "Toscanische und oberitalienische," p. 103. Percopo, "Nuovi Documenti," *ASPN, 19,* 380–82, gives the wrong date, December 19. Cf. Lucia Ciapponi, "Appunti . . . Giovanni Giocondo," p. 141.

95. Fabriczy, "Toscanische und oberitalienische," p. 103. An elegy (II, 9) written by Sannazaro after a similar trip, to Cuma, is cited in Antonio Altamura, *Jacopo Sannazaro* (Naples, 1951), p. 173.

96. Fabriczy, "Toscanische und oberitalienische," p. 104.

97. Ibid., pp. 103–05. One further architectural influence came into Alfonso's life at this point. Barone records a document dated February 25, 1492 ("Cedole," *ASPN, 10,* 1885, 12–13), in which Salvatore de Nastasi, libraio, is paid for binding a copy of Filarete's treatise for the ducal library. The manuscript is, or was, in the library of the University of Valencia, cod. lat. 837. Cf. Tammaro De Marinis, *La Biblioteca napoletana dei re d'Aragona, 2* (Milan, 1947), 72–73. But this source of inspiration would, I should think, have been pretty much drowned out by the presence in Naples of Francesco di Giorgio and of a royal copy (now apparently lost) of his own treatise.

98. Brenzoni, *Fra Giovanni,* p. 24. He and the other artists imported by Charles probably stayed at Amboise until Charles' death in 1498.

99. For Giuliano see H. Redtenbacher, "Beiträge zu Kenntniss des Lebens des florentinen Architekt Giuliano da San Gallo," *Allgemeine Bauzeitung, 44*

(1879), 1–10; Gustave Clausse, *Les San Gallo, 1* (Paris, 1900); C. von Fabriczy, "Chronologischen Prospekt über Giuliano da Sangallo," *Jahrbuch der preussischen Kunstsammlungen, 23* (1902), Supplement, 1–42; Rodolfo Falb, ed., *Il Taccuino senese di Giuliano da San Gallo* (Siena, 1902); Hermann Egger, "Entwürfe Baldassare Peruzzis für den Einzug Karl V. in Rom," *Jahrbuch des kunsthistorischen Sammlungen, 23,* pt. 1, *1* (Vienna, 1902), 1–44; G. K. Lukomski, *Les Sangallo* (Paris, 1934); Giuseppe Marchini, *Giuliano da Sangallo* (Florence, 1942); and H. Saalman, "The Authorship of the Pazzi Palace," *Art Bulletin, 46* (1964), 388–94. For the palace for Ferrante see Clausse, *Les Sangallo, 1,* 109–12; C. Huelsen, ed., *Il Libro di Giuliano da San Gallo* (Leipzig, 1910), esp. *1,* 16; Lukomski, pp. 143–45; Schreiber, *Poggio-Reale Variationen,* pp. 12–14; R. Filangieri, "Rassegna critica," *ASPN, 63* (1938), 278; Armando Schiavo, "I Progetti berniniani per il Louvre," *Emporium, 1* (1940), 15–26, esp. 15; Marchini, *Giuliano da Sangallo,* pp. 88, 99, 101; and L. H. Heydenreich, "Leonardo da Vinci, Architect of Francis I," *Burlington Magazine, 94* (1952), 277–85. Dr. Hartmut Biermann of the Bibliotheca Hertziana has prepared a study entitled "Das Haus eines vornehmen Römers—Das Modell Giuliano da Sangallos für den König von Neapel Ferdinand I," the manuscript of which he has very kindly let me read. This deals with Albertian and Roman influences on the design.

proved abortive. Vasari tells us that he had been commissioned to rebuild the whole town of Poggio Imperiale near Florence (1483) as a monument to Lorenzo, an undertaking that remained incomplete.[100] Giuliano also went to Milan to design a palace for Lodovico Sforza, a very ornate conception, we are told, but this too was never finished. He is said to have built or projected another palace for Charles VIII, and Vasari adds that Giuliano earned his nickname with a fourth large project, a monastery for a hundred friars outside the Porta San Gallo in Florence, consisting of a cloister and church (this was at least partly erected) built around a piazza. Clausse indicates that he had also been responsible for military architecture at Castellina and Ostia.[101] Thus Sangallo, far more than Giuliano da Maiano, had a reputation as an urbanist and designer of large buildings. This was presumably why he came to Naples for Alfonso's great structure, just as he was summoned to Rome in 1505 when his old patron Giuliano della Rovere, now Julius II, decided to build the greatest of all Renaissance cities.[102]

Giuliano da Sangallo's name is connected with three sketchbooks, one in the Vatican, one in the Biblioteca Comunale in Siena, and one in the Escorial, as well as with various loose drawings. These contain proof that he was indeed able to conceive intelligently on a large scale.[103] What is even more interesting is that when we look at the palace for Ferrante we see that it is actually a vast variation of Poggioreale.[104]

Vasari declares that the Neapolitan palace was designed in 1487 or 1488 on a commission from Lorenzo and that it was for Alfonso rather than for Ferrante. He adds that Giuliano spent a great deal of time on it, that he went to Naples with a model, and that construction was actually begun on a site near the Castel Nuovo. We are told that Alfonso showered Giuliano da Sangallo with gifts and invited him to remain, but that the architect was loyal to Lorenzo and returned to Florence.[105] There are documents that bear Vasari out: on February 27, 1488, the Duke paid 100 ducats to Giuliano da Sangallo in Naples.[106] And the main version of the palace plan in the Vatican *Libro* is inscribed: "This is the plan of the

100. Vasari, *4*, 275–76, 280. Cf. also Marchini, *Sangallo*, p. 88 and pl. xvia. Later (p. 281) Vasari says that after 1502 Antonio da Sangallo the Elder, Giuliano's brother, worked with Giuliano and that it was Antonio who made the model for the new fortifications here. The palace for Charles VIII was to have been either in Avignon or Lyons, and based on the Della Rovere palace at Savona (which was actually begun).

101. For the monastery at Porta San Gallo see Vasari, *4*, 274–75; for the other works see Clausse, *San Gallo*, *1*, 59–109.

102. Vasari, *4*, 278, 281. Giuliano da Sangallo followed Giuliano da Maiano not only in Naples but in Loreto, where Vasari says he was called upon to complete the latter's work on the piers of the dome (*4*, 277–78).

103. Huelsen, *Libro* (Vatican Library, Codice Barberiniano MS Lat. 4424), and Falb, *Taccuino* (Biblioteca Comunale, Siena, MS S.IV.8).

104. A related plan is on 8v of the Barberini sketchbook, a possible palace for (or by?) Lorenzo de' Medici. For the version of Ferrante's palace on 39v cf. Huelsen, *Libro*, *1*, 56. Other related drawings are mentioned in the following pages. For the link between the palace for Ferrante and Poggioreale cf. Redtenbacher, "Beiträge," p. 5, and Pane, *Architettura*, p. 36. Schreiber suggests that the palace in Lyon may also have been based on Poggioreale (*Poggio-Reale Variationen*, pp. 12–14).

105. Vasari, *4*, 271–74.

106. Fabriczy, "Toscanische und oberitalienische," p. 98. There was an earlier document that would relate Giuliano da Sangallo to Neapolitan royal patronage. This is dated 1483 and refers to "lo prezzo de uno quatro de li Maye haveva da fare in la Sagrestia dell'Annunziata." Cf. G. Filangieri, *Documenti*, *6*, 416. No price is mentioned, and no trace of the work is known to me.

model of a palace that the Magnifico Lorenzo de' Medici sent to King Ferrante of Naples, and I, Giuliano da San Gallo, as soon as I had finished it, went [there] with the model above mentioned. This was in 1488."[107]

The palace was to have been immense, of High Renaissance or, better, Romantic Classical scale. The central courtyard inside its colonnade is 160 x 90 braccia. (The figures written inside the court itself, "B cxxxv" and "B LX" do not correspond to any rectangular shape in the design. The closest is that formed by the outside bank of seats, which is 135 x 80 braccia. I conclude that B LX is an error for B LXXX.) The whole palace is approximately 270 braccia square, i.e. 157 meters or 517 feet, almost exactly the depth of St. Paul's, London, and the Duomo in Milan. Ferrante's palace was thus quite possibly the largest civic building planned during the Early Renaissance.[108]

Set into this great outer rectangle are smaller square room-blocks at the corners and in the middle of the sides parallel to the main axis. The front stands on a monumental base with flights of lateral steps and a staircase 60 to 65 braccia wide set into it. These steps are lacking on the other three sides, which suggests that the palace was designed for a sloping site. The main facade is preceded by a five-bay, cross-vaulted porch leading into a triple-arched, columned vestibule and out to another cross-vaulted loggia, six bays wide, which fronts on the immense courtyard. This is screened by square, coupled piers alternately open and filled with pairs of what I take to be columns. At the rear is a large rectangular indentation, around which the columnar screen continues, with a fountain or statue in the center. This leads into a laterally placed rectangular niched hall, 25 x 75 braccia. Beyond the hall, terminating the major axis of the building, is a small, round, niched and columned room, a kind of holy of holies, which projects beyond the square formed by the outer walls of the palace. Flanking the rectangular niched hall, which is marked S, there are two suites of large chambers in each of which are other rectangular niched halls, also marked S. The front and back towers and the arms are filled with smaller suites of rooms with independent staircases. Each arm is also provided with its own loggias. There seem to be no entrances except those at the front. The building therefore would have possessed a hierarchical progression of spaces leading from a broad open entrance front, through a series of internal ceremonial rooms and courts flanked by utilitarian honeycombs, to a small terminal climax.

The central court is an amphitheater like that at Poggioreale, but much larger, and shaped like a T. On the other hand, the monumental base with its projecting portico suggests Poggio a Caiano. The combination of numerous small rooms with such enormous central spaces is so far as I know unique in the period.

Regarding classical antecedents, one thinks first of Diocletian's Palace at Split, with its

107. Huelsen, *Libro, 2,* 39v: QUESTA E LA PIANTA DVNO MODELO DVNO PALAZO CHELMAGNIFICO LORENZO DEMEDICI MANDO ARE / FERNDO DINAPOLI EIO GIULIANO DA S° G° POIHE IO LEBBI FINITO ANADAI COLO M° SOPRA DETO / LE BRACA DAMISURARE [giving the scale] / FU NEL MCCCCLXXXVIII. Cf. also ibid.,

1, 56.

108. With the exception of Nicholas V's projected new Vatican Palace of c. 1450, as reconstructed by Magnuson, *Studies in Roman Quattrocento Architecture* (Rome/Stockholm, 1958), pp. 98–162.

corner towers, honeycombed arms, loggias, and interior processional axes. The Vatican *Libro* contains the plans of other Roman buildings of this same great scale (though not of Dio-cletian's Palace), e.g. the Baths of Caracalla. Other possibilities exist, especially for the T-form atrium, in Roman houses that might have been known to Giuliano.

Finally, there are related plans by Giuliano himself: actual copies in the Vatican *Libro* (8v) and in the *Taccuino senese* (17r and v) and two plans on 11r of the *Libro* (Fig. 98). These sketches with their inscription "M° L°" probably relate to the palaces Giuliano designed for Lorenzo.[109] They too are for very large buildings. Huelsen measures the lower as 150 braccia square, with the corner room-blocks 40 and the central hall 70 x 30 braccia. The basement, says an inscription, will be 10 braccia high. The upper building is even larger: 180 braccia square according to Giuliano's rough scale, and the room-blocks 30. Once again both conceptions involve the juxtaposition of small and large rooms.

All of Giuliano's schemes are based on stock spaces with internal variations. In the upper Taccuino conception is a Greek cross of circulation space: the arms terminate in room-blocks and the intersection consists of an enormous octagonal niched salon. The latter is based on Giuliano's plan of the "Bath of Viterbo" on fol. 8 in the *Taccuino senese*. In each arm of the cross the columnar screen is handled differently: on the left a lateral procession is backed by staircases; in the upper center is a rectangular arrangement around the three inner walls; on the right is a processional way with flanking aisles; and on the bottom is a kind of apse. The corner room-blocks are also varied in plan, but with no independent stairs or loggias. (Pal-ladio's Villa Rotonda here comes to mind.) In the lower sketch there is a similar Greek cross of circulation space, twice as wide as the corner blocks and lateral arms.

These plans seem to be laid out in accordance with a large modular grid (Fig. 100a–f). That is, with a few exceptions, the circulation spaces are standard squares or multiples of them, while the room suites are subdivisions. The Palace of Ferrante is designed on roughly 50-braccia coordinates: the horizontals generate, in order, the front podium, the front wall, the two back seats of the amphitheater, an inner partition, and the back of the main block of the building. The vertical coordinates create the outer and inner walls of the two arms, the returned front seats of the amphitheater, and the central axis. Within this the room-blocks are divided into subgrids.

In the upper plan in *Libro* 11r, the horizontal and vertical coordinates also neatly slice the main volumes of the building, and the lower right corner tower is again a subgrid. The lower plan is based on an irregular grid, and the tower or room-block subgrids are split into thirds. Even Poggio a Caiano seems to have been laid out in this manner: the splitting is fairly clear in the front, though it is violated toward the back. One cannot make such a claim for the

109. The "G" I take for "Giardino" and the "S" for "sala" or "salone." What the "R" and the "H" stand for I do not know. The lower plan is almost ex-actly repeated in Uffizi A7792. Filangieri, in "Rassegna critica," *ASPN, 63* (1938), 278, says Alfonso wanted *two* palaces for Naples, one being the Palazzo Tribunali mentioned by Pietro Summonte and the other a house for Lorenzo himself. This is repeated by De Marinis, *Biblioteca napoletana, 1,* 114, n. 61.

Peruzzi sketch of Poggioreale because it is too rough, but no particular grid is even hinted at in the drawing. The first Serlio variation of Poggioreale, however, is definitely based on a grid, an irregular one, as is the second; and it is highly likely that Poggioreale itself was created on the same principle.

The first person to write about this layout technique was probably Francesco di Giorgio. Filarete mentions something vaguely like it (Book VI), but Francesco speaks of it at length.[110] Unfortunately his discussion is hard to follow, but what he seems to mean is that palaces should be designed with a large *three-dimensional,* rather than merely two-dimensional module, corresponding to the shape and size of actual rooms in the building. These module-rooms he calls "cubiculi." The plan of a cubiculum is a "quadratum," i.e. a square. In the manuscript of his treatise in the Florence Biblioteca Nazionale there are no fewer than 69 house and palace plans on this principle.

Francesco tells us that intermediate measurements are obtained as follows. The architect begins by dividing the outer square or rectangle of his building into quadrata. He then sets the court or courts within them; these courts may be square, circular, or octagonal, and may measure $1\frac{1}{3}$, $1\frac{1}{2}$, or $1\frac{2}{3}$ quadrata. Around them, in turn, the cubiculi are set. These can be square, or they can measure $1\frac{1}{3}$ or $1\frac{1}{2}$ quadrata. Larger rooms, "salocti" or "triclini," can be longer in proportion, 2 quadrata in plan, or else $1\frac{1}{2}$ or even $1\frac{2}{3}$. Similar formulas are given for lesser rooms, kitchens and workrooms, and even for gardens.[111] Room heights are created from the diagonal of the quadratum; and thus does the original two-dimensional module become a cube or parallelepiped of volume.

Francesco's system involved geometrical rather than harmonic proportions and is therefore somewhat different from the Palladian principles that Wittkower discusses in the second part of *Architectural Principles in the Age of Humanism.* But the system is rather like the subdivision into giant squares that Wittkower notes in the facade of Santa Maria Novella. The difference is that with Francesco we have complete modularity dictating volumes throughout the building. Francesco's system thus forms part of a Quattrocento tendency toward an architecture of volumes and surfaces rather than articulated planes; an astylar architecture, vast in scale.

As for Ferrante's palace, one question remains. What was its purpose? I propose that it was not to be a personal residence, as is often assumed, but an office building or courthouse. In other words, I assume that Giuliano's "palace for Ferrante" is identical with Pietro Summonte's "great palace near the Castel Nuovo, in the Piazza dell'Incoronata, where the various

---

110. For Francesco di Giorgio's teaching on proportions cf. Henry Millon, "Architectural Theory," and Gunter Hellmann, "Proportionsverfahren des Francesco di Giorgio Martini," *Miscellanea Bibliothecae Hertzianae* [*Römische Forschungen, 16*] (1961), pp. 157–66. Both articles discuss church architecture almost exclusively, and Hellmann's deals with the influence on it of medieval quadratura. But neither church architecture

nor quadratura comes into Francesco's discussion of civil palaces.

111. Cf. Francesco di Giorgio, manuscript cited, and and the text published in Promis, esp. pp. 56–59. For other manuscripts see ibid., pp. 89–122. Francesco, however, uses the word "module" in describing a different geometrical system of producing measures (II, 4, in Promis, pp. 179–80).

tribunals would have been located." As mentioned, Vasari, like Summonte, tells us San-gallo's project was commissioned for Alfonso; i.e. it was a part of the renewal and that it was begun near the Castel Nuovo (Fig. 1). (It is interesting that the present Palazzo Muni-cipio, by Stefano Gasse, 1819–25, is on approximately this same sloping site.)

Ferrante and Alfonso had good reason to desire such a building. The Neapolitan bureauc-racy in 1488 was disjointed and mutinous.[112] At the top, headed by the King, was the Council of State with twenty members, which administered what we would probably call the depart-ments of state, war, and the interior. This met at the Castel Nuovo and its secretary was the Grand Chancellor of the kingdom. Under him was a numerous staff of scribes. There was also the Tribunal of the Sacred Council, a sort of superior circuit court, with a president and seventeen members; then there were the criminal and civil courts of the Vicaria, headed by the Chief Magistrate, with thirteen legal assistants, as well as their scribes and examiners, etc. The Vicaria, which created notaries and judges throughout the kingdom, met in the Convent of Santa Chiara. The Tribunal of the Regia Camera della Sommaria, headed by the Grand Chamberlain, had many officials and dealt with royal incomes, the sale of fiefs, and the super-vision of the royal militia, forts, jails, and artillery. There were other smaller tribunals for trade groups such as the silk and wool guilds, and still others for monastic orders, ecclesi-astical appointments, and the like. The seggi had a tribunal of their own with numerous em-ployees, and there were the professional organizations—the colleges of doctors, theologians, lawyers, etc.

These tribunals exercised great power, and yet were exceedingly independent of the throne. Some were almost completely controlled by the barons. Often they met in private houses belonging to their hereditary presidents—for example the Sommaria's headquarters was the palace of the Marchesi of Pescara. The paymaster's office also had its own seat, as did the Vicaria. Some, like the Hunting Tribunal, maintained small standing armies. The diffu-sion of powers among these independent bodies was expressed architecturally by the fact that Naples had no regular city hall where they all met. In 1540 Don Pietro of Toledo partly remedied the situation, as I have noted, by gathering a number of these tribunals into the Castel Capuano.

I believe the palace designed in 1488 for Ferrante and Alfonso was an earlier attempt to achieve the same thing. This would explain the many suites of small rooms, often with in-dependent access, which surrounded the impressive sequence of larger halls and chambers. The latter would have been used for the greater tribunals, and the amphitheater would have been devoted to public spectacles. Indeed Giuliano's palace can be seen as a public version of Poggioreale in more than just its plan. Where the villa was a private celebration of the

---

112. The ensuing account is based on G. A. Sum-monte, *Historia, 1,* 191–234; Nicola Toppi, *De origine omnium tribunalium* (Naples, 1655); B. Capasso, "La Vicaria Vecchia. II. La Vicaria Vecchia, palazzo di giu-stizia in Napoli," *ASPN, 15* (1890), 388–417; and Felice De Filippis, *Castelcapuano, reggia e fortezza* (Naples, 1956), pp. 61–65.

military victories of the Crown over the barons, the Palazzo dei Tribunali would have been the public expression of a legal and juridical victory.

At least two of the buildings we have discussed thus far, Poggioreale and the Palazzo dei Tribunali, seem to have been planned on the principle of the cubical grid, an aspect of the late Quattrocento sensibility for an astylar architecture of volumes. The same thing can be sensed in prospettiva legittima and even in the rectangles of latitude and longitude of the globe itself. They are part of the age's concern for infinity and ubiquity. These conceptions added a "modern" voice, neutral both in terms of the Gothic and the Antique, to the chorus of stylistic languages that were present on the Neapolitan scene.

Chapter 6: THE WESTERN DEFENSES AND THE HYDRAULIC SYSTEM

FRANCESCO DI GIORGIO AND THE NEW MILITARY ARCHITECTURE   The largest feature of Alfonso's renewal was the new western defense system. Though construction began in 1494, it was not finished until 1540 or possibly later. It involved a complete remodeling of the Castel Sant'Elmo, the Castel Nuovo, and the Castel dell'Ovo, and a new set of walls, linking all three, along the western side of the city and harbor front (Fig. 1). Unlike the eastern walls, these later structures made use of the revolutionary principles of defense warfare which were being developed throughout Italy.

Francesco di Giorgio was the main figure in this aspect of the renewal. He visited Naples between February and June 1491 and from June to November 1492. Later he made two other visits, but it was probably during his stay in the summer and fall of 1492 that the plans for the new defenses were drawn up.[1]

Francesco's supervision of these projects was intermittent. After he returned to Siena in 1492, it was always difficult to get him back. In March 1493 he was given permission by the Balía to return to Naples but apparently did not go. On the following April 19 he was ordered to do so, but was still in his native city on February 18, 1494, when he was again granted permission to leave.[2] Even then it is not certain he actually went. The much-postponed third visit was probably intended as a long one, however, since in 1494 the Balía asked Francesco to close out his accounts as the city's hydraulic engineer.[3]

We cannot be sure that Francesco di Giorgio actually returned to Naples until January 1495,[4] but he remained there as military engineer throughout the following year with its dramatic events: abdication, French invasion, recapture by Ferrandino, and the death in exile of Alfonso II. Unlike Fra Giocondo, Francesco remained loyal to the Aragonese and was of great service to Ferrandino in his victories of 1495. His fourth and last visit to Naples, early in 1497, was also concerned with the new defense system.

1. Giovanni Gaye, *Carteggio inedito d'artisti dei secoli XIV, XV, XVI, I* (Florence, 1839), 305–19. Cf. also Fabriczy, "Toscanische und oberitalienische," p. 102; and Allen S. Weller, *Francesco di Giorgio* (Chicago, 1943), pp. 29–30; 35–36; 382–89.

2. Gaye, *I*, 317–19, which mentions the "edificii quali si fanno per la Maestà del Re e delo Illo. S. D. di Calabria, acciò quelli si traghino a perfectione." The letter is from the Balia in Siena to Francesco in Naples, dated July 7, 1492. Cf. also Weller, *Francesco di Giorgio*, pp. 33–36.

3. F. Donati, "Francesco di Giorgio Martini in Siena," *Bollettino senese di storia patria*, 9 (1902),

149–85, esp. 179.

4. R. Filangieri, *Cronaca figurata*, p. 112. This reference, dated January 13, has not hitherto been noted so far as I know. Earlier writers have accordingly dated Francesco's 1495 stay as beginning around August 26 (e.g. Weller, *Francesco di Giorgio*, p. 390; I myself have done the same: cf. my "Porta Reale," p. 92). Erring on the other side, R. Filangieri, in "Rassegna critica," *ASPN*, 63 (1938), 273, and n. 1, says Francesco arrived in February *1494*. But I have found no document for this nor does Filangieri cite one, so I assume it is a slip of the pen.

Francesco was not the only architect whose military knowledge was called upon by Alfonso in the 1490s. Fra Giocondo's trips to Nola and elsewhere to "oversee certain construction" may well have been military in purpose,[5] and in June 1492 he was asked to make drawings to illustrate two treatises by Francesco, one on architecture and the other on artillery. Just before this he had made designs of his own for forts.[6] Other military architects who worked for Alfonso in the 1490s were a certain Maestro Vincenzo de Cortona, who was paid 30 ducats in 1493 for making models of forts; and Antonio Marchese, a Florentine associate of Francesco di Giorgio's, who in 1494 was told to secure the Castel Ponte Santa Croce.[7] On November 4 of that same year, Alfonso, by now king, summoned a fifth, unidentified, Florentine architect:

> Baccio: we need you to serve us in certain works which we do not see how any other architect could complete satisfactorily. Once you have received this, for our love come as quickly as you can without delay. . . . We will be in Siena.[8]

This letter reflects the passionate, disorganized preparations that Alfonso undertook in the mid-1490s as he watched his father's network of alliances break apart. The architect he wrote to may have been Baccio Pontelli, another expert in military architecture, to whom various forts—Osimo, Offida, and Senigallia—have been ascribed.[9] At the same time, however, Alfonso planned to go personally to Siena, which may reflect still another attempt to get hold of Francesco di Giorgio.

Alfonso's desire to secure foreign specialists in military building was, for him, unprecedented. Earlier, as the Duke of Calabria, he had been his own military architect. Thus in 1485, in Capua, Alfonso "looked over the city walls, laid them out in a new manner, and toured around with the leading citizens re-doing everything in his wise spirit of invention."[10] We have already seen how likely it was that in 1487 Alfonso personally laid out the eastern walls of Naples. After the Barons' Revolt he himself refortified the castles seized from the rebels. Thus on October 10, 1487, he wrote from Diano to his librarian and secretary, Albino:

5. Fabriczy, "Toscanische und oberitalienische," pp. 103–05.

6. He may also have been asked to restore the ancient street pattern. Cf. Per Hamberg, "Vitruvius, Fra Giocondo and the City Plan of Naples," *Acta archaeologica, 36* (1965), 105–25; also n. 38 below.

7. Barone, "Cedole," *ASPN, 10* (1885), 23; ibid., *14* (1889), 398.

8. From G. Ceci, "Nuovi Documenti," *NN, 9* (1900), 83: "Rex Siciliae, etc. / Baccio: ad noi occorre havere ad servirece de voi in certe opere le quali non vedemo che per altro mastro ne potesse essere ben satisfacto: et però per nostro amore ricevuta la presente ce venerete ad ritrovare senza indugiarve: et per nostro gran servicio vengate lo più presto sera possibele senza perdere de tempo: noi ce trovarimo in lo territorio de Sena. / Dat. in Castris prope Terracinae IIII Nov. MCCCCLXXXXIIII. / Rex Alfonsus. / Jo. Pont. / Magistro Baccio florentino."

9. Though it is possible that Baccio Pontelli was then no longer alive. Cf. Paolo Giordani, "Baccio Pontelli a Roma," *L'Arte, 11* (1908), 96–112; P. Gianuizzi, "Documenti relativi a Baccio Pontelli," *Archivio storico dell'arte* [i.e. *L'Arte*], *3* (1890), 296–99, and Gaspare De Fiore, *Baccio Pontelli, Architetto fiorentino* (Rome, 1963). De Fiore gives the date of Baccio's death as 1494 (pp. 94, 99); but even if Baccio were dead Alfonso may not have known this.

10. "Vide le mura de la cipta et quelle designo cum modo nouello: et li principali homini de dicta Cipta et sua I.S. andaua reassectando ogni cosa cum suo sagacissimo ingegno," Leostello, *Effemeridi*, p. 50.

We have made a tour through these lands that belonged to the former Prince of Salerno [Antonello Sanseverino, one of the leaders of the revolt], and we have provided for the strengthening and rebuilding of the principal castles of this estate so that they will remain secure for all time. Today we find ourselves again in Diano; tomorrow we will go and furnish the castle at Sala, and the day after we will be on the way home. We hope within four days to be in Naples.[11]

On other occasions the Duke supervised fortifications in Capua, Longano, and Baia.[12] In 1490, Leostello says, he "designavit Menia" at Longano. Other forts or mural defenses apparently built to his directions were at Rocca di Cilento, Gaeta, Manfredonia, and Chieti, where Alfonso "desegnò le mure future."[13]

Leostello's attributions may of course be mere conventional phraseology. And, it is true that military engineers do appear during the 1480s, for example the Turk Maestro Calasa, and Diego Portoghese and Giovanni de Petrizza.[14] But none of these earlier men seems to have had the unique knowledge of the "Baccio" of Alfonso's letter. In any case, the rapidity of Alfonso's movements in the 1480s suggests that the architectural and military problems raised were fairly easily solved. The Duke's attitude to military architecture after the Barons' Revolt in 1486–90 is therefore in considerable contrast to his attitude later when he issued his importunate summonses to Francesco di Giorgio and "Baccio."

Alfonso's earlier fortifications—those of Otranto, Poggio Imperiale, and the eastern walls of Naples (Fig. 60)—had been the traditional ones of Italian defensive warfare.[15] Such structures were designed for missiles that were lobbed or hurled in elliptical trajectories—hence the higher the walls the better. The buildings are tall and thin, perching like crowns on hilltops or dipping along the contours at the edges of the towns. This kind of fortification was rapidly passing out of favor during the latter part of the Quattrocento. As larger cannon were built, and fired with heavy gunpowder charges, missiles could travel with great velocity over flat trajectories. It became possible, even easy, to breach the walls of these traditional forts.

11. From Giovanni Albino, *Lettere, istruzioni ed altre memorie de' re aragonesi*, Gravier, *Raccolta*, 5, 150–51: "Nui hauemo fatto uno discurso per queste Terre, che foro del olim Principe de Salerno, et hauemo proueduto ala fortificatione, et reedificatione dele principale castelle de questo stato, in modo che per ogne tempo se ne porrà stare securo. Hogi ne retrouamo qui in Diano, domane anderimo ad prouedere lo castello dela Sala, et posdomane serimo in cammino de retorno, et speramo fra quattro di essermo in Napoli."

12. Morisani, *Letteratura*, pp. 37–38.

13. Leostello, *Effemeridi*, p. 285.

14. R. Filangieri, "Rassegna critica," *ASPN*, 63 (1938), 273. Filangieri adds that Giuliano da Maiano built military structures for Alfonso but cites no evidence.

15. Cf. E. Rocchi, *Le Origini della fortificazione moderna*, 1 (Rome, 1894), 1–140; Mariano Borgatti, *Castel Sant' Angelo in Roma* (Rome, 1931); Romeo Mella, "Fortificazione," s.v., *Enciclopedia italiana* (Rome, 1931); R. Filangieri, "Rassegna critica," *ASPN*, 64 (1939), 249–54; Vincent Scully, "Michelangelo's Fortification Drawings: A Study of the Reflex Diagonal," *Actes du XVIIᵉ Congrès international d'histoire de l'art* (The Hague, 1955), pp. 323–32; Horst De la Croix, "Military Architecture and the Radial City Plan in Sixteenth Century Italy," *Art Bulletin*, 42 (1960), 263–90; J. S. Ackerman, *The Architecture of Michelangelo*, 1 (London, 1961), 45–53, 2, 43–48; A. Cassi Ramelli, *Dalle Caverne ai rifugi blindati*, (Milan, 1964), pp. 309–84; and J. R. Hale, "The Development of the Bastion, 1440–1534," in J. R. Hale, J. R. L. Highfield, B. Smalley, eds., *Europe in the Late Middle Ages* (London, 1965), pp. 466–94. For the political repercussions of the new military techniques see Piero Pieri, *Il Rinascimento e la crisi militare italiana* (Turin, 1952), pp. 320–98.

Similarly, the defenders could not use the new weapons effectively from their high, narrow firing platforms. The type of fort Alfonso was erecting throughout Calabria and Apulia in the wake of the Barons' Revolt was obsolescent. New structures, designed on entirely different principles, were needed.

Ironically, the Aragonese had done a great deal to develop the monster cannon responsible for this architectural revolution.[16] Riccardo Filangieri informs us that in 1442 Alfonso I's mobile "bombardes grosses" were effective in destroying the Angevin keep that had stood on the site of the Castel Nuovo.[17] Not much later, a certain Giovanni Bruno developed a secret process for making stone cannonballs for the king's bombards and trabucchi.[18] These newer pieces were often designed as works of art. When Pisanello came to Naples in 1448, he or an assistant left behind him in the Codex Vallardi some handsome sketches for heavy artillery pieces, which may have been cast by Guglielmo Lo Monaco.[19] In 1472 Luciano Laurana was made artillery master of the Castel Nuovo at 300 ducats a year. His salary payments were continued through March 1474. But apparently the manufacture of artillery pieces in Naples fell off during the next two decades. Since numbers of monster field pieces are shown by Ferraiolo in his illustration of the expedition to Otranto, Alfonso of Calabria was presumably familiar with the offensive possibilities of these cannon in 1481; and in 1492, when the new western walls of Naples were being planned, he ordered forty new iron bombards to be transported from San Nicola to the Castel Nuovo magazine. The cannon founder at this time was Maestro Francesco de Mantova, who received the noble annual stipend of 400 ducats.[20]

Alfonso's arms buildup was also a reflection of the French forces' great reputation for artillery. Much of Charles' success during the Italian invasion of 1495 is attributed to his use of large guns.[21] But despite these French weapons and despite their faint-hearted defense in 1495, the Neapolitans actually possessed the superior firepower.[22] The author of *Le Vergier d'honneur,* before seeing the guns of Castel Nuovo, marveled:

> on avait, ainsi qu'on peut entendre,
> La plus terrible et grosse artillerie
> Qu'on vit jamais, et la mieux accomplie.[23]

16. R. Filangieri, "Rassegna critica," *ASPN, 64* (1939), 249–54; and Iole Mazzoleni, "Gli Apprestamenti difensivi nei castelli di Calabria ultra alla fine del regno aragonese," *ASPN, 69* (1944–46), 132–44.

17. R. Filangieri, "Rassegna critica," *ASPN, 63* (1938), 324.

18. Ibid. A bombard was a short, shallow gun like a mortar but with a two-piece barrel. A trabucco was a more old-fashioned mechanical siege machine. These, and even hand guns, were often called "artiglieria." The bombards described by Francesco di Giorgio in his treatise (V, 1) were about 5 meters long, weighing about 225 lbs., and fired a stone ball. The longest gun was the basilisco, about 8.45 meters long. It fired a bronze or iron ball.

19. R. Filangieri, "Rassegna," *ASPN, 63* (1938),

325. These were mostly of the long, one-piece types— basilische and passavolanti—20–25 piedi in length. Cf. E. Rocchi, "Le Artiglierie italiane del rinascimento e l'arte del getto," *L'Arte, 2* (1899), 347–72.

20. R. Filangieri, op. cit., p. 327.

21. Iole Mazzoleni, "Gli apprestamenti."

22. L. Volpicella, "Le Artiglierie di Castel Nuovo nell' anno 1500," *ASPN, 35* (1910), 308–48. Giucciardini, Paolo Giovio, and Biringuccio all seem to have overpraised French artillery. Cf. Rocchi, "Le Artiglierie," p. 356. The French use of iron cannonballs was perhaps their real source of superiority (Biringuccio, Smith-Gnudi ed., p. 319). These seem first to have been used in Italy by the French against Ferrandino.

23. Quoted by R. Filangieri, "Rassegna critica," *ASPN, 63* (1938), 328.

On October 28, 1495, Ferraiolo tells us that bombardments from cannon in the Castel Nuovo, then held by the French, reached as far as Santa Maria la Nova and even to the Piazza Sellaria (now Piazza Nicola Amore), i.e. across the greatest width of the city—a claim reaffirmed by Riccardo Filangieri.[24]

Meanwhile various solutions to the architectural problems raised by these new cannon were being tried out. The massive tower scarps, surmounted by cantilevered balconies, called ravelins in Naples, and the antemural fortification of the main portal, completed in 1453, had been Alfonso I's contribution to the changeover (Fig. 101). Transitional fortifications, halfway between the old and the new, were also begun by Biagio Rossetti in the early 1490s in Ferrara for Ercole I d'Este.[25] Here for perhaps the first time the curtain was completely abandoned. Rossetti built low ramparts, fronted by deep scarps and counterscarps, and composed of wide terrepleins and low parapets. There were low round towers, also, the sort called torrioni, which rose only to the height of the walls. The defenses of Ferrara thus became a geometrical ring-shaped hill, forming a lap or valley for the city and flowing out into projections and dropping back according to the patterns of defense fire that were envisaged.

Such transitional ideas had for long been competing with even fuller realizations of the new needs. The chief figure here was Francesco di Giorgio's mentor, the Sienese military engineer Mariano di Jacopo, called Taccola (1381–1458?).[26] Taccola set forth his ideas in a treatise called *De machinis libri decem,* written about 1449. He also used some of his new principles in the defenses of Rome, which were erected by Calixtus III in the 1450s. In 1461 Lodovico of Savoy is said to have fortified Turin in the same manner, though this work was not actually finished until 1536. In the war between Venice and the Este of 1482–84, the Senate called for marble-sheathed walls of the new type at Pontelagoscuro on the Po. Such new structures were also built at Ostia in 1483 (probably by Baccio Pontelli), and quite a bit later at Civitavecchia for Cardinal Della Rovere from designs by Bramante. The latter fort was very like the contemporaneous remodeling of the Castel Nuovo by Francesco di Giorgio.[27]

The governing feature of these new fortifications ultimately became the polyhedral bastion. This was a gun platform rather than a tower, and allowed for maximum crossfire at advanced, low positions and even for long-range attacks, with cannon, on the besiegers. Various candidates have been mentioned for the honor of inventing this device. It is even possible that it grew out of the old "puntoni" of the Middle Ages, the hexagonal towers that were set against the walls of forts. One imagines such a bastion being created in the modern-

24. R. Filangieri, *Cronaca figurata,* p. 194.

25. For the place of Castel Nuovo in fortification history see R. Filangieri, *Castel Nuovo* (Naples, 1964), pp. 47–58. For Ferrara see Bruno Zevi, *Biagio Rossetti Architetto ferrarese* (Florence, 1960), pp. 150–57. For other defenses of this same type (deep round torrioni but no angular bastions) cf. R. Filangieri, "La Citadella aragonese e il recinto bastionato di Castelnuovo," *Atti dell'Accademia Pontaniana,* ser. 2, 34 (1929), 49–73.

26. See the biographical article in *Enciclopedia italiana,* E. Rocchi, "Le artiglierie italiane," p. 351, and Luigi Michelini Tocci, "Disegni e appunti autografi di Francesco di Giorgio in un codice del Taccola," *Scritti di storia dell'arte in onore di Mario Salmi,* 2 (Rome, 1962), 203–12, with other bibliography; also n. 36 below.

27. Romeo Mella, "Fortificazione."

izing of structures like Frederick II Hohenstaufen's forts at Prato or Augusta (Fig. 95).[28] At first the new forms were probably carried out in earthworks and only later translated into masonry. Filarete, in Book VI of his treatise, anticipates the zigzag plans that resulted from these bastions, but this layout does not really embody the new principles. The walls are too narrow, and their ramparts would never allow room for maneuvering passavolanti and basilische.[29] Verbal descriptions of the polyhedral bastion apparently first appear in Taccola.[30] By designing his building as a complex of such bastions, sometimes working it dramatically into and out of the site, an architect could create a fort that was literally unapproachable when its guns were firing.

The resulting forms had a cold, solid immensity (Fig. 102). The deep ramparts lay behind an array of polygonal, faceted shapes, massive and steeply raked. The torrioni, bastions, and outer scarped ditches flanked inner rising volumes—cylinders and pentagons—that twisted up from among the outworks, constantly turning away from them. The older medieval elements—the wooden hoardings and roofs and the cantilevered machicolations—began to shrink and disappear. Construction now called for thin masonry shells over vast earth, tufa, or brushwood cores, vaulted above, crouching and massive below, gripping the site with molding, penetrative force. Low, brown, swelling, and harsh, the new forts sailed like warships across the hills and probed and settled deeply into their contours. To the startled contemporary eye such structures must have seemed the work of giants.

The large cannon and their trajectories not only dictated the character of the solids that contained them but also established a new kind of space around those solids. Approaches, streets, and squares were conceived as alleys and fields for cannon fire. Exterior space adjacent to these structures was thus suddenly active, alive, paramount. The guns were in large part the reason for the linked sequences of spaces that were opened up by Renaissance planners through medieval labyrinths: for example it was for defense purposes that Nicholas V (it is said on Ferrante's advice) called for the new streets and piazza in the Borgo Leonino.[31]

This new space-positiveness, and the sort of angular volumes that went with it, was, I believe, partly responsible for the increased consciousness of volume and space that typifies High Renaissance architecture and urbanism. It would thus not be accidental that some of the chief begetters of the new movement, Francesco di Giorgio, Giuliano da Sangallo, and Bramante, were involved in military engineering. Furthermore, like the cubical grids of Francesco di Giorgio's palaces, the new military shapes were a neutral element in the play of styles. By no definition could the new forms be called Roman, Greek, or Gothic; yet they

28. H. Hahn, *Hohenstaufenburgen in Süditalien* (Munich, 1961), pp. 25–27.

29. Cf. John R. Spencer, *Filarete's Treatise on Architecture*, 1 (New Haven, 1966), 66, n. 1. In this connection the zigzags that Sepe (*La Murazione,* p. 9), thinks were built into the northern sector of the eastern walls of Naples are perhaps relevant. Sepe says they were probably due to the placement of existing structures, but

they may instead (or also) have been an attempt to echo the Filarete pattern. It was not until two years after these eastern walls were complete (1492), however, that a copy of Filarete's treatise was made for the ducal library (Chapter 5, n. 102).

30. Michelini Tocci, "Disegni e appunti."

31. Stefano Infessura, *Diario della città di Roma* [1475], ed. Oreste Tommasini (Rome, 1890), p. 79.

could be considered purely artistic entities apart from their military function. This is shown above all in Michelangelo's use of them in his 1528–29 fortifications for Florence. Here, indeed, the stretching, faceted solids are carried to their ultimate, and perhaps militarily useless, climax.[32]

The first architect (as opposed to Taccola the technologist) to write on this new architecture was probably Francesco di Giorgio. His work, written in an urgent, incoherent Italian, dwells much on the new principles.[33] It ends with descriptions of the actual forts, in the new manner, that he built for Federigo da Montefeltro in the Marches. An example of Francesco's approach is San Leo (Fig. 102). Sasso di Montefeltro, Tavoleto, and Serra di Sant'Abondio are others. One notices too that Francesco speaks with equal pride of his hydraulic works for the city of Siena.[34] It is clear indeed that he looks upon the architect as far more than a builder of palaces and churches. To him as to Vitruvius, or even Leonardo, the architect was a kind of titan, the founder of cities, the shaper of the earth, the governor of its torrents, and the winner of battles. He was the ideal person to build at the new Cyclopean scale.[35]

We can sometimes see nonmilitary forms, apparently generated by this attitude, in contemporaneous architecture. Thus there is the massive raked buttress, really a scarp, on the south wall of Francesco's little monastic church, San Bernardino (after 1482), just outside Urbino. The three-part layering and the general effect of the squat cylinder housing the dome also contribute to the effect of a fort. And, bound with the Florence Nazionale manuscript of Francesco's treatise, is a sheet on which some Quattrocento designer (possibly Francesco himself) has made a fort from a gigantic molded base (Fig. 107) such as one might design for a pier. Here indeed is a Cyclops-image, the building as colossus.

BUILDING THE WESTERN DEFENSES   The first specific record that Francesco's new principles were applied in the southern capital has already been mentioned: it comes on June 30, 1492, when the painter Antonello da Capua was paid for binding manuscripts of

---

32. Scully, "Michelangelo's Drawings."

33. For Francesco's military and engineering accomplishments see the bibliography in Gustina Scaglia, "Drawings of Machines for Architecture from the Early Quattrocento in Italy," *Journal of the Society of Architectural Historians*, 25 (1966), 90–114, esp. 90–91, 111–12, nn. 1, 71. See also Luigi Serra, *L'Arte nelle Marche*, 2 (Rome, 1934), 116–37; E. Lavagnino, "L'Architetto di Sisto IV," *L'Arte*, 27 (1924), 4–13; Selwyn Brinton, *Francesco di Giorgio Martini of Siena*, etc. (London, 1934–35); and Weller, *Francesco di Giorgio*, pp. 206–10. The possibility that Fra Giocondo may have had a hand in the new type of fortifications at Naples is discouraged by the illustrations in his later edition of Vitruvius; they are thoroughly medieval (*M. Vitruvius per Iocundum solito castigatior factus cum figuris et tabula ut iam legi et intellegi possit* [1513]

(Florence, 1522). Other authorities, like Valturio in *De re militari* (Verona, 1472), also preferred antique revivalism to the new ideas; nor is there anything even in Alberti suggesting that he was "modern" in this respect, though he may have known Mariano di Jacopo in Rome in the 1450s.

34. *Trattato,* Promis ed., pp. 288–93.

35. For Francesco's work in the Marches, besides the bibliography cited in Chapter 5, n. 93, and in this chapter, n. 33, see "Francesco di Giorgio nel Montefeltro," *Il Marzocco, 32* (July 3, 1927) and in *La Balzana, 1* (1927), 135–36; and Luigi Serra, "Le Rocche di Mondavio e di Cagli e le altre fortezze di Francesco di Giorgio Martini nella Marca," *Miscellanea di storia dell'arte in onore di Igino Benvenuto Supino* (Florence, 1933), 435–55.

treatises by Francesco, one on architecture and the other on artillery, with 126 illustrations by Fra Giocondo.[36] (Earlier in the same month, as noted, Alfonso had paid Biase Crescuonno de la Costa for twenty vellum sheets, again given to Fra Giocondo, to make designs for forts; but we do not know whether these were of the traditional type or not.)[37] Nothing is known of the fate of this copy of Francesco's treatise. Fabriczy has suggested that some of Fra Giocondo's drawings for the architectural part are now in the Uffizi, but there is no evidence of the treatise on artillery.[38]

It was not until seventeen months later, in January 1494, that measures were taken to put Francesco's ideas into effect.[39] Eventually, indeed, Alfonso had to settle for the services of Francesco's assistant, Marchese, designated in the documents as "proto-architect."[40] In January 1494 Antonio signed a contract at a salary of 200 ducats a year to build the new western defense system.[41] At the same time Alfonso, by now king, levied a tax of 60,000 ducats to pay for it.[42]

36. Fabriczy, "Toscanische und oberitalienische," p. 107. For the question of the *Trattato* manuscripts cf. Michelini Tocci, "Disegni e appunti"; Gustina Scaglia, "Drawings of Machines"; De Marinis, *Biblioteca napoletana, 2* (Milan, 1947), doc. 830; A. Panatelli, *Di Francesco di Giorgio Martini* (Siena, 1870), p. 128; Weller, review of Brinton's *Francesco di Giorgio*, in *Art Bulletin, 18* (1936), 120–22; and Mario Salmi, *Disegni di Francesco di Giorgio nella collezione Chigi Saracini* [Siena; Accademia Chigiana. *Quaderni, 2*] (Siena, 1947); and James H. Beck, "The Historical 'Taccola' and Emperor Sigismund in Siena," *Art Bulletin, 50* (1968), 309–19.

37. De Marinis, *La Biblioteca napoletana, 2*, doc. 826.

38. Fabriczy, "Toscanische und oberitalienische," p. 107. Philip Foster has pointed out to me a fifteenth-century manuscript of Francesco's treatise in the Spencer Collection of the New York Public Library. On fol. 3v is a passage in which the author contrasts himself to the sort of architect who solicits patronage—which is something Francesco certainly cannot be accused of doing in his relations with Alfonso. He then adds: "pero ho io determinato servire alla tua Ex.tia si non in tutto in parte le ragione di essa Architettura." In the left-hand margin at this point is the rubric: "Ad Alfonso." This person is not further identified, but he may have been the Duke of Calabria, and the New York codex may therefore be related to the two that were bound in 1492. For other views on the fate of the Neapolitan manuscripts see G. Mancini, ed., Giorgio Vasari, *Vite cinque* (Florence, 1917), p. 57. Mancini says the 126 drawings were probably copied by Fra Giocondo from the *Opusculum de architectura*, MS 383, Biblioteca del Re (now in the Biblioteca Nazionale), Turin, and from the Magliabecchiana manuscript, i.e. II.1.141, Bib. Naz., Florence. Heinrich von Geymüller, in *Cento Disegni di architettura, d'ornato e di figure di Fra Giovanni Giocondo* (Florence, 1882), pp. 22–24, also suggests the Florence Magliabecchiana manuscript as model. In view of these possibilities it would be interesting to do further work on the New York manuscript, especially since the 1492 Neapolitan payment record is the earliest document, so far as I know, for the existence of Francesco's treatise.

39. G. A. Summonte, *Historia, 4*, 623, says the work began in 1493: "[Ferrante] si diede a fortificar di nuovo le fortezze della Città, e quelle del Regno, & a ben munirle di necessarj prefidj."

40. G. Filangieri, *Documenti, 6*, 102. Cf. also Vasari, *4*, 476, n. 4. The design of Castel Sant'Elmo is sometimes given to a certain Pierluigi Escriva, Scrivà, or Scribà, a Valencian architect who also worked for Francesco Maria della Rovere and who built a fortress at L'Aquila in 1543 (E. Rocchi, *Le Fonti storiche dell' architettura militare*, Rome, 1908, pp. 336–37). However the work at L'Aquila is completely unlike Sant'Elmo, and the absence of contemporary documentation makes it probable that Escriva worked under Don Pietro in the 1540s, i.e. that he merely completed the fort Francesco had designed. Rocchi cites a writing of Escriva's, *Apologia en excusaciòn y favor de las fabricas del reino de Nàpoles*, which I have not as yet come across, but which might throw light on the question.

41. For Marchese see G. Ceci, "Nuovi Documenti," *NN, 9* (1900), 84, and R. Filangieri, "Antonio Marchese da Settignano, Architetto militare del Rinascimento," *Rivista di artiglieria e del genio, 70* (1931), 473–79.

42. Passero, *Giornali*, p. 62: "In questo anno 1494 nello mese de maio se ei puosto l'impruonto in Napoli per fare le mura de Santa Chiara per si a lo castiello de Sant' Eramo, & per pare lo castiello del ovo & questo impruonto ei da sessanta milia docati." Cf. also Lodovico Bianchini, *Della Storia delle finanze del regno di Napoli, 2* (Naples, 1834), 132.

Even with these new funds and an architect now available, the actual construction does not seem to have begun until the following October 2, when Polla dela Martino, "intagliatore di pietre," provided stone for the new walls.[43] Again on October 7, Giordano di Fabrizio di Cava sold a certain Berardino de Lambrosio enough stone to build forty *canne* of new walls in the Salita de Sant'Erasmo, i.e. the approach to the Castel Sant'Elmo. I assume that this was a part of the linkage between the town and the castle shown in Lafrery (Fig. 106). On October 31, 15,000 palmi of pietre dolci were purchased for the same purpose, no doubt for the wall cores.[44] On the following December 18, all the stone necessary for 200 canne of new walls, also along the salita, was bought.[45] Perhaps slightly less than a mile of new walls was therefore constructed before Alfonso's abdication.

In January 1495 an event that has not been properly incorporated into Francesco di Giorgio's story occurred: his arrival in Naples and the immediate beginning of work on the two castles. On January 13, according to Ferraiolo, the Sienese architect began tearing down the two gate towers of Sant'Elmo. Ferraiolo says this was to become the finest fort in Italy. He goes on:

> and at this time His Majesty the King caused the bastion above Baia to be built for the defense of that place, which was a handsome structure, with casemates and defenses all well arranged.
>
> And in this same year, in October [Ferraiolo means 1494], His Majesty had a bastion built, called a casemate [sic], at the bridge over the moat of the Castel Nuovo, at the foot of the Torre Beverello; and if this casemate had ever been completed it would have been the destruction of the city in the war [i.e. when the French held Castel Nuovo and Ferrandino occupied the rest of the city].

In other words, Alfonso began the erection at Baia and at the Castel Nuovo of the low, thrusting bastions, or *torrioni*, topped with vaulted gun chambers that distinguish the new type of fortification. On the following day, January 14, Ferraiolo wrote:

> On this day His Majesty began to have ditches made, and outer ditches, and casemates around the Castel Nuovo, and he also built defenses at the citadella [i.e. barbican, in Neapolitan usage] to repair the castle. He created great buildings and ramparts because he believed he could hold out [against the French] and that what eventually happened was not going to take place.[46]

Thus the whole western defense system, even including an outpost at Baia, was under construction in the days just before Alfonso's abdication on January 23. These facts, brought to light by Riccardo Filangieri only after he had completed his documentary history of Castel

---

43. G. Filangieri, *Documenti, 6,* 301; ibid., *5,* 315.

44. Ibid., *5,* 230. Giannone, *Historia, 3,* 445, says the stretch from the Porta San Gennaro to Monte San Martino was completed by Charles V, using "pietra dolce del monte del paese con nuovo modo di fortifica-zione, non con Torri, ma con baloardi; e questa fu l'ultima ampliazione per cio che riguarda il giro delle mura" [written c. 1687].

45. G. Filangieri, *Documenti, 6,* 45.

46. R. Filangieri, *Cronaca figurata,* pp. 112–14.

Nuovo, make it certain that Francesco di Giorgio created the plans for the new western defenses and that he began building them during the reign of Alfonso II.[47]

No documents for any immediate further work survive, but more structures may have been finished before Charles' arrival, for Sanudo speaks of "a fortress [at San Martino] newly built. It surrounds Naples for three miles, and takes the form of a scorpion, embracing the Bay with its claws, and twisting its tail towards land."[48] Sanudo confirms earlier that the walls between the Castel Sant'Elmo and the city were in place during Alfonso's reign.

But Francesco di Giorgio and his assistant Marchese soon found themselves more occupied with demolition than construction. About five months after Ferrandino's reentry on July 7, 1495, a French garrison still held the Castel Nuovo. To drive them out Francesco made use of what was probably the first successfully exploded military mine in history.[49] Once again the inventor of the principle was Taccola, apparently,[50] though Passero gives the credit to Federigo:

> Today [November 27, 1495] they say that that vessel of wisdom, Don Federigo, had a passageway dug under the citadel . . . and inside the tunnel a large barrel of powder was placed. He then set it afire, and it made such an explosion that the whole castle blew up, and the walls fell in at once. No sooner had they done so than the King's men were all about, and took the citadel without losing a single man. But many Frenchmen were killed because they were inside the castle on guard, suspecting nothing.[51]

Drawings attributed to Francesco show precisely this mechanism (Fig. 108),[52] and we also know that it was Francesco's assistant Marchese who dug the tunnel. Marchese put his knowl-

47. Of course Filangieri recognized that this discovery modified his earlier conclusions, especially as in "La citadella," *Atti accademia pontaniana*, pp. 56–57, and in "Rassegna critica," *ASPN*, 63 (1938), 275. In the former he had said that Marchese made the design for the new bastioned outworks of Castel Nuovo, and that it was not begun until the reign of Federigo, being completed between 1509 and 1519. In the "Rassegna critica" he had said that the work was left unfinished on the east. But only my interpretation accords with Pietro Summonte's letter to Michiel, which says the new walls were mostly built by, or during Alfonso II's reign. (Nicolini, *L'Arte napoletana*, p. 171; cf. also above, Chapter 2, n. 28.) Summonte's phrase "Le gran mura della città, in buona parte già facte" (during or before Alfonso's reign) would more probably refer to the western rather than the eastern walls in any case, for we have seen that the latter were completely finished in 1490, four full years before the new reign began, while the western walls only had been commenced at Alfonso's succession. For further information on the outer defenses see Giorgio Rosi, "La Cinta bastionata cinquecentesca di Castel Nuovo," *Atti del V. congresso di storia dell' architettura*, 1948 (Florence, 1957), 317–26, which publishes two nineteenth-century plans of Francesco's structure. On April 12, 1493, a certain Vincenzo de Cortona

made models for other forts in the kingdom, possibly again in the new manner (Barone, "Cedole," *ASPN*, 10, 1885, 23). The author of *Le Vergier d'honneur* in 1494–95 commented on the bastioned outworks of Castel Nuovo, referring to its "boulevars . . . et d'aultres efforts rude [sic] et vehemens." and to the fact that they were partly of wood (i.e. a brushwood core?) and partly stone (M. L. Cimber, ed., *Archives curieuses de l'histoire de France*, ser. 1, 1, Paris, 1834, 332).

48. Sanudo, "La Spedizione," pp. 238; 121.

49. E. Percopo, "Nuovi Documenti," *ASPN*, 20 (1895), 301, and R. Filangieri, "Rassegna critica," *ASPN*, 63 (1938), 266–67.

50. But cf. E. Rocchi, "Francesco di Giorgio Martini," *Bollettino senese di storia patria*, 7 (1900), 186–201; and idem, *Le Fonti storiche*, pp. 243–53.

51. Passero, *Giornali*, pp. 89–90. See also R. Filangieri, *Cronaca figurata*, pp. 198–99, 205, n. 149. Paolo Giovio, in *Dell'Istorie del suo tempo*, 1 (Venice, 1560), 120, says the author of the mine was a certain "Narciso toscano." Conceivably he meant Antonio. Ferraiolo, in R. Filangieri, *Cronaca figurata*, pp. 198–99, gives the date as November 9.

52. Mario Salmi, *Disegni di Francesco di Giorgio*, p. 9, n. 1.

edge to use again in a second mining of the Castel Nuovo in 1501. According to Riccardo Filangieri, the earlier mine destroyed the front wall of the citadel, and badly damaged the portal.[53] Francesco may have been troubled in his conscience about this. In the treatise he refers to a secret process, which may well have been the mine (used as an antisiege weapon), in a way that sounds strangely modern: "I keep silent, in order not to weigh down my conscience, on a mode of defense which can suddenly end the lives of a great multitude of men."[54]

In any case, it was with such help that Ferrandino regained his kingdom, except for a few pockets here and there, by September 12, 1496. This was just a year and two months after his entry into his capital. I know of no public works undertaken by the young monarch before his untimely death the following October 7.[55]

In the spring of 1497, however, Federigo took up where Alfonso II had left off. On March 13 he wrote directly to Francesco, who had recently returned to Siena from his third sojourn in Naples. "We are ready to make the same financial provision," said the new king, "that our beloved brother the Most Serene King Don Alfonso of happy memory made for you." Federigo specified that Francesco was to rebuild the Castel Nuovo and other damaged defenses. So anxious was he to secure Francesco's services that he simultaneously wrote to several important citizens of Siena.[56] In a second letter, on March 16, 1497, Federigo suggested that Francesco take Marchese, then in Siena, along with him. But Francesco was prevented from returning by new duties in his homeland;[57] and so in this same month of March 1497, Antonio Marchese was reestablished as architect for the western defense system.[58] He was granted citizenship, and in July was given a house.[59]

I assume that, as carried out, the construction of the two castles followed Francesco di Giorgio's original plans of 1492 and that Lafrery's map of 1566 shows the whole complex after it was completed (Fig. 106).[60] As justification I can point out that Marchese himself was almost continuously in charge of the work until his death in 1522.[61] Also, early sources tell us that Don Pietro of Toledo, who ruled and rebuilt Naples from 1532 to 1553, is said

53. R. Filangieri, "Rassegna Critica," *ASPN, 63* (1938), 274, 266.

54. Saluzzo and Promis, *Trattato,* p. 260.

55. Passero, *Giornali,* pp. 106, 114. Federigo was crowned in Capua by Cesare Borgia, Cardinal of Valencia and oldest son of Alexander VI, on August 10, 1497.

56. G. Ceci, "Nuovi Documenti," *ASPN, 9* (1900), 81–84, esp. 83.

57. Ibid., and also R. Filangieri, "Rassegna Critica," *ASPN, 63* (1938), 274.

58. The contract is dated March 12, the day before Federigo's letter to Francesco di Giorgio. In it Antonio is again called proto-architect. E. Tormo, in a facsimile of Francisco de Hollanda's 1539–40 sketchbook in the Escorial, *Os Desenhos das antigualhas que vio Francisco d'Ollanda* (Madrid, 1940), mentions the attribution of

the Castel Sant' Elmo to Pedro Luis de Scriva, and dates the whole structure 1537–46 (p. 197). But this is belied by Francisco's own description of the fort, which mentions a certain "Antonio" as architect (ibid., p. 199). This would be Marchese. See above, n. 40; also Giovanni Bresciano, "Documenti inediti concernenti artisti napoletani del quattro e cinquecento," *ASPN, 52* (1927), 374; and Bartolommeo Capasso, *La Circoscrizione,* p. 23.

59. Bresciano, "Documenti," p. 374.

60. Pontano mentions this new complex in "De magnificentia" (126v), rather unfairly citing it as an example of the unjust attainment of this quality, on the grounds that the work was supported by public taxes.

61. Cf. R. Filangieri, "Rassegna critica," *ASPN, 64* (1939), 253, and Vasari, *3,* 570, n. 3.

to have contented himself, in these western structures, with carrying out Alfonso's intentions.[62]

There are not many documents for this phase of the renewal. From those published by Gaetano Filangieri, it seems the new walls were recommenced in September 1500. At that time five more canne were built, enclosing the garden of Monteoliveto.[63] However, Capasso states that new walls were erected along what is now the via Toledo by Marchese in 1499. They were torn down to create that street in 1528.[64]

According to Capasso's reconstruction of them (cf. Fig. 1), the new walls led from the Porta Reale down the Calata Trinità Maggiore and through Piazza Monteoliveto to include that monastery and its garden. Then they turned down the present via Toledo to cover its long, straight length as far as the via Santa Brigida, where they turned at right angles to join the Castel Nuovo. The old Porta del Castello was moved to this point. It was also planned to carry out the new walls along the harbor front.[65]

There seem to be no significant published documents on the reconstruction of the Castel Sant'Elmo. We only know that it indubitably was transformed between 1495 and about 1540 from a smallish castle overbuilt with residential blocks, a shapeless compound as we see it in the Strozzi panel, into that aggressive complex of sharp, high bastions, bristling above the monastery of San Martino, which can be seen in Stoopendael and Lafrery (Figs. 105, 106): a building clearly embodying the type of architecture that Francesco had pioneered and that would transform a rocky hilltop into an immense geometrical cliff with buttresses plunging down to merge with the base of the hill. Indeed some of the sketches in Francesco's book could almost be preliminary thoughts for Sant'Elmo (Fig. 104).

The most important part of the program, all the more so after its partial destruction in 1495, was the new outer defenses of the Castel Nuovo. Unlike Sant'Elmo, the Castel Nuovo is fully documented in published sources. Aside from printed documents and the Aragonese archives (now destroyed), Filangieri has used intarsia views of the building executed about 1510 in Monteoliveto, and Francisco de Hollanda's famous drawing of about 1540 (Fig. 103).[66] The new fortifications extended far out from the old castle, presumably so that

62. De la Ville sur-Yllon, "Le Mura," p. 54. However the plaque over the main gate of Castel Sant' Elmo reads: IMP CAROLUS V INVICTI AUG CAES IUSSU / AC PETRI TOLETTI VILLAE FRANCAE MARCHION / IUSTISS [?] PROPEGIS AUSPICIS.

63. G. Filangieri, Documenti, 6, 41. Work was also done on the eastern walls. Thus on June 22, 1501, Pietro Marzano, builder, with Maestro Panunzio Ferraro, was told to demolish the chapel of Sant'Agnese in the garden of the late Cola di Toraldo near San Pietro ad Aram (i.e. in the vicinity of the Porta Nolana) and to rebuild these walls in the Orto Santa Marta near Porta Petruccia. Cf. G. Filangieri, Documenti, 6, 141. On October 13, 1500, Franco de Giovanni sold stone to Maso di Mariconda, of Cava, for walls and towers of

the Porta Capuana (ibid., 5, 231). Other work of the period on the city walls (at unspecified places) took place on March 3, 1501 (ibid., 5, 231) and on the following July 3, when maestri Natalello and Giulio de Alfiero, fabbricatori, were asked to make the "regi fossi" of the city for the Curia (ibid., 6, 188).

64. B. Capasso, La Circoscrizione, p. 23, G. A. Summonte, Historia, 5, 272–73, and De la Ville, "Le Mura," pp. 49–56.

65. Capasso, La Circoscrizione, p. 23, and A. Colombo, "I Porti e gli arsenali di Napoli. III. Epoca aragonese e viceregnale," NN, 3 (1894), 72–74, 89–92.

66. Cf. Francisco de Hollanda, Os Desenhos, 45r and p. 198, for the entrance to Sant' Elmo, which is portrayed with curious rounded casemates. The intarsia

enemy fire could not reach it effectively. Like Sant'Elmo, they were designed in the transitional style of Biagio Rossetti's Ferrarese walls and Francesco's own work in the Marches: low, round torrioni instead of angular bastions, and continuous casemates. In the Castel Nuovo these were segmentally vaulted, giving a scalloped silhouette. Even the towers of the inner castle were treated in this way. The general effect of the northeast front, with its powerful wall stretched between massive torrioni, was like an enlarged version of San Leo (Fig. 102). The torrioni of Castel Nuovo also possessed ramlike triangular buttresses, however, below the level of the parapet.[67]

According to Filangieri, the great pentagonal bastion, the Baluardo dello Santo Spirito (on the right in Fig. 103), was originally a torrione. Then, in 1517, Marchese went to Rome to a conference called by Leo X on the defense of Civitavecchia. There the younger Antonio da Sangallo presented plans for a polyhedral bastion, and on seeing them Marchese decided to rebuild the northern corner of the Castel Nuovo in the same fashion. The work was completed only about 1537,[68] and with it the Castel Nuovo was brought even further up to date.[69] Now, indeed, the older central portion of it became a corps de logis whose defenses were largely symbolic. It became in fact a medieval and antique-revival castle in a protective "modern" setting. Once again there is the expressive juxtaposition of styles in Naples.

Federigo followed out the implications of this shift with perfect logic: he remodeled parts of the interior of the Castel Nuovo in a Gothic style. The new apartments he built for himself on the second floor between the Sala dei Baroni and the Torre del Mare were designed "alla Catalana" by a certain Pere Marza, commencing in 1496.[70] In doing this Federigo behaved, in fact, as if he wished to maintain the stylistic balance of the building, that delicate adjustment of the Gothic, Antique, and now a neutral modernism, which had been created over the years. The result was that he made over the Castel Nuovo into a kind of towered, fortified palace, or even an urban Poggioreale, a heraldic restatement of its former self.[71]

We must here add to these completed works Alfonso's intention to "extend all the main streets in straight lines from wall to wall, removing all projections . . . and then to lay out transversely, also in straight lines, the cross streets from one end of the city to the other," as

scenes in Monteoliveto, once thought the work of Fra Giocondo (E. Percopo, "Nuovi Documenti," ASPN, 19, 1894, 378–79), are by a certain Fra Giovanni da Verona (R. Filangieri, "Rassegna Critica," ASPN, 62, 1937, 298–99, and Ciapponi, "Appunti per una biografia di Giovanni Giocondo da Verona," Italia medioevale e umanistica, 4, 1961, 139).

67. Such buttresses are also seen in Late Gothic French fortifications, e.g. at La Ferté-Milon, near Paris (1382–1407). But in this case they seem to have risen all the way to the top.

68. R. Filangieri, "Rassegna Critica," ASPN, 64 (1939), 252–59.

69. R. Filangieri, "La Citadella aragonese," p. 66. See also G. Rosi, "La Cinta bastionata," p. 321. This

outer set of ditches was exceedingly deep according to Fichard (August Schmarsow, ed., "Excerpte aus Joh. Fichard's 'Italia' von 1536," Repertorium für Kunstwissenschaft, 14, 1891, p. 374).

70. R. Filangieri, "La Casa di Federigo d'Aragona in Castel Nuovo," Studi di storia napoletana in onore di Michelangelo Schipa (Naples, 1926), pp. 353–64, esp. p. 356; idem, "Rassegna Critica," ASPN, 63 (1938), 306–07. Cf. also J. R. Hale, "The Early Development of the Bastion," p. 476.

71. Filangieri, "La Casa," pp. 307–12. Marchese built other fortifications besides Castel Nuovo and Castel Sant' Elmo, e.g. in 1498 in Calabria (G. Filangieri, Documenti, 6, 102).

Pietro Summonte put it. Although Summonte speaks only of the ease with which the city could be cleaned, and we have noted the antiquarian impulse behind the idea, there was I think also a military one as well. If the plan had been achieved, therefore, we would probably have been able to see in Naples, as in Ferrara and elsewhere, a city whose public spaces were shaped according to cannon trajectories, i.e. a Naples crisscrossed by boulevards controlled from the great bulwarks (even the words are related) that rose on the west.

THE HYDRAULIC SYSTEM   If the new fortifications of red piperno and golden tufa represented Pontano's "garland woven with gold and coral branches," the new hydraulic system was Parthenope's bloodstream, the waters of life that would cleanse and restore her. The renewal was above all things aqueous. Naples was practically afloat, what with its moats, its labyrinth of rumbling underground conduits, its fountains flowing in squares and court-yards, and its harbor.[72] Furthermore, there was plenty of support, both archaeological and literary, for seeing aqueducts and fountains as forms of magnificentia. Apart from the stunning remains of antiquity and the admiring descriptions of Pliny and Vitruvius, one thinks of Frontinus, and especially of Fra Giocondo's edition of that author.[73] Alberti emphasized aqueducts and fountains as major civic elements (IV, 6) and Pontano in "De magnificentia," even suggested that they can be the main expression of a ruler's moral greatness:

> Certain great lords among the Romans got praise for their water system above all else, which, as it was intended solely for use did not require any ornament. Nevertheless, the very amplitude, spaciousness, and solidity of the work may commend the magnificentia of the man who commissions it, and though the conduits are not covered with carvings, they are no mean ornament to the city.[74]

Here again is praise for a vast "astylar" set of forms though, unlike the new fortifications, these had been known and built in antiquity.

For most of its history Naples had had two main aqueduct systems. Vestiges of one, the Ponti Rossi, still exist.[75] This carried water from Serino, 46 miles to the west, and had probably been built by Nero. Summonte says this aqueduct entered Naples from the north, near

72. Cf. Roberto di Stefano, "Napoli sotterranea," *NN,* ser. 3, *1* (1962), 101–12, which deals with the various aqueducts and contains a map of the conduits, p. 108. Di Stefano is working on a definitive bibliography of the subject. Cf. also G. A. Summonte, *Historia, 1,* 268–304; Celano, *Notizie, 2,* 407–35; Luigi Cangiano, *Su le Acque publiche potabili della città di Napoli* (Naples, 1843), esp. pp. 9–20; Beloch, *Campanien,* pp. 70–72; de la Ville, "Il Sebeto," *NN, 11* (1902), 113–16; R. Filangieri, "Rassegna Critica," *ASPN,* 63 (1938), 321–22; Gino Doria, *Le Strade,* p. 379; and Raffaelle Mormone, "Contributo ad una storia delle fontane napoletane," *Bollettino di storia*

d'arte dell' istituto universitario di magistero, Salerno, 3 (Sept./Dec. 1953), 108–14.

73. A letter from Francesco Morosini to the Council of Ten in Venice, dated November 18, 1504, affirms that Fra Giocondo was a hydraulic engineer and had designed waterworks at Blois (R. Brenzoni, *Fra Giovanni Giocondo Veronese,* pp. 26–29).

74. *De magnificentia,* VIII. According to Cangiano, *Su le Acque,* pp. 34–35, Piero Antonio Lettieri also designed a large-scale remodeling of the Bolla system under Don Pietro of Toledo, but this was shelved.

75. Cf. De la Ville, "Il Sebeto," and Di Stefano, "Napoli sotterranea," pp. 104–06.

the Porta di Costantinopoli, and supplied fountains in that part of the city. At various places along its course the water flowed into great storage tanks which were among the wonders of the age. The one at Miseno was called the "piscina mirabilis" and others, notably a castello d'acqua not far from the city walls, were still visible in Summonte's own day. There was one at a place called Pertugio built in opus reticulatum.[76] But most of the Serino system had been abandoned in Summonte's time and seems to have been unused during the Quattrocento as well. It is now once again active.

The Duke's efforts were centered on the Bolla system which, as already observed, entered the city to the east, at the shore (Fig. 1). This was fed by the Sebeto, rising on the flanks of Mount Somma, and by the more northerly River Sarno. Summonte describes it as follows:

> Issuing from the storage tanks at Bolla it slowly gains size with new and copious sources and springs which it finds in its course, and, ever increasing, it comes to a place called the Fosso di Sant'Antonio where there is a strainer like the others, and where the water is cleansed. From here it passes into another place called Fosso del Casaro, where there is a second strainer, and where one sees it swollen with other streams which come together at this point. From here it goes to Poggioreale, where the water is collected in an uncovered cistern that supplies the delightful fountains there. From the overflow two mills, further downstream, are operated.

One can get an idea of a castellum from a woodcut in Fra Giocondo's Frontinus (Fig. 109). Figure 82 shows what the system at Poggioreale looked like at the beginning of the eighteenth century. I have included this arrangement on my map (Fig. 1).

Summonte goes on to describe the aqueduct's progress to the city itself and to various squares and private houses. It forms the moat for the Porta Capuana, he says, where there are also public spouts (bronzi) as well as underground conduits running to nearby palaces and gardens:

> One sees in the Convent of Sant'Anna near the Capuana moat an uncovered conduit, four palmi wide, with the water three-and-a-half palmi deep. These conduits are made in such a way that one can easily clean them without removing the water. There is inside them a walkway consisting of little balconies, and one can pass along the whole without getting wet. They are as tortuous as possible so that, as Pontano says in Book VI of *De bello neapolitano,* by splashing the water and agitating it often at the corners, one makes it healthier, and as experience shows, cooler, and besides, going straight its pressure would damage the foundations of the buildings it passed under.[77]

Summonte traces the possible origins of the Acqua della Bolla as far back as the time of

---

76. G. A. Summonte, *Historia, 1,* 269–75.

77. G. A. Summonte, *Historia, 1,* 281–82. Pontano may also have had this system in mind, with its noisy splashing waters, in "Ad musam, de conversione Sebethi in fluvium," Parthenopaeus, XIV, ll. 33ff.:

"[Nerea] illa autem, irato properans / ad litora curru, / coerula coeruleis per vada currit equis; / cuius ob adventum resonant Tritones in antris, / Candidaque in scopulis laes remugit aqua."

Virgil and refers to the work done on it by Giovanna I, Charles III, and other rulers. It was through this aqueduct that in 1442 Alfonso I secretly entered the city. He himself later restored it and provided fountains called formali (from formulae or formellae, meaning aqueducts supplied by the king but administered by the nobili and popoli).[78]

Most of the fountains in Naples were simple spouts and basins as in Figure 109. Sometimes the spouts were made of cannon, as in the famous fountain on the via Mezzocannone which gave that street its name.[79] But others were elaborate sculptural realizations of the *Lepidina* metaphor, exploiting in water and marble the idea of life flowing through Parthenope's stone body. The Parthenope fountains at La Duchesca and Poggioreale, discussed in the last chapter, were examples. But this tradition had already been established with the famous fountain of the Quattro del Molo, dating from the time of Alfonso I, where a statue of Parthenope stood in the midst of a group of river gods. Under Don Pedro a fountain was built in the Piazza Portanova, representing in sculptured form, over its two spouts, a flaming mountain. Above this was a siren from whose nipples water poured. On her lyre was written: "While the fires of Vesuvius burn, the Siren soothes." Vestiges of one of the most important of the great civic fountains still stand in the Piazza Capuana. Its ancestry can be traced back at least to the days of Giovanna I.[80] It had been enlarged and decorated by the Spanish and given an inscription directly recalling *Lepidina*.[81]

The question of the engineers responsible for the system is difficult. Giuliano da Maiano, says Vasari, "designed many fountains with handsome and imaginative ornaments for the houses of the nobles and the city squares of Naples."[82] His language is so close to Pontano's and Pietro Summonte's that one is tempted to believe Giuliano was originally involved. In any case, we have a document showing that after Giuliano's death in 1490 Alfonso of Calabria required other fountains from Francesco di Giorgio.[83] In June 1491 Francesco also made an "edificio" to pump water from the moat to the barbican of the Castel Nuovo, so that it could be distributed through the living apartments.[84] Both he and Fra Giocondo were famous as hydraulic engineers; in fact, on November 24, 1492, in a letter to the Balía of Siena, Alfonso referred to Francesco as the irreplaceable "Camerlingo de le fonti di questa cità."[85] It therefore seems likely that these two rather than Giuliano carried out most of the new water system. If this is true it would be most logical to date Alfonso's restoration of the Acqua della Bolla about from 1490 to 1493, i.e. just before the campaign to build the new western defenses.

78. G. A. Summonte, *Historia*, 1, 292.

79. The inscription read: ALFONSUS FERD. RE / GIS FIL. ARAGONIUS / DUX CALABR. EX JUS / SU PATRIS FAC. CUR. Cf. Luigi Conforti, "Le Fontane di Napoli. I. Mezzocannone," *NN*, 1 (1892), 44–45; and G. Doria, *Le Strade*, p. 317. There are no documents for this fountain, and the statue of the king which stood upon it was unrecognizable. It is lithographed in D'Ambra, *Napoli antica*, pl. LVII.

80. Bartolommeo Capasso, "La Fontana dei quattro del molo di Napoli," *ASPN*, 5 (1880), 158–94; and G. A. Summonte, *Historia*, 1, 284–85; 292.

81. Quoted in ibid., 1, 287.

82. Vasari, 2, 470.

83. Dated July 7, 1492, and quoted in Weller, *Francesco di Giorgio*, p. 382.

84. R. Filangieri, "Rassegna critica," *ASPN*, 63 (1938), 265–66.

85. Gaye, *Carteggio*, 1, 317–18.

Chapter 7: THE PORTA REALE

THE EARLIER GATES On January 25, 1494, just as Antonio Marchese was about to begin building the western walls, Ferrante died. With his death the meaning of the renewal changed, and Alfonso became patron of it in name as well as fact. The one monument directly associated with Alfonso's kingship is the Porta Reale. This was planned and partly executed as the principal feature of the new western walls and as a pendant to the Porta Capuana on the other side of the city. In many ways it would have been the renewal's psychological climax.

In 1494 the existing Porta Reale stood on or near the site of an even earlier gate, the Porta Cumana, in the middle of what is now the Piazza Gesù (Fig. 1).[1] This Porta Reale had been erected either by Charles I or Charles II of Anjou.[2] Sculpture decorated it, of what sort we do not know, and it was inscribed: "I am the royal gate of the excellent Seggio al Nido, adorning the walls of this, Parthenope's city."[3]

The Porta Reale quarter was an aristocratic one in the fifteenth century. It contained Santa Chiara with its convent, the Palazzo Sanseverino, and to the west, Santa Maria di Monteoliveto.[4] Circulation had been improved in 1456 when Alfonso I widened one of the approach streets.[5] The Porta Reale also stood across the central decumanus of the city, what Pietro Summonte called the "umbilicus urbis," the Via San Biagio dei Librai. Thus even more than the Porta Capuana, it was a major urban element in a nucleus of important buildings grouped around a central avenue. In name, history, and location the Porta Reale was the appropriate gate to transform into a western version of the Porta Capuana.[6] With Alfonso's accession occurring at the very moment work on the adjacent walls was begun, it was equally appropriate to make the Porta Reale a monument to the new king.

However it is quite possible that already in 1487, during his second and final sojourn in

1. For the pre-Viceregal Porta Reale see C. Foucard, ed., "Descrizione della città di Napoli e statistica del Regno nel 1444," *ASPN*, 2 (1877), 731–57, esp. 733; De la Ville, "Le Mura e le porte," p. 52; and F. Nicolini, "Dalla Porta Reale al Palazzo degli Studii," *NN*, 14 (1905), 114–18, 129–35, esp. 130–35.

2. G. A. Summonte, *Historia, 1*, 46; De la Ville, "Le Mura."

3. De la Ville, "Le Mura," p. 52: EGREGIAE NIDI SUM REGIA PORTA PLATEAE, / MOENIA NOBILITA[N]S HUIUS URBIS PARTHENOPEAE.

4. Nicolini, in *L'Arte napoletana*, pp. 182–83, notes Vasari's tale in which King Robert desired to make his friend Giotto "the first man of Naples." At this the artist asked if that was why he had been given lodgings near the Porta Reale. For Santa Chiara see A. De Rinaldis, *Santa Chiara. Il Convento delle chiarisse, il convento dei minori, la chiesa* (Naples, 1920).

5. Camillo Minieri-Riccio, "Alcuni Fatti di Alfonso I di Aragona," *ASPN*, 6 (1881), 449.

6. In L. Salazar, ed., "Racconti di storia napoletana," *ASPN*, 33 (1908), 514, we hear that when Charles VIII entered the city on February 22, 1495, he was given the keys to the two principal gates, the Porta Capuana and the Porta Reale, "E li dissero che erano le due porte principali dell'un capo della terra all'altro, e queste sono nominate le porte Reali." But I do not feel that "reale" here was actually a name, as opposed to a description, of the Porta Capuana. With the Western gate, of course, it was both.

Naples, Giuliano da Maiano had designed a new Porta Reale on the model of his eastern gate. This would explain Vasari's saying that on Giuliano's return to Naples that year,

> King Alfonso commissioned from him a gate near the castle where there were to be more than eighty figures which Benedetto was to make in Florence. But the whole remained unfinished because of the King's death. There are still fragments of it in Florence, in the Misericordia, and others were at Canto alle Macine in our own day, but I don't know where they are now.[7]

For a long time it was thought that this "gate near the castle" was either the Arch of Alfonso I or the Porta Capuana.[8] But no one who had lived in Naples, as Vasari had, would have referred to either of these monuments as being near the castle. "The castle" tout court would have to be the Castel Nuovo,[9] and neither the Porta Capuana nor the Arch of Alfonso was "near" that building: the Arch of Alfonso is actually in it, and the Porta Capuana is at the far end of the city from it.[10]

To put a different interpretation on Vasari's remarks, let us say that in 1487 Giuliano did design a new western gate, and that some time after Ferrante's death and before Alfonso's abdication this proposed Porta Reale was redesigned by one of Giuliano's successors as a monument to the coronation of 1494; this would account for Vasari's referring to Alfonso as King. Let us also assume that, as Vasari says, work was abandoned when Alfonso died.

There is evidence to justify all three of these assumptions. First, the idea of erecting a triumphal arch marking the events of 1494 was discussed at the time of Ferrante's death. It was suggested that a temporary funeral arch be put up in front of the cathedral.[11] There is no evidence that this was done, but on the other hand such a temporary arch was erected in front of the mint, for Alfonso's coronation. Thus by May 1494 the emphasis had changed from funerary to festive: "The King is dead, long live the King!" It is not difficult to imagine Alfonso's deciding to make a permanent arch out of the appropriately named Porta Reale,

7. "Gli [Giuliano] fu allogata dal re Alfonso una porta vicina al Castello, dove andavano piu d'ottanta figure, le quali aveva Benedetto a lavorar in Fiorenza: ma il tutto per la morte de quel re rimase imperfetto, e ne sono ancora alcune reliquie in Fiorenza nella Misericordia e alcune altre n'erano al Canto alla Macine ai tempi nostri, le quali non so dove oggi si ritrovino." Vasari, 2, 473 and n. 2; see also ibid., 2, 482–86, and 3, 337, n. 3.

8. Fabriczy, "Toscanische und oberitalienische," p. 98; E. Bertaux, "L'Arco e la porta trionfale di Alfonso e di Ferdinando d'Aragona al Castel Nuovo," ASPN, 25 (1900), 48; "Don Ferrante" [Benedetto Croce], note in NN, 12 (1903), 48; Pope-Hennessy, Italian Renaissance Sculpture, p. 307.

9. The Castel Capuano had by Vasari's time been transformed into the Palazzo Tribunali. Since the physical transformation (by Giovanni Benincasa and Ferdi-

nando Manlio) had begun only in 1530 it is possible that the old name still stuck. But Castel Capuano would never have been known simply as "the Castle."

10. In another passage (2, 470) Vasari says Giuliano created the sculpture of the Porta del Trionfo in the Castel Nuovo's gran sala, and of the Arch of Alfonso I, as well as that of the Porta Capuana. Such errors are understandable inasmuch as these works were a hundred years old by Vasari's time. As we have seen with Pietro Summonte there was confusion about their authorship even among earlier antiquarians. For Vasari's sojourn in Naples in the 1540s see Paola Barocchi, Vasari pittore (Milan, 1964), pp. 24–27.

11. G. A. Summonte, Historia, 4, 624. Presumably this would have acted as a facade, like the temporary arch erected in front of Santa Maria del Fiore for Leo X's triumphal entry into Florence, Nov. 30–Dec. 2, 1513.

which was already a monument to one of his illustrious predecessors and in need of re-building.

In 1875 Giovanni Baroni published a document supporting these assumptions.[12] This is an inventory of the contents of Benedetto da Maiano's studio, made after his death in 1497 by the painter Cosimo Rosselli and others. It lists a group of marbles in the woodworking shop including:

> 1 piece with the sketch of the Duke, about 3 braccia; 1 finished bishop, 3 braccia; 1 juggler, sketched, 3 braccia; 1 Don Federigo, sketched, 3 braccia; 1 musician, finished, 2 1/1; 1 piece of frieze with the architrave finished, 3¼ braccia; 1 cornice belonging to the above frieze, and a piece 2⅓ braccia, finished; 1 piece of a pavilion, which was for the Porta Reale, that is in Naples.

In another part of the shop, the "bottega dei marmi," was a second group of marbles: "1 figure belonging to the Porta Reale; 1 [figure], 3 braccia; 1 king and a bishop, 2⅓ braccia; 1 ring, finished; 2 pieces and 4 trumpeters, finished; 1 other single trumpeter." Various fragments of architectural ornament are also named. Of all of these, only the "piece of a pavilion" and the "figure" are specifically connected with the Porta Reale. But it seems at least conceivable that all of the figures, which were of the same material and size, belonged together as a frieze, quite possibly depicting a coronation, for the Porta Reale.[13]

There is still more evidence: in 1903 the "king and a bishop, 2⅓ braccia" of Benedetto's inventory were identified with a relief in the Bargello (Figs. 110, 111, 112).[14] This has the right measurements. Although it is 1.56 meters high (and 2⅓ braccia would be only 1.36

---

12. G. Baroni, *La Parrocchia di San Martino a Majano* (Florence, 1875), pp. lxvii–lxxvi, 88–95. Cf. also L. Céndali, *Giuliano e Benedetto da Maiano* (Florence, 1926), pp. 178–86.

13. A copy of the will is now in the Archivio di Stato di Firenze, Bigallo n. 1219, anno 1497, pp. 99–109, dated July 3. The relevant text is as follows (beginning at the top of p. 100):

1° pezzo con la bozza dl Duca di br 3.m c̄c̄ā.
1° vescovo finito di br 3.
1° ludiere bozzato di br 3.
1° Don Federigo bozzato di br 3.
1° sonatore finito di br 2 1/1.
1° pezzo di fregio con l'architrave finito. di br 3¼.
1ª cornice appartenete a d[etto] fregio et pezzo di br. 2⅓ finito.
1° pezzo di padiglione che fue alla porta reale cioe, à Napoli.

Another section (p. 103) is headed "Queste sono le cose ch sono in bottega de marmi cioe, dove si lavora e marmi" and the relevant part (p. 104) reads:

1ª figura appartenete alla porta reale.
1ª di br 3.
1° Re ed un vescovo di br 2⅓.
1° anello finito.

2. pezzi ed 4. trombetti finiti.
1° altro trombetto solo.

The list continues:

1° tondo bozzato di nrā Dona di br 1° ¼.
2 pezzi di pilastri à canaletti di 4. pezzi alto br 3¾ finiti.
1° pezzo di cornicione di br 3.
2 pezzi di cornice finite di br 3¾
1° pezzo d'architrave di br 3¼.
1° pezzo di cornice di br 3¾ intagliata.
2 pezzi d'architrave [sopradetti] pilastri.

Of course, not all of these items are necessarily part of the Neapolitan project, and others that I have not transcribed may have belonged to it; we shall see later why my groupings seem right.

14. I. B. Supino, *L'Incoronazione di Ferdinando d'Aragona* (Florence, 1903). Cf. also note by Don Ferrante [B. Croce], *NN, 12* (1903), 48; C. von Fabriczy, "Das Marmorrelief der Krönung eines Kaisers in Museo Nazionale zu Florenz," *Repertorium für Kunstwissenschaft, 26* (1903), 262–63; Jacob Burckhardt, *Der Cicerone*, ed. W. Bode, 2 (Leipzig, 1879), 330, 881; and Marcel Reymond, *La Sculpture florentine, 1* (Florence, 1897), 158.

meters), the upper part of the relief, including the bishop's head and hands and the crown—everything beyond about 1.36 meters in fact—is modern.[15] There is even a document linking it to Benedetto: he had provided that should his heirs die out his sculpture would go to the Compagnia del Bigallo, a religious order. In 1555 Benedetto's line did come to an end, and the Bargello piece was duly discovered three hundred years later on one of the Order's properties.[16]

Thus my reading of Vasari's tale is confirmed: in 1487 a monumental gateway "near the castle" was due for rebuilding; sculpture for it was begun in Florence by Benedetto da Maiano and then abandoned; and at least one fragment survived not only into Vasari's day but into our own. We also know, from Benedetto's will, that this proposed gate was the Porta Reale.

THE BARGELLO RELIEF   The Bargello relief clearly belongs to the oeuvre of Benedetto's shop and was executed late in the artist's career; about this there is now no disagreement.[17] It is carved from a marble that has taken on a coffee-colored patina, in relief so high that the two figures are almost freestanding. The king sits on a throne with lion-headed arms and a tall back. Massive yet weak, he is vested as a priest in an alb, tunicle, stole, and cingulum. The fringed ends of the stole hang evenly and severely down over his knees. The drapery in both figures is smooth and polished though the king's head and hands are not. In his right hand he holds the remains of a scepter and in his left an orb; the nose is broken off and the right eye seems to have been damaged. The bishop is vested in a long, soft alb and a chasuble that falls in heavy, supple folds.

Up to Giuliano's death, as we have seen, Benedetto's career had been closely linked with his brother's, and at the same time he had drawn much of his style from the slim oval forms of Antonio Rossellino. But in the 1490s Benedetto's work became different. Now the sculptor exploited a more vigorously rotund language constructed out of rough solids. Gestures became resolute, drapery heavy and broad-edged.[18] We can most usefully compare the Bargello group to one of the genuflecting angels in Benedetto's San Bartolo altar, in the Church of Sant'Agostino, San Gimignano, of 1492–94 (Fig. 113).[19] Both have the same rounded,

15. Charles Seymour has suggested to me that the original hands of the bishop, his head, and the crown, may have been fastened to an upper section of the relief, perhaps to the "padiglione" mentioned in the inventory.

16. Baroni, *La Parrocchia,* p. 90. In my "Porta Reale," p. 78, the date is misprinted as 1575.

17. For earlier attributions see my "Porta Reale," pp. 78–80 and nn. 8–11. (August von Schmarsow gave it to Luca della Robbia; Bode, in the editions of the *Cicerone* earlier than that cited above, said it was by a follower of G. Pisano; Robert Vischer and Marcel Reymond thought it was medieval.) Cf. also Antonio Igual Ubeda, *Iconografía de Alfonso el Magnánimo* (Valencia, 1950), pp. 21–22.

18. G. Galassi, in *La Scultura fiorentina del quattro-*

cento (Milan, 1949), p. 194, has well evoked the character of the Bargello piece: "Nel tempo stesso arcaistica e anticipatrice appare l'incompiuta 'Incoronazione' che doveva ornare la 'Porta Reale' a Napoli ed ora è, in quello stato quasi amorfo e non esente da rimaneggiamenti, nel Museo del Bargello, altro ed ultimo esempio delle incertezze in cui si dibatteva un autore che aveva già in corpo il Cinquecento, ma fu tenuto in iscacco nell'avanzare dell'età, dalle mode imperanti e dal proprio difetto di coraggio." Cf. also, but with caution, H. Gottschalk, *Antonio Rossellino* (Leignitz, 1930), pp. 66–67, where the earlier influence of Rossellino on Benedetto is discussed, and Luitpold Dussler, *Benedetto da Maiano* (Munich, 1924), pp. 72–75.

19. Ibid., pp. 45–46.

expectant velocity. The king's garments are inflated with slow, heavy volumes like those of the San Bartolo allegorical figures. The little Charity is especially relevant (Fig. 114). Ovals still play a role in this later sculpture, however; the bodies of both figures are formed from them, but now they are large, dominant, abstract—a half-oval for the king's torso, clearly stated around the shoulders, and a smaller oval for the legs below. The heads also are basically ovals, although the king's is overgrown by his fat features while the Charity's is kept taut and hollow. One observes in both, too, the characteristic weightlessness of the arms and the leathery plane of drapery below the knees. The king's face is in turn related to the marble life-size bust of Onofrio di Pietro in the Museo dell'Arte Sacra, San Gimignano, usually dated 1493 and given to Benedetto (Fig. 115). There are the same heavy, vertical furrows and the same flat, soft outer panels of the faces within which the central features flow together. Indeed from the San Gimignano bust we can imagine how the finished head of the Bargello king might have emerged from its present cloudy incompleteness.

Yet for all their likeness to the work of Benedetto's late period, the two Bargello figures inhabit different worlds. They are very nearly in two different styles. The bishop rushes toward the king in a manner completely at odds with the latter's motionless solemnity. The bishop's posture is helical, his silhouette amorphous, as if diffused by his energy and motion. The king in contrast has a strongly bounded linear symmetry. What force he has is in his stillness. The bishop's vestments twist actively around him, anticipating or lagging behind the movements of his body; the king's vestments descend archaically in flat ripples to his feet, like a deposit of time and dust. One understands how earlier students could evoke the name of Giotto in looking at this king, just as one sees a later Florentine style, muscular and kinetic, in the bishop.[20] Here again, for Naples, even in the work of a Florentine sculptor, there is the expressive juxtaposition of styles.

THE ROYAL PORTRAIT TYPE   The king himself, portrayed in this retrospective and traditional manner, belongs to a sequence of royal portraits that goes back continuously at least as far as the early Middle Ages.[21] Such state figures are common in seals, medallions,

20. For the bishop's face the restorer seems to have adapted the portrait of Giotto attributed to Benedetto in the Florence Cathedral. (Incidentally this latter attribution can be buttressed by the inventory, which on p. 106 lists "2 teste di giotto senza busto" possibly terra-cotta models.) See also R. Vischer, *Studien zur Kunstgeschichte* (Stuttgart, 1886), p. 81.

21. Cf. Erwin Panofsky, *Tomb Sculpture* (New York, 1964), pp. 85–87, where he discusses the "image in majesty" which "remained exceptional until the very end of the Quattrocento" (p. 85). He lists a number of relevant tombs: those of Philippe de Courtenay, titular King of Constantinople, in the lower church at Assisi; the tomb of Henry VII, d. 1313, in the Camposanto, Pisa, by Tino da Camaino; that of Charles of Calabria, d. 1328, in Santa Chiara, Naples, also by Tino; the tomb of Robert the Wise, d. 1343, in the same church,

by Giovanni and Pacio da Firenze; that of Cino dei Sinibaldi, d. 1337, in the Cathedral at Pistoia; that of Antonio degli Orsi, d. 1521, by Tino, in the Florence Cathedral (with a seated bishop instead of a king); and the tomb of William the Silent, in the New Church, Delft, by Hendrik de Keyser (seventeenth century). Another important type of seated figure in majesty is of course found in papal iconography, e.g. Jacopino da Tradate's tomb of Martin V in the Cathedral at Milan (1435–40?), or the Pollaiolo tomb of Innocent VIII (1498) in St. Peter's. For scenes of actual coronation, there is Filarete's panel of the Emperor Sigismund on the bronze doors of St. Peter's (finished 1445), and Matteo da Campione's "Teodolinda and Agilulfo offering the Iron Crown to St. John the Baptist" in the cathedral at Monza (discussed by Schmarsow, in "Die Kaiserkrönung in Museo Nazionale," *Festschrift zu*

and manuscripts.[22] In large-scale sculpture, an early example is the great seated figure of Frederick II Hohenstaufen, thought to be Barbarossa in the fifteenth century when it was still visible on the Porta Romana at Capua (Fig. 116). This statue was especially important because it was so near Naples and so antique in appearance, and above all because it was set into a city gate.[23] Indeed the famous sketch of the Porta Romana attributed to Francesco di Giorgio (Uffizi, 333v) may even have been made during his 1495 visit to Capua, as part of a plan to revamp Giuliano's original design for the Porta Reale.[24] Of almost equal antiquity, in fact and appearance, is the statue of one of the possible builders of the medieval Porta Reale, Charles I of Anjou, now in the Palazzo dei Conservatori in Rome (Fig. 117). Here we see a colossus, flattened yet rigidly urging himself forward, probably made for a high niche, as is the case with the Bargello relief. In 1481 this famous statue was set up in the Palazzo Senatorio in a conspicuous place.[25] This portrait of an earlier Neapolitan king would have been one of the latest novelties during Alfonso's visit to Rome in 1486.

Such statues were particularly common in Neapolitan tombs. Charles I's own tomb, formerly in the cathedral in Naples and now destroyed, contained one. There were others, some of them now lost. One that still exists is King Robert, Charles' grandson and successor, seated on his tomb in Santa Chiara (Fig. 118).[26] Here however there is a variation. Once again we see, as in the statue of Charles I, the throne with its lion-headed arms, the careful, severe arrangement of drapery, the massive V-shaped gatherings in the lap, and the immovable hands. Now, however, the monarch is vested as a deacon, with the two ends of his stole hanging straight down over his dalmatic beneath. The sense of a consecration, as well as of royal rule, is therefore expressed. In the seated statues of Ladislas and Giovanna (Fig. 119) on the former's tomb in San Giovanni a Carbonara, the relationship of style and content to the earlier figures is again strong, but now the rulers are dressed as priests, not deacons.[27]

The priestly garb of these later statues suggests that one was crowned a king, as one was

---

Ehren des Kunsthistorisches Instituts in Florenz, Leipzig, 1897, p. 63). This scene occupies part of a long frieze, as was probably meant to be the case with Benedetto's fragment. Elena Romano has an interesting essay on the seated idol-cadaver, ruling in majesty, in her *Saggio d'iconografia dei reali angioini di Napoli* (Naples, 1920), see esp. p. 52; and finally cf. Harald Keller, "Die Entstehung des Bildnisses am Ende des Hochmittelalters," *Römische Jahrbuch für Kunstgeschichte, 3* (1939), 229–334, esp. 302–16.

22. They appear on the Neapolitan coins of René of Anjou, Charles II, Robert the Wise, Charles III Durazzo, Ladislas, and Alfonso I (cf. *Corpus nummorum italicorum, 19,* Rome, 1940, pl. iv.

23. Cf. Cresswell Shearer, *The Renaissance of Architecture in Southern Italy* (Cambridge, England, 1935), and Ottavio Morisani, "Considerazioni sulle sculture della Porta di Capua," *Bollettino di storia dell'arte dell' istituto universitario di magistero, Salerno, 3* (Jan. 1953), 1–20; (March 1953), 1–4; (Sept.-Dec. 1953), 1–76. The gate was not dismantled until 1557.

24. Cf. Chapter 4, n. 67.

25. Cf. Mario Salmi, "Arnolfiana," *Rivista d'Arte, 22* (1940), 133–77. Salmi dates the statue c. 1277 and relates it to that on the Porta Romana. Peter Meller interestingly discusses it as a commemoration of Charles' Roman senatorship in "Physiognomical Theory in Heroic Portraits," *Acts of the XXth Congress of the History of Art, 2* (1963), p. 64.

26. For this, in addition to the bibliography cited in n. 21 above, see E. Bertaux, "Magistri Johannes et Pacius de Florentia marmorarii fratres," *NN, 4* (1895), 134–38, 147–52.

27. Cf. Bertaux, "Magistri Johannes et Pacius," p. 137. Theodor Klauser, *Die Cathedra im Totenkult der heidnischen und christlichen Antike* (Münster, 1927), discusses seated figures in tomb art, and says that in antiquity cathedras were also supplied for mourners, both in pagan and Christian tombs; in this connection one thinks of the cathedra in the Chapel of the Cardinal of Portugal, San Miniato, Florence.

consecrated a priest, forever; that once the ceremony had been performed not even death could end one's reign. Indeed, medieval kings were often literally consecrated priests during their coronation ceremonies. It was said that the king was a mixta persona, part clergyman and part layman. Similarly the formula "sit rex atque sacerdos" was applied to Charlemagne and his successors. Alfonso was not only vested as a priest at his coronation, he read the Gospel of the Mass, an unequivocally sacerdotal act.[28]

The idea of the priest-king had another aspect in Aragonese times. This can be seen in the triumphal frieze of Alfonso I (Fig. 120). Here, it is true, the king has shed some of the trappings of his coronation, including the vestments and crown, but not the orb, nor the scepter his missing right hand once held. Nevertheless, he strikes the eye, amid the swirling costumes and marching feet of the procession, as a still, hieratic figure, as it were introduced from some earlier world. He is almost an idol, yet at the same time he is rotund, distended, and full of that life force one senses in the statues of Ladislas and Giovanna. While Alfonso I has translated the seated maiestas image from the earlier tomb context into that of a pagan triumph, he has allowed it to recall its old self. Even the setting in which this occurs is not so completely changed as one at first thinks. Apart from the architectural relationships between Alfonso's arch and the earlier Neapolitan tombs, there was a functional one, for at one time Alfonso's arch was intended to be its hero's cenotaph.[29]

Ferrante developed these ideas of stylistic contrast for expressive purposes in his own inner arch, but at the same time he went back to the earlier tradition of the priestly portrait. This was natural enough, given the special importance to him of affirming his investiture. The original program of Ferrante's relief is not hard to reconstruct. Its flanking figures are still present (Fig. 121). Probably the central panel with Ferrante's portrait was removed on the occasion of Charles V's entry in 1535, as was his equestrian portrait on the Porta Capuana.[30] We know from documents, nevertheless, that the figure of Ferrante in the Castel Nuovo

28. See Edouard Eichmann, "Studien zur Geschichte der abendländischen Kaiser-Krönung," Historisches Jahrbuch, 45 (1925), 21–56, esp. 41; idem, Die Kaiser-Krönung in Abendland, 1 (Würzburg, 1942), 105–08; Marc Bloch, Les Rois thaumaturges (Strassburg, 1924), pp. 185–215; and Ernst Kantorowicz, The King's Two Bodies (Princeton, 1957), pp. 314–450. Scipione Mazzella, in Descrittione del Regno di Napoli (Naples, 1586), pp. 342–46, confirms that Alfonso wore a dalmatic and pluvial, and speaks of a "Regno perpetuo." There is also the Coronation Mass prayer quoted by G. A. Summonte, Historia, 5, 14: "et in Regnum aeternum secum [Alfonso] regnare faciat Jesus Christus Dominus noster Rex Regum." This concept of the king reigning forever with Christ in Heaven is precisely what is embodied in the seated "majesty figures" of the Neapolitan tombs. The idea that the king's "dignitas non moritur" was also common (Kantorowicz, The King's Two Bodies, pp. 314–450).

29. C. von Fabriczy, "Der Triumphbogen Alphonsos I," Jahrbuch der preussischen Kunstsammlungen, 20

(1899), 150, documents for April 2, 1466, and June 30, 1466. At the same time the earlier royal tombs of Santa Chiara and elsewhere functioned as gates. Thus the monument to Ladislas is the entrance to the Caracciolo del Sole Chapel, and (less certainly) the tomb of Robert opened into a room beyond. (For the latter see Costanza Gradara, "Isolamento del sepolcro di Re Roberto d' Angiò," Bollettino d'Arte, ser. 1, 11, 1917, 99.)

30. That a relief was there at one time is quite certain (Fabriczy, "Triumphbogen," p. 151). The Bargello relief would in any case not fit into Ferrante's arch, as is shown by Rolfs' measurements (Franz Laurana, 1, 160), which give the empty panel as 0.94 m wide, between the existing figures, 1.45 m high, and 0.86 m deep. The Bargello piece (with its modern extensions on the top), is 1.56 m high and 1.23 m wide, not counting the base. Assuming that Benedetto's original conception was for a group of about this same height, the piece would be 11 cm too high and 29 cm too wide for the inner arch. On the other hand the Bargello fragment

portal wore a crown and held an orb and scepter, these having been gilded in 1468 and 1471.[31] A cardinal's hat carried by the man on the far left makes it obvious that an ecclesiastical figure is also missing. That it was in fact a coronation scene is shown unequivocally by the inscription: "I succeeded to my anointed father's kingdom and, proved in every way, I received the kingdom's robe and holy crown."[32]

The best evidence, however, for the missing part of Pietro's scene, as Bertaux has suggested, is a relief that appears on Ferrante's coins.[33] This shows him vested as a priest in the manner of Robert and Ladislas. But there is one critical difference: unlike these earlier figures, in the coin Ferrante is *actually being crowned*. On the right, a bishop places the crown on the new king's head; on the left, another bishop in pontifical hat holds a book which could be the Scriptures, the *Ordo coronationis*, or possibly even the investiture itself.[34] So it seems almost certain that this coin scene was derived from Pietro da Milano's missing panel. It is unusual as a formula and does not appear in any earlier recorded Neapolitan currency.[35]

Moreover, the scene is the perfect statement of Ferrante's aims. He uses the tradition of the priest-king seated in state but has built that time-honored image into a more modern context, one suggested by the triumphal frieze of Alfonso I. For like the latter, Ferrante's relief depicts an actual moment in history, a procession in which the barons walk docilely in the royal presence. At the same time the pagan implications of his father's famous triumph are removed, and the historical moment chosen is far more central to the illegitimate king's claim: the coronation-consecration itself. Like his father, Ferrante would rule from the gate of his fortress-palace in the midst of a documented, irrevocable historical action. But like Ladislas and Robert, he would equally be shown as a consecrated priest-king, entitled to rule forever.

It is my opinion that Alfonso II intended to display a similar scene showing his own coronation on the Porta Reale, thus carrying on this tradition with its cumulative modifications. It would have been impossible to add another gate to the Castel Nuovo. What therefore could be more logical than to transform this earlier monument to another great king? What

---

would be much too small for the Porta Capuana, whose blank attic is approximately 2.1 m high (cf. Francesco de Cesare, *Le più belle Fabbriche del millecinquecento ed altri monumenti di architettura esistenti in Napoli*, Naples, 1845, pls. 1, 2). In any case we have seen in Chapter 4 that the attic ornament for this gate was completed and actually installed—something of course that could not be true of the unfinished Bargello fragment, which has always remained in Tuscany.

31. C. von Fabriczy, "Der Triumphbogen," p. 151, docs. 20, 25.

32. SUCCESSI REGNO PATRIO CUNCTIS QUE PROBATUS / ET TRABEAM ET REGNI SACRUM DIADEMA RECEPI.

33. Bertaux, "L'Arco e la Porta," p. 47. Rolfs, in *Franz Laurana, 1, 163*, rather oddly denies that the scene could have been a coronation, such being too static a cen-

ter to account for the movement in the flanking figures: "der Richtung von Rechts nach links gehende Bewegung (der einige nach vorn gekehrte Gesichter nicht widersprechen) gestatten die Vermutung, dass es sich um einen feierlichen Zug, eine Prozession handelt."

34. *Corpus nummorum italicorum, 19*, 211, and pl. ix, fig. 7. The composition appears both on ducats and coronati. Cf. Memmo Cagiati, *Le Monete del reame delle Due Sicilie*, fasc. 2 (Naples, 1911), p. 114, no. 1.

35. Somewhat similar scenes were of course common on papal coins and medallions, e.g. Hill 807, which portrays Sixtus IV seated on his throne flanked by St. Francis on the left, and St. Anthony. Similarly there could be allegorical coronations, e.g. Hill 560 (by Giulio della Torre, c. 1534): Daniel Renier flanked by Justice (left) and Prudence, who crown him, and with the motto VIRTUTEM INSIGNEM MERITO DAMUS ECCE CORONAM.

more convenient act of magnificentia could there be? As evidence that Alfonso II did apply this paternal coronation formula to himself, I can cite the coins of his reign, on which the identical scene of an enthroned monarch being crowned by bishops appears (Fig. 122).[36] But a far more striking piece of evidence that Alfonso reused the formula is of course Benedetto's fragment. Though here the royal figure is weathered and its features broken, it is a perfectly believable portrait of Alfonso (Figs. 110, 111, 112). Even the ambiguity of the sitter's identity, noted by Fabriczy,[37] is significant. In it one sees another instance of that anonymous royal Neapolitan image of majesty, an image that was transferred from person to person and whose marble carapaces, as each king died, were deposited on their tombs.

RECONSTRUCTING THE PORTA REALE   We can even gather some idea of the intended appearance of the Porta Reale. In June 1494 Alfonso II provided funds for new buildings for one of his favorite monasteries, the Benedictine foundation of SS Severino e Sossio. This was about a month after the coronation. The actual construction however occurred only after 1537. Recently the interior of the church has been stripped of some of its Baroque encrustation. The handsome nave flanked by shallow arched chapels recalls the style of Giuliano da Maiano, though it is probably the work of his pupil, Giovanni Donadio, called Mormando (Fig. 125).[38] There are sturdy double pilasters and simplified detail, tight and linear, a high-friezed entablature with sharp tiny dentils, and stubby fish-scaled consoles for keystones. It all recalls the Porta Capuana (Fig. 70).

Probably at the same time the church was redesigned, a series of frescoes was planned for one of the new cloisters, the Chiostro del Platano. The series still exists, though in a ruinous state. It is the work of Antonio Solario and assistants, and although the dates of execution are in dispute, clearly the frescoes were conceived in 1494–95. They depict events in the life of St. Benedict.[39] In one of the scenes, St. Benedict Being Welcomed to Affile (Figs. 123,

36. Alfonso also used the state figure, with regalia but without the two clergy, on his mezzo-carlino. Cf. *Corpus nummorum italicorum*, *19*, pl. ix.

37. C. von Fabriczy, "Das Marmorrelief," *Repertorium für Kunstwissenschaft*, 26 (1903), 262–63.

38. For this see Notar Giacomo, *Cronica*, p. 184; Gallo, *Diurnali*, p. 36; Celano, *Notizie, 3*, 720; G. Filangieri, *Documenti, 5*, 231, 267, 330, 6, 151; N. F. Faraglia, "Memorie artistiche della chiesa benedettina de' SS Severino e Sossio di Napoli," *ASPN, 3* (1878), 235–52; Bartolommeo Capasso, "Appunti per la storia delle arti in Napoli," *ASPN, 6* (1881), 535–37; G. Filangieri, "Prospetto cronologico della vita e delle opere di Mastro Giovanni Donadio di Mormanno organista ed architetto," *ASPN, 9* (1884), 297–300; G. Ceci, "Una Famiglia di architetti napoletani del rinascimento: i Mormanno," *NN, 9* (1900), 167–72, 182–85; Pane, *Architettura*, pp. 260–64; and Iole Mazzoleni, *Il Monastero benedettino dei SS Severino e Sossio* (Naples, 1964), pp. 24–62. Alfonso's is the old church

attached to the south side of the present main building (the latter being by Giovanni Del Caizo and dating from after 1731). While the facts that emerge from all this are not consistent it can be said that: (1) in the mid 90s Alfonso bequeathed possibly as much as 17,000 ducats for rebuilding the church; (2) a design was made around this time, and construction possibly begun; (3) in all probability the architect was Giovanni Mormando; and (4) most of the actual construction took place after 1537, with Mormando's son-in-law Giovanni Francesco di Palma, also called Mormando, in charge. In his will, interestingly enough, the elder Mormando identifies Giuliano da Maiano as his teacher (Faraglia, "Memorie artistiche").

39. The cloister is now part of the Archivio di Stato building. For the frescoes see Stanislao D'Aloe, *Le Pitture dello Zingaro nel chiostro di San Severino in Napoli*, etc. (Naples, 1846); Jacob Burckhardt, *Cicerone*, 10th ed., 2, (Leipzig, 1909), 3; N. F. Faraglia, "Due pittore per amore," *NN, 3* (1894), 113–17; idem, "I

124), we see the young saint just after he has fled with his nurse from the temptations of Rome, as he goes into the hills west of the city to realize his vocation. In the background is the Church of St. Peter, Affile, where Benedict remained for a time.[40]

Next to the church is an object not mentioned in the legend: a gate much resembling the Porta Capuana (Fig. 124). Thus the artist has made a topical allusion, resetting in Naples Benedict's conversion and his resolve to go into a monastic life. In my opinion this was done in honor of the frescoes' donor. In other words, I assume the scene was planned after January 1495, when Alfonso had also taken up the Benedictine life, preferring like Benedict "to endure the evils of the world rather than its praise, and to fatigue himself with God's work rather than to be exalted by the favors of this life."[41] The splendid Renaissance city in the background would symbolize the new Naples Alfonso now will never see, as well as the Rome that Benedict was leaving: it would be the World both were giving up. The scene of pagan sacrifice on the frieze over the gate echoes the same idea.

The gate in Solario's fresco, however, is not quite the Porta Capuana. In the latter there are massive low towers, almost torrioni, which rise straight from the ground. The vertical sense of the pilasters is continued upward, across the ends of the attic, by the niches. On the other hand the frescoed gate's towers are scarped, and they contain keyhole gun embrasures at ground level. The towers themselves are thin and of brick, like those at Urbino. The Montefeltro palace also supplies a precedent for the gentle outward flow of these scarps. Many of the changes suggest Francesco di Giorgio or Marchese, and it may therefore have been one of them who in 1494 recast Giuliano's proposed western gate as a coronation monument. The church in the fresco is also in Francesco's manner.

With all this in mind, in addition to Benedetto's inventory of fourteen figures, and the description by G. A. Summonte of the coronation ceremony itself, it is not difficult to reconstruct the frieze of which the Bargello relief was to have been the centerpiece. We remove the pagan sacrifice that Solario has placed in the attic of his arch and the inscription EFIDE

Dipinti a fresco dell'atrio del platano in S. Severino," *NN*, 5 (1896), 49–52, 135–37, 167–68; 6 (1897), 56–58, 103–06; Benedetto Croce, "Antonio da Solario Autore degli affreschi nell'atrio di S. Severino," *NN*, 6 (1897), 122–24; Luigi Serra, "Nota sugli affreschi dell'ex convento dei SS Severino e Sossio a Napoli," *NN*, 9 (1906), 206–12; Rolfs, *Geschichte der Malerei Neapels* (Leipzig, 1910), pp. 123–35, and Carlo Astolfi, "Quando è vissuto Antonio Solario detto lo Zingaro?" *Rassegna bibliografica dell'arte italiana*, anno 10 (1907), 38–39. E. Modigliani's "A Madonna by Antonio da Solario and the Frescoes of SS Severino e Sosio at Naples," *Burlington Magazine, 11* (1907), 376–82, shows fairly conclusively that the series was executed under Antonio Solario's direction in the last years of the Quattrocento. The Chiostro del Platano cycle is carried out in a hard, graceful Venetian style, with compact, active figures against sumptuous architectural and land-

scape backgrounds. The style and composition approach those of the scenes from Benedict's life in Monteoliveto Maggiore, near Siena, begun by Signorelli (1497–98) and completed by Sodoma and others (1505–08). The relationship of these cycles has not been analyzed so far as I know; it might be useful to undertake the task before the Neapolitan paintings completely disappear.

40. "Enfide," as it appears over the city gate in the fresco, is also known in the literature as Alfadena, Effida, Offida, and Ensida. Nowadays it is the town of Affile, south of Subiaco. Cf. George Kaftal, *Iconography of the Saints in Central and South Italian Schools of Painting* (Florence, 1965), p. 167, where in the S. Severino fresco the left-hand, more distant city is interpreted as the Rome St. Benedict is leaving.

41. Gregory the Great, *Dialogi libri IV*, ed. U. Moricca (Rome, 1924), p. 75.

below. The latter becomes a dedication to Alfonso II. Above this in the center we set the Bargello fragment surmounted by the "padiglione" mentioned in the inventory. This may have resembled the canopy over the king in Alfonso's arch. The bishop on the left will be Giovanni Borgia, the papal legate who crowned Alfonso, and the other bishop, holding the book, will be the "finished bishop" of the inventory, i.e. Alessandro Carafa, Archbishop of Naples. Flanking this group, perhaps in the manner of Pietro da Milano's and Francesco Laurana's courtiers on the inner arch (Fig. 121), would be the "Duke," the newly created Duke of Calabria, Ferrandino; and "Don Federigo," would be Alfonso's brother. The two unnamed figures of the inventory may also have stood near the throne. Perhaps they represented two of the ambassadors; or perhaps one of them was Goffrè Borgio, son of Alexander VI, whose marriage to Alfonso's natural daughter Sancia was being celebrated as part of the coronation festivities. The other parts of the frieze would be peopled with the musicians and juggler also mentioned in the inventory.[42]

When Antonio Marchese's western defenses were resumed in 1497, they may still have had a place for this coronation arch. Francesco di Giorgio was back in Naples early in this year, and we have seen that Federigo later wrote to Francesco about his intention to go on with his brother's program. In fact, at the same time he sent to Siena for Francesco (i.e. in March), Federigo sent to Florence for Benedetto da Maiano. In the extant letter Federigo merely asks the artist to bring certain books and writings left by Giuliano, which seem to have had to do with Loreto rather than Naples.[43] But it is quite possible that there was other correspondence on the subject of the coronation pieces then in the artist's shop. However, although Benedetto did seek permission to make the trip, he died before he could do so, on April 24 of that same year, 1497.

Whatever Federigo's plans were in 1497, he never actually did rebuild the Porta Reale as a monumental gate. "The whole," as Vasari says, "remained unfinished." Benedetto's frieze stayed in Florence, and the design for the new gate was transferred to a Benedictine setting— like its begetter. The Porta Reale, after being moved from its old site to a new one outside the gardens of Monteoliveto in 1528, was rebuilt as an ordinary city portal very much like the earlier eastern gates.[44]

42. I assume that some or all of the architectural fragments listed above in n. 13 were also intended for the Porta Reale. The large ones could have been samples, to be duplicated in Naples in order to make enough lastre to complete the design. The small ones would have been part of the frieze architecture, similar to that in the Arch of Alfonso I.

43. Published in Céndali, *Giuliano e Benedetto da Maiano*, pp. 176–80.

44. It appears as no. 8 on Lafrery's plan (Fig. 106), and formed the entrance to the via Toledo. The Church of Santo Spirito now stands on its site. Don Pedro there erected a plaque detailing the history of the Porta Reale, and when the gate was demolished in 1775 the plaque was preserved for a time in the adjacent Palazzo De Rosa. The inscription was also preserved, according to De la Ville Sur-Yllon ("Le Mura e le porte," p. 52). Cf. Vincenzo Florio, *Memorie istoriche o siano annali napolitani*, MS XXVI. D. 13–14, Biblioteca Società Napoletana per la Storia Patria, Naples, pt. 1, 191–94; G. Russo, *La Città di Napoli dalle origini al 1860* (Naples, 1960), fig. 53; G. Doria, *Le Strade di Napoli*, p. 379; Celano, *Notizie, 3*, 39–40, A. Colombo, "La Strada di Toledo," *NN, 4* (1895), 58–62; and F. Nicolini, "Dalla Porta Reale al Palazzo degli Studi," *NN, 14* (1905), 132.

Chapter 8: THE TOMB SCULPTURE

ONTEOLIVETO   Alfonso's will provided for the reconstruction of two major churches, SS Severino e Sossio and Santa Caterina a Formello. A third church, rebuilt during the Duke's actual lifetime, is Santa Maria di Monteoliveto, known now as Sant'Anna dei Lombardi. This belonged to Alfonso's favorite Olivetan order, the White Benedictines, and it was located just inside the new western walls not far from the old Porta Reale (Fig. 1).[1] Only four chapels remain more or less as they were in Alfonso's period, and three of these, though built during the renewal, were at least technically under the patronage of others. Nevertheless, I believe the Duke intended to transform Monteoliveto into a royal pantheon, i.e. to make it the "most sumptuous church" mentioned by Pietro Summonte.

Alfonso's connection with Monteoliveto had always been close. According to Leostello, he frequently dined and heard mass there. His chaplain in 1482 was Fra Giovanni Mirabella, an Olivetan monk;[2] and on his abdication it was to another Olivetan monastery, in Mazara del Vallo, Sicily, that Alfonso fled. Just before leaving Naples he gave the Neapolitan house three fiefs and other gifts.[3] In fact, Alfonso virtually refounded Monteoliveto; accordingly behind the high altar on the presbytery wall are memorial tablets, one to the church's original founder, Gurello Orilia, who began the structure in 1411, and the other to Alfonso II.[4] The large southern chapel, now containing the Mazzoni Lamentation, also became a joint memorial to Orilia and Alfonso.

The church was already something of an Aragonese pantheon. Francesco and Carlo d'Aragona, illegitimate brothers, and Alfonso's illegitimate son Pietro all lie, or once lay, there.[5] The building contained the magnificent chapel of yet another illegitimate relative, Alfonso's sister Maria Piccolomini, Duchess of Amalfi. Giuliano da Maiano had also asked to be buried in this church.[6] And then there is Vasari's reference to a tomb for an unspecified infant brother of Alfonso's, made in Florence by Luca della Robbia and Agostino di Duccio, of marble with terra-cotta ornaments.[7] However, Vasari does not say this was destined for

1. Cf. L. Catalani, *Le Chiese di Napoli*, *1* (Naples, 1845), 47–67; Cesare D'Engenio, *Napoli sacra* (Naples, 1624), pp. 501–17; Pane, *Architettura*, pp. 186–99; G. Ceci, "Nella Chiesa di Monteoliveto," *Rassegna storica napoletana*, 2 (1934), 205–12, especially for the sixteenth-century alterations; and Franco Strazzulo, "La Fondazione di Monteoliveto di Napoli," *NN*, ser. 3, 3 (1963–64), 103–11.

2. Barone, "Cedole," *ASPN*, 9 (1884), 423.

3. Celano, *Notizie*, 3, 315.

4. D'Engenio, *Napoli sacra*, p. 503. Another plaque to Alfonso was placed in the refectory (Celano, loc.

cit.). Cf. Pompeo Sarnelli, *Guida de' Forastieri . . .* (Naples, 1697), p. 277.

5. Celano, *Notizie*, 3, 338; Passero, *Giornali*, pp. 47–53; and Tristano Caracciolo, "Opuscula historica," in Gravier, *Raccolta*, 6, 147.

6. Celano, *Notizie*, 3, 338. According to Giovanni Mormando's will, however, Giuliano was actually buried in SS Severino e Sossio. Cf. G. Ceci, "Nuovi documenti," *ASPN*, 29 (1904), 791–92.

7. Vasari, 2, 175 (Vasari here wrongly identifies Agostino as Luca's brother).

Monteoliveto, and it must be admitted that other more important relatives of Alfonso lie elsewhere. Thus Ippolita's coffin was placed (though perhaps only temporarily) in the Annunziata,[8] and Ferrante is in San Domenico Maggiore along with other members of the family; but they too lack tombs, and they lie in simple wooden cases in the sacristy. The coffins of Ferrandino and (I think) of his queen, Giovanna, were added later. So at one time it may actually have been the intention to bury them all in this projected pantheon.[9]

Alfonso's new construction at Monteoliveto apparently began on February 10, 1487, with a payment of 200 ducats to Gaspare de Ruggieri.[10] This was for a new cloister, which I presume to be the large one now used by the Carabinieri and which unfortunately I have not been allowed to enter. It is said to contain a fountain at the center with portrait sculptures of Gurello Orilia and Alfonso. The cloister itself, with two stories of arcades supported on marble columns, is handsome but not novel.[11]

It is usually assumed, though without documentation, that the interior of Monteoliveto was remodeled by Giuliano da Maiano. (It was again rebuilt in the mid-seventeenth century by Gennaro Scacco.) Pane envisages a series of chapels lining the main aisle similar to the two present western chapels, i.e. with lunettes, small finestre a squarcio, and handkerchief vaults. He also sees narrower Corinthian pilasters and wider arches down the nave than at present, but otherwise a similar parti. Such a composition, with heavy subdivided volumes massively framed, would have given the interior an Albertian character, as in the design by the two Mormando for the interior of SS Severino e Sossio (Fig. 125), or Santa Caterina a Formello (Fig. 127).

Another part of the church related to Alfonso's patronage is the Cappella Tolosa in the northeast corner (Fig. 128). This is reminiscent of the Pazzi Chapel in Santa Croce, consisting as it does of a small vaulted chancel and a delicate umbrella vault over a main square chamber.[12] Unlike the Pazzi Chapel, however, this was frescoed. It is now being restored; the artist is said to have been Cristoforo Scacco and the date about 1499. An early student has claimed that one of the scenes included a portrait (not now discernible) of Alfonso.[13]

8. R. Filangieri, *Cronaca figurata*, p. 76. Beatrice (d. 1508) was buried in San Pietro Martire, and her tomb is still visible in that church along with those of an earlier Pietro d'Aragona (d. 1439) and of Ferrante's first wife, Isabella di Chiaromonte (d. 1465). Cf. G. Cosenza, "La Chiesa e il convento di San Pietro Martire," *NN*, 9 (1900), 104–09.

9. A fire in 1506 burned the original coffins of Ferrante and Ferrandino (Cosenza, "San Pietro Martire," p. 109). Against my suggestion it must be admitted that it was normal, on the principle of *ubi tumulus, ibi funus*, to bury a body in the place where the funeral was held. Cf. Antoine Bernard, *La Sépulture en droit canonique du décret de Gratien au concile de Trente* (Paris, 1933), pp. 95–97.

10. Barone, "Cedole," *ASPN*, 9 (1884), 619.

11. T. C. I., *Napoli e dintorni* (Milan, 1960), s. v.

12. Cf. Pane, *Architettura*, pp. 186–99. Ceci, "Nella Chiesa di Monteoliveto," reconstructs the original fifteenth-century plan as a single nave on each side of which were pairs of chapels communicating with each other and with the exterior by means of corridors. G. Filangieri (*Documenti, 6, 359*) mentions, without a document, four majolica roundels in Monteoliveto, presumably those now in the Cappella Tolosa. He attributes them to Andrea della Robbia.

13. Camillo Guerra, "Dei Dipinti di recente scoperti nella cappella della famiglia Tolosa in Monteoliveto di Napoli," *Atti della reale accademia di archeologia lettere e belle arti di Napoli*, 1 (1865), 212–22. Guerra attributes the scenes to Pinturicchio and rejects an earlier attribution (which I have not found in print) to Antonio Solario, though he does liken them to the SS Severino e Sossio scenes. Guerra also found portraits of

THE PICCOLOMINI CHAPEL   The two most interesting parts of Monteoliveto are linked to Alfonso more directly. These are the two double-roomed chapels flanking the vestibule on the west. They function as outsize bays symmetrically added on either side of the main axis of the church, rather like the Old and New Sacristies (though these of course are on the east) in San Lorenzo, Florence. Indeed, San Lorenzo, as an older church being transformed into a family pantheon, may well have inspired Alfonso's work at Monteoliveto. Giuliano da Maiano's Faenza Cathedral (begun 1474), with its two richly decorated, projecting, cubical transeptal chapels, would also be related.

Both these western chapels, the Piccolomini on the north and the Terranuova on the south, were founded by important supporters of the Aragonese cause. Maria d'Aragona, the chief occupant of the Piccolomini Chapel, was Ferrante's daughter, born in 1452. At age 16 she married Antonio Piccolomini, the son of Nanni Todeschini of Siena and of Pius II's sister Laudonia. Antonio Piccolomini, who commissioned the chapel, had distinguished himself as a military leader for the Aragonese and in 1461 was made Duke of Amalfi.[14] He was also Chief Magistrate of the kingdom, i.e. President of the Great Court of the Vicaria. He took the name of Aragon so that he like his wife became part of the "Aragonese progeny," which Pietro Summonte says the proposed pantheon was destined for. Maria herself died in 1470 leaving three daughters, one of whom married Marco Coppola, son of the Count of Sarno, whose engagement was the occasion of the famous arrests after the Barons' Revolt on August 13, 1486.[15]

Maria's epitaph expresses the sense of death as a living sleep, so popular in Renaissance funeral poetry:[16]

> You who read these words, do so in a low voice lest you wake the sleeper. Mary of Aragon, a child of King Ferdinand, is enclosed within. She married the stalwart Duke of Amalfi, Antonio Piccolomini, to whom she left three daughters as a witness of their mutual love. One can believe she is sleeping, for she little deserved to die.

The tomb and altarpiece (Fig. 130), standing respectively on the south and west walls of the chapel, were commissioned in about 1470 from Antonio Rossellino in Florence.[17] Three or four years later, when Rossellino died, he and his assistants had completed only parts of

---

Blessed Bernardo Tolomei, founder of the Olivetans, and St. Benedict. Alfonso II, he says, was dressed in a yellow hood and black suit with wide sleeves, and knelt before St. Peter.

14. Cf. R. Filangieri, *Cronaca figurata*, p. 49, n. 16. Capaccio, in *Il Forastiero* (Naples, 1634), p. 259, says Maria had earlier been married to Giovan Giordano Orsino. Pandolfo Collenuccio, in his *Compendio dell' istoria del regno di Napoli* (Venice, 1613), I, pp. 272–73, adds that after Maria Piccolomini's death in 1470 Antonio married another Maria, the daughter of Marino Marzano, former Prince of Rossano. It was this later

marriage of Antonio's that produced the son, Alfonso, who became the husband of John Webster's infamous Duchess.

15. Ferraiolo, in R. Filangieri, *Cronaca figurata*, pp. 49–50.

16. Croce says it is by Pontano (*Storie e leggende*, p. 253).

17. See O. H. Giglioli, "Tre Capolavori di scultura fiorentina in una chiesa di Napoli," *Rivista d'Italia*, 5, tome 2 (1902), 1030–44; C. von Fabriczy, "Documenti su due opere di Antonio Rossellino," *Rivista d'arte*, ser. 1, 5 (1907), 162–65; and Rolfs, *Laurana*, I, 236–38.

the tomb and probably most of the altarpiece.[18] For eight years or so things languished. Then in 1481 Antonio Piccolomini got in touch with Fra Bartolommeo di Firenze, the abbot of the Olivetan Monastery of San Miniato al Monte in Florence. Fra Bartolommeo had been charged with commissioning the work,[19] and Antonio Piccolomini now asked that some of the money paid for the unfinished tomb be returned. This was done, and the new artist selected by Fra Bartolommeo was Benedetto da Maiano. This, by the way, was probably the first Neapolitan commission for either of the Maiano brothers.

Other documents may bear on the history of this chapel. One, dated May 24, 1488, records a payment of just over 79 ducats by the Duke to Benedetto for procuring 1,015 tiles.[20] Their destination is not mentioned, and they may have been intended for one of the villas or for the Castel Capuano. But it is also possible that they were for the magnificent tile floor of this chapel. Another document, dated December 31, 1488, records a payment of 24 ducats by Alfonso to Giuliano da Maiano as part of a fee for an altarpiece, which Giuliano was having made for the Duke in Florence. I suggest that this was for Benedetto's work on the Nativity altar (Fig. 143).[21] As substantiation we know that Benedetto was in fact charged with finishing the work and that it was set in place the following year, 1489. If my reading of either of these documents is accepted, Alfonso must be thought of as a patron of his half-sister's chapel. The chronology helps confirm this: after languishing for eighteen years, the work was completed in 1488–89, at the peak of the renewal, and just after Antonio Piccolomini's daughter had played an important role in settling the Barons' Revolt.[22]

It is true that the tomb of Maria Piccolomini (Fig. 131) and to a lesser extent its chapel are copies of Rossellino's chapel and tomb for the Cardinal of Portugal (1461–66) in San Miniato, Florence (Figs. 129, 132).[23] They are therefore of no great intrinsic interest in the general history of Italian art. It is true, too, that in comparison with its prototype the Nea-

---

18. Heinz Gottschalk, *Antonio Rossellino* (Leipzig, 1930), pp. 58–67, esp. p. 60, n. 60, with bibliography; Leo Planiscig, *Bernardo und Antonio Rossellino* (Vienna, 1942), p. 58; John Pope-Hennessy, "The Martelli David," *Burlington Magazine*, 101 (1959), 134–39; Frederick Hartt, Gino Corti, and Clarence Kennedy, *The Chapel of the Cardinal of Portugal, 1434–1459* (Philadelphia, 1964), pp. 62–63.

19. Fabriczy, "Documenti . . . Rossellino."

20. Barone, "Cedole," *ASPN*, 20 (1895), 327–28.

21. Fabriczy, "Toscanische und oberitalienische," p. 94. I do not see why Fabriczy assumes the altarpiece, described as a "cona," must have been a painting.

22. For the finishing of the chapel see Fabriczy, "Documenti . . . Rossellino," and F. Schottmüller, "Benedetto da Maiano," Thieme-Becker, s.v.

23. Vasari, *3*, 95. The Florentine church was also an Olivetan monastery at the time, and the occupant of the tomb, Cardinal James of Portugal (d. 1459), grandson of John I of Portugal, was, like Alfonso II, particularly fond of the order. See Hartt et al., *The Chapel*, passim,

and Panofsky, *Tomb Sculpture*, p. 74. It is possible that a loose sheet of drawings now in the British Museum (Fig. 129) was made for Antonio Piccolomini. Cf. Hartt, pp. 68–72 and Fritz Burger, *Geschichte des florentinischen Grabmals* (Strassburg, 1904), p. 169. Hartt et al., however, think it was not this but another drawing, now in the Buonaccorso Ghiberti codex, Biblioteca Nazionale, Florence, that was made for the Duke, by Benedetto, c. 1475. But this latter sketch is of the tomb only, and Giuliano da Maiano (or perhaps a different, original architect, c. 1470) in Naples would have required more information about the chapel as a whole, as on the British Museum sheet. Indeed, this latter sheet was probably in Vasari's collection (for which see Hartt et al., p. 68); and Vasari could have acquired it when he was living at Monteoliveto in the 1540s. Cf. also Martin Weinberger and Ulrich Middeldorf, "Unbeachtete Werke der Brüder Rossellino," *Münchner Jahrbuch der bildenden Kunst*, ser. 2, 5 (1928), 85–110.

politan tomb seems rather flat, even unpleasantly convex. The Cardinal's monument is set into impressive steps that jut forward and down from its containing arch. This bulk is matched on the other side of the room by the cathedra. Thus with the altar and its richly colored, painted altarpiece, an inward tension is created that reaches equilibrium in the center of the Florentine chapel under the dome. Such equilateral tension is lacking in the Neapolitan chapel which, because of its vestibule, has an axial effect. Even the tomb itself is inferior to the original, e.g. in the carving of the base frieze (Figs. 134, 136), in its encased columnar effigy (Figs. 133, 135), and in its relatively flaccid supernatural population.[24]

Yet if Maria's tomb is contrasted with a Neapolitan monument, that of Malizia Carafa (Fig. 17), we see that it is a radical departure from local tradition. Although Malizia's tomb was executed at about the time of Maria's death in 1470, it goes back in style and composition to the tombs of Ladislas and Cardinal Brancacci.[25] Despite their size these earlier monuments are essentially pavilions, miniature tabernacles whose architecture is at considerably smaller scale than the buildings in which they are set. In Maria's tomb this housing, or pavilion, has been scaled up to become an enlarged bay of the church. It is composed of four thick arches with wide, continuous archivolts (as in the Porta Capuana), whose intradoses are coffered and decorated with rosettes, angels, and symbols. Fragments of gilt still adhere to them. In this sense the Piccolomini Chapel is another example of that big new scale also seen in the western fortifications and in the proposed Palazzo dei Tribunali.

One can thus interpret the chapel as a quadrifrons arch, which the viewer actually enters, the center of a triumphal crossroads with vestibule and entrance on the east, sarcophagus on the south, altar on the west, and a fourth arch on the north which is empty but could have been made for another tomb (e.g. for Maria's husband). Thus while the means to achieve it are now different and more grandiose, the sense of procession experienced in the earlier Neapolitan tombs, with their biers borne forward by caryatids, is still present in the Piccolomini Chapel; in fact it has increased. This effect is something specifically lacking in Rossellino's more centralized chapel in Florence.

In the tomb itself, in place of the normal Neapolitan caryatids, there is a solid compressed base carved as a slightly flattened antique sarcophagus, with reclining winged genii bearing cornucopias, and with unicorns, lamps, and a garland of fruit. In the center a skull sprouts vegetation (Fig. 134). This base supports a sarcophagus on a stand. The angels, who on the older tombs held back curtains, have become putti removing the pall from Maria's body and displaying it to the viewer (Figs. 133, 137, 138). Maria is archaic; her stiff horizontal rigor, her gown with its architectural folds, and her curiously Pre-Raphaelite face are, in context, "Gothic," like the "Gothic" seated maiestas figures of the royal tombs. There is a great dif-

24. On the influence of the tomb of the Cardinal of Portugal in Benedetto's work see Hartt et al., *The Chapel of the Cardinal,* pp. 71–72.

25. Curiously enough Celano, *Notizie, 3,* 320, quite gratuitously endows Maria's tomb with putti pulling back curtains, a more typically Neapolitan feature (e.g. Fig. 17).

ference between this effigy and the naturalistic ease with which the Cardinal of Portugal (Fig. 135) lies on his bier. Finally, as the epitaph implies, Maria's tomb is also her marriage bed. Her rich brocaided bridal gown and her flowered veil evoke the spirit of Laurana's epithalamic portraits: once again we have the association of death and marriage.

Above and behind her, against the dark blue wall like a diorama, is a divine tableau, as in the Brancacci tomb, which transforms the more earthly and pagan meanings of the lower part of the monument. The sarcophagus stands before what seems to be a sharply ornate, delicate mantelpiece. On it is a square-framed, tabernacle-like panel, carved with a tondo relief of the Ascension (Fig. 142). Angels that are miniatures of those holding the wreath above attend the standing Christ as if to assure us of the passage of Maria's soul. On either side of the tabernacle, angels kneel like acolytes (Figs. 139, 140), carrying jars of burning incense. All this suggests the ceremony that takes place when a nun, dressed for marriage but covered with a pall, makes her profession lying on a bier in front of the altar.[26]

Above this tableau, in a sweeping descent, two angels carry down the beautiful wreathed tondo surrounding the Blessed Virgin and the Infant Christ (Fig. 141). Thus the point of contact between divine and human is sealed, one rising and the other descending, in a momentary, explosive touch. The tomb is a sculptured drama based on the liturgical facts of the funeral chapel: an eternal but fictional embodiment of the upward procession that takes place in reality (but therefore only temporarily) when mass is said.

The other important work of sculpture in the chapel is the altarpiece (Fig. 143). This is quite different from its Florentine counterpart, which was a painting of the Madonna and standing saints by Antonio and Piero Pollaiolo (the original is now in the Uffizi). The Neapolitan panel is set within the wide arch of the western wall beneath an oculus, which corresponds to the Madonna's tondo on the south. In the center is a marble Nativity. It is taut and elegant, looking worn rather than carved to its fragile thinness, as by the action of water (Figs. 148, 149, 150). On either side of this joyful scene, separated by pilasters, is a niched statue with a roundel above, from which another head leans out. On the Gospel side stands St. James (Fig. 144) with a prophet above (Fig. 146); on the Epistle side is St. John the Evangelist (Fig. 145) beneath a younger, yearning prophet (Fig. 147).[27] Architecturally the altarpiece is a miniature triumphal arch—a model in two dimensions of the idea of the

26. Notar Giacomo (*Cronica di Napoli,* p. 167) thus describes Ippolita's funeral in 1488, which also had a bridal aspect: "In la bara, era una coltra di brocato: ipsa era vestita de una camorra de brocato bianco, con un circhio de oro in testa con più ioge." The similarities to a nun's profession could of course be prefigurings: I have not been able to find a fifteenth-century ceremonial for Benedictine nuns that gives such directions. But counter-reformation books confirm their later existence with phrases like "et ipsa virginibus preparata, te [i.e. Christ] perducente, ad sempiternae foelicitatis Nuptias introire mereatur." When the nun's veil is asperged the clergyman says: "sponsa Christi virginitatis propositum custodiat." The abbess then places the veil on the new nun's head and a wedding ring on her finger. The nun lies on a bier, and the four youngest nuns of the house place a pall over her, while the sacristine puts candles at the head and feet of the "corpse." Later the abbess says: "Surge qui dormis, et exsurge a mortuis, et illuminabit te Christus." All this is from the *Cérémonial des réligieuses de l'abbaye de Notre-Dame de Montier-Villiers,* 2 (Paris, 1626), pp. 31–40.

27. Gottschalk, *Rossellino,* p. 60, curiously identifies these four as Matthew, Mark, Luke, and John.

chapel as a whole. It stands on a rich, gay base carved with symbols of the Evangelists and rises to an entablature consisting of cherub heads between cornucopias. Above the cornice large, free-standing putti hold a thick garland that falls on either side of the panel and suggests the tomb Madonna's wreath unfurled (Figs. 151, 152).

Above the oculus is a blessing God surrounded by adoring angels, in much-renewed fresco. In the spandrels, as on all the walls, are the arms of the Piccolomini quartered with those of Aragon. The pendentives of the domed roof contain frescoed capricci and heavy moldings that follow the joints of the spandrels and dome.

In the altarpiece, I take the upper putti, except possibly for the one on the extreme right (Fig. 152), as the work of Benedetto's assistants.[28] The two statues could well be by Rossellino, but the roundels are more problematical. The Moses on the left has a good deal of the arched thrust and elegance of Rossellino's hand (Fig. 146). The bony, intense figure on the right (Fig. 147) is also probably his. The main scene (Fig. 148), with its choreographic elegance sharply pressed by spatulate edges, is at the least purely Rossellinesque. The only figures possibly by Benedetto's hand are the two shepherds on the right and the two central, broad-faced angels dancing above the roof (Fig. 150).

As to the tomb, I follow the general opinion that Benedetto and his shop were responsible for most of the upper half, and that the lower parts are the work of Rossellino's assistants. However, the Madonna tondo is probably by Rossellino (Fig. 141). It and the altar Madonna are set softly and fluidly back into themselves, placid, milky, pretty, with none of the broad masculinity of Benedetto's late style.[29]

THE TERRANUOVA CHAPEL   The pendant chapel on the south was founded in the late 1480s by Marino Curiale, Count of Terranuova. It was about the same size and almost of the same design as its model until it was taken over by the Mastrogiudice family, a collateral line of the Curiale. Their sixteenth-century tombs by Girolamo d'Auria and others now fill the room and its antechamber.[30] Unlike the Piccolomini Chapel the important sculpture here consists only of the altarpiece; it is entirely by Benedetto and his shop.

Marino Curiale of Sorrento was made Count of Terranuova after the death of his brother Gabriele.[31] The inscription on Marino's tomb, dated 1490, proclaims his importance to Fer-

28. For other attributions, cf. Gottschalk, *Rossellino,* pp. 60, 65–66, also Planiscig, *Rossellino,* pp. 57–58. Planiscig attributes all the statues in the altarpiece to Matteo del Pollaiolo. As to the tomb, Gottschalk finds in it no certain work by Rossellino. He gives the tondo, the angels holding it, the putti, and the acolyte-angels all to Benedetto.

29. According to Celano (*Notizie, 3,* 337) the marble crucifixion panel in the antechapel is also by Rossellino, but it is now given to Giulio Mazzoni of Piacenza (1525–1618). There is a copy of the Rossellino Nativity in the vestibule of the Cappella del Tesoro in the Annunziata; the small marble tondo of the Madonna

adoring the Child, with St. Joseph and Shepherds, in the Bargello, and a terra-cotta sketch in the Staatliche Museen, Berlin, are also related (Gottschalk, *Rossellino,* pp. 63–64).

30. The altar itself is also sixteenth-century. For this see Dussler, *Benedetto da Maiano,* pp. 39–42. He says the predella scenes and the Virgin in the *Annunciation* are all workshop. Rolfs, *Laurana, 1,* 236–38, gives practically all the usual "Benedetto da Maiano" attributions in the Cappella Piccolomini to Matteo del Pollaiolo.

31. I have not been able to find out precisely when this occurred. See G. A. Summonte, *Historia, 4,* 425–26.

rante.[32] Marino may also have been related to the Corrado Curiale, who was one of the judges of the rebel barons. He was certainly majordomo to the elder Queen Giovanna, and his wife was one of the matrons Ferrante sent north to examine Isabella.[33] Like the chapel of Maria Piccolomini, therefore, that of Marino Curiale was a monument to an important royalist supporter.

It is generally agreed that the Terranuova Chapel, like the Piccolomini, was finished in 1489.[34] Certain documents may be relevant to it. On August 23, 1488, the Duke paid 200 ducats to Benedetto da Maiano in Florence for unspecified work.[35] This could refer to the Porta Capuana or to one of the villas, but I would like to think that it was for the Terranuova and the Piccolomini altarpieces. A more persuasive bit of evidence that royal patronage (if not specifically the Duke's) was involved in the Terranuova Chapel is a letter written by Queen Giovanna to Lorenzo de'Medici in Florence in 1489. In it she asked that the two marble "tabole" for the Monteoliveto chapel of Count Terranuova, who is characterized as "la principale homo de nostra casa," be shipped to Naples free of duty.[36]

The only architectural difference between the two chapels is that in the one belonging to Marino Curiale the pilasters are wider, and fold at the inside corners of the principal room (as in the Chapel of the Cardinal of Portugal). The walls therefore do not read quite so much as distinct panels. The altarpiece is very much like its opposite number architecturally, but in the center is a magnificent Annunciation set in a cruciform vaulted building, a kind of open-air church that leads back to a garden with a well (Fig. 153), thus continuing the idea of procession in the room. Flanking this scene are, on the Gospel side, a statue of St. John the Baptist (Fig. 155) with the head and shoulders of a female martyr or sibyl above, and, on the Epistle side, St. John the Evangelist (Fig. 156) beneath a similar bust.

This sculpture, except for the Annunciation, upper putti, and predella scenes, is withered and toughly classicizing compared to that in the other chapel. But on the other hand, there

32. It reads:QUI FUIT ALFONSI QUODAM PARS MAXIMA REGIS / MARINUS HAC MODICA / NUNC TUMULAT[UR] HUMO. (Cf. Celano, Notizie, 3, 321, for a different version.) The present inscription is a variant of one composed by Alfonso I for Gabriele Curiale, Marino's brother (Angelo di Costanzo, Istoria del regno di Napoli, 3 (Milan, 1805), 128–29.

33. Corrado Curiale is mentioned by Ferraiolo in R. Filangieri, Cronaca figurata [1486], pp. 60, 62. For the Duchess' trip to Milan see Notar Giacomo, Cronica, p. 169.

34. Fabriczy, "Documenti . . . Rossellino." F. Schottmüller, Thieme-Becker, s.v.

35. Fabriczy, "Toscanische und oberitalienische," pp. 96–98: "A Juliano et herede D'Antonio Gondi mercanti fiorentinj a di 19 del presente ducento ducati per banco de Luysi de Gayeta et Franc° de Palmer et sonno per altretanti ne hanno pagati in Firenza a Benedetto de Leonardo da Mayano per ordine del prefato S. duca di Calabria al quale li dona graciosamente CCd."

36. Cf. Milanesi, Nuovi Documenti per la storia dell'arte toscana (Florence, 1901, Rome, 1893), p. 155, also published in Giglioli, "Tre Capolavori," p. 1043. The original is in the Archivio di Stato, Florence. As published by Giglioli it reads: "Regina Sicilie, etc., Magnifice vir amice noster carissime lo spectabile conte de Terra Nova nostro maior domo fa venire de Fiorenza dui tabole de marmoro per lo besogno de una sua cappella che fa fare in questa cita ad Sancta Maria de Monte Oliveto. . . ." I cannot see any evidence that the Annunciation panel is in two pieces, and this leads me to think that Queen Giovanna while interceding in the name of her own servant only, and mentioning only his chapel, actually meant both the Terranuova Annunciation and the Piccolomini Nativity, which would have been together in Benedetto's shop awaiting shipment to Naples. Even this does not connect the chapels directly with Alfonso of course; that must remain for now only a probability.

is a grandiosity of figure scale, absent in Rossellino's design, and a developed rendering of architectural voids. The predella sequence is exquisite: The Adoration of the Shepherds (Fig. 160), The Adoration of the Magi (Fig. 161), The Resurrection, The Entombment (Fig. 162)—out of order chronologically but in the center for obvious reasons—The Appearance of Christ to the Virgin and Apostles (Fig. 163), The Pentecost with the Virgin (Fig. 164), and The Death of the Virgin (Fig. 165). One also sees the Annunciation, of course, as part of this sequence (Fig. 153) in a special relationship with the Entombment directly beneath. Although these interesting little reliefs are mainly by assistants, they are fully influenced by the High Renaissance proclivities of Benedetto da Maiano and illustrate the pre-Michelangelesque atmosphere of his shop: big, broad, blade-like faces, powerful bodies even for the women (Fig. 164), old men's faces downcast into shadow, flowing into their beards. The two left-hand scenes (Figs. 160, 161) may be by Benedetto himself.

The entablature frieze is filled with baskets of grain and grape garlands. Above stand two of what I take to have been an original group of four putti, holding another garland (Figs. 158, 159).[37]

Benedetto's procedure in working out the main scene is recorded in a well-known clay model.[38] The powerful contoured plane of the Annunciate's robe (Fig. 157) is fully in the manner of the San Bartolo figures or of the Bargello relief (Figs. 110, 113, 115), while the twisting, fluttering contrast of the angel makes one think of the bishop in the latter work. There is a kind of muscular shapeliness, too, in the putti, which recalls the master and, again, the early Michelangelo.[39]

Taken together, the two chapels fulfill those aspects of the renewal that could be expressed in liturgical sculpture. The Piccolomini Chapel, especially, with its processional movement and dramatic tableau of death and resurrection, touches on the familiar Alfonsine themes of the recumbent stone body brought to life, of family solidarity, and of marriage, death, and resurrection.

With the construction of these rooms, furthermore, the Neapolitan funeral monument entered a new phase, the most grandiose realization of which is the Carafa Chapel in the basement of the cathedral, the famous "soccorpo" of 1497–1506 by Tommaso and Giantomaso

---

37. Cf. Dussler, *Benedetto da Maiano*, pp. 39–42. The sequence of small predella-like scenes, possibly by Andrea dell' Aquila, over the portal of the Chapel of Santa Barbara in Castle Nuovo, is almost exactly the same, and is even similar in style. Here we have, from the left, The Annunciation, The Nativity, The Adoration of Magi, The Resurrection, (no Entombment as is found in the Terranuova predella), Christ's Appearance to the Apostles (without the Virgin), the Pentecost (ditto), and The Death of the Virgin.

38. Cf. L. Dussler, "A Clay Model by Benedetto da Maiano for the Altar in Monte Oliveto, Naples," *Burlington Magazine, 45* (1924), 21–22. The sketch was then in the collection of Oscar Bondy, Vienna, and in-

cludes the God the Father, the Annunciate, and the Angel. A drawing for the Terranuova altarpiece in the Uffizi is noted by Céndali, *Giuliano e Benedetto da Maiano*, p. 157. Gigetta Dalli Regoli, in "Problemi di grafica crediana," *Critica d'Arte, 12* (1965), fasc. 76, 25–45, publishes designs for altars similar to those in Monteoliveto, including Uffizi 1436 E (attributed to Lorenzo di Credi), where there is an Annunciation scene and a John the Baptist, much like Benedetto's in the Terranuova Chapel (Fig. 154).

39. Margrit Lisner, in "Zu Benedetto da Maiano und Michelangelo," *Zeitschrift für Kunstwissenschaft, 12* (1958), 141–56, boldly attributes the right-hand putto to Michelangelo himself.

Malvito. This is a veritable funeral basilica, perhaps quite consciously an adaptation of Alfonso's plans for Monteoliveto.[40] Other examples are the Carafa di Santa Severina (now Saluzzo) Chapel in San Domenico Maggiore, of 1512–16 (Fig. 166), and the Nativity Chapel (of the Carafa Conti di Ruvo) in the same church with its massive Albertian architecture, perhaps like that of SS Severino e Sossio partly derived from the Porta Capuana or from Giuliano's Monteoliveto.

At the same time the smooth, heavyish, attractive but torpid style of early sixteenth-century sculpture in Naples, as seen in the work of Giovanni da Nola and Girolamo Santacroce, owes a good deal to the two Monteoliveto chapels. Certainly these artists' weightier, broader, more deliberate style has little to do with Laurana's lilting art. A not dissimilar Romanness, also perhaps owing something to Benedetto's Neapolitan work, appeared in Roman commissions by other Florentines working in that city, e.g. in Andrea Sansovino's two tombs in Santa Maria del Popolo, for Ascanio Sforza and Girolamo Basso (1505ff.). Sansovino had used this manner earlier in a design even more like the Monteoliveto altarpieces for the Sacrament or Corbinelli altar (probably c. 1490) in Santo Spirito, Florence (Fig. 167). But here the inner surface of the roundels and flanking arches has thickened and filled the front plane to emphasize a triumphal-arch shape; and the standing saints are more secure on their axes and in their dry heroic confidence. Also related are two earlier altars by Andrea Ferrucci, one in the Duomo, Fiesole (1493), and the other now in the Victoria and Albert Museum, London (1493–97): both of these were begun just after Ferrucci had returned from Naples.[41]

MAZZONI'S LAMENTATION   There is one more work of sculpture in Monteoliveto, slightly later than the Rossellino/Maiano chapels, which is a kind of aftermath to the renewal. It is in fact the plastic expression of Alfonso's agony and death: Guido Mazzoni's

40. Cf. A. Miola, "Il Soccorpo di S. Gennaro descritto da un frate del Quattrocento," *NN*, 6 (1897), 161–66, 180–88; Franco Strazzullo, "La Cappella Carafa del duomo di Napoli in un poemetto del primo cinquecento," *NN*, ser. 3, 5 (March/April 1966), 59–71; A. Muñoz, "Studii sulla scultura napoletana," p. 87; and Ottavio Morisani, "Considerazioni sui Malvito di Como," in Edoardo Arslan, ed., *Arte e artisti dei laghi lombardi, 1* (Como, n.d.), 265–74. When Cardinal Oliviero Carafa resumed his position as Archbishop of Naples in 1497 he brought to the cathedral the relics of San Gennaro, hitherto kept in the Sanctuary of Montevergine near Avellino. His plan was to make a great underground chapel for them. This was built, but the relics are now kept in the famous seventeenth-century chapel by Francesco Grimaldi on the main floor of the cathedral. Originally the Carafa Chapel was to contain a tomb for San Gennaro in the center, sustained by four harpies. A sculptured effigy was to lie on a sarcophagus, with two angels, one at the head and one at the feet. Above the sarcophagus was to be an altar, and a super-

structure including reliefs or groups of David beheading the Philistine and of Judith and Holofernes, and four triumphal cars for Sol, Luna, Mercury, and Jove, with figures from the Zodiac. The whole was to be surrounded by a decorative iron grating. The marble kneeling statue of the Cardinal that we now see in the apse was to have been placed before the altar-tomb. We have all this from the poem written in 1503 by Fra Bernardino Siciliano, published in Miola, "Il Soccorpo." Another example of the influence of the Monteoliveto chapels is the tomb of Tommaso Brancacci (1492) in San Domenico Maggiore, which borrows the framing arch and Virgin and Child tondo of the Piccolomini monument; also the first and fifth chapels to the left in San Pietro Martire, both probably by Pila.

41. John Pope-Hennessy, *Catalogue of Italian Sculpture in the Victoria and Albert Museum, 1* (London, 1964), 180. Cf. also inv. 303 and 304 in the same collection, related to my Figs. 17 and 18, and possibly the work of Jacopo della Pila's shop.

famous Lamentation (Fig. 169) in the chapel dedicated to the monastery's two patrons.[42] It belongs to the mood of fearful self-accusation that built up in Alfonso between 1492 and 1494. It complements his self-abasements of the latter year when the Duke was "much given to devotion, conversed as much as possible with monks, and read the Greater Office."[43] This sort of melodramatic penitence was apparently characteristic of the family. Thus on October 6, 1496 (the feast of San Gennaro), as a procession with the Host went past the Castel Capuano, the wailing Queen Mother Giovanna greeted it on her bare knees like one of Mazzoni's figures.[44]

Artistically the Lamentation belongs to a different current, darker and older than that which created the Piccolomini and Terranuova chapels. It rejects their small white humanist world, marble and remote, for a life-size crowd of naturalistic figures. Where the Piccolomini Chapel is a theater for the observer, here the observer is denied the propriety of distance, of that gap between himself and the scene which sharpens but also reduces it for him. With Mazzoni's figures there is only overwhelming closeness. Their grief floods the space around them (Figs. 169, 170).[45]

In much of this, Mazzoni's sculpture can be linked with the polychromed wood-carving of the International Style. Such art had had an earlier sculptural expression in the exquisite presepio of wooden figures, just under life size, now in San Giovanni a Carbonara and made by Giovanni and Pietro Alemanni in 1478.[46] The latter figures have a roughly similar stylized idiosyncrasy, e.g. in the jumble of grotesque detail around egglike volumes. But Guido Mazzoni was not a wood-carver; his art fully exploits the pastier, more continuous surfaces of terra-cotta, and produces textures that when colored have the coarse viscosity of theatrical makeup.

Mazzoni was born in Modena about 1450 and was trained by his uncle, a goldsmith. He became a specialist in terra-cotta groups, portraits, and theatrical masks.[47] The great artistic

42. Celano, *Notizie*, 3, 331–32.

43. Sanudo, "La Spedizione," p. 176. Sanudo says he can hardly describe the intensity of the King's piety, that he used to wait on 12 paupers at table, feed 47 other poor men (one for each year of his age), wash and kiss their feet, give them clothes, etc. Croce well describes Alfonso's situation: "Ed ecco che si osa gettare obbrobrio su quel principe sventurato che, all'inoltrarsi degli invasori, disertato dai suoi popoli vaghi di cose nuove, rinunziò il trono al figlio e, poco stante, morì a soli quaranta sette anni. Che cosa doveva egli fare, a mente degli accusatori? Lasciarsi ammazzare per sostenere la loro brama di gesti smisurati? Aggiungere con questo atto smisurato la propria persona alla serie di coloro che non provvedono già alla salute del loro paese, ma cercano 'inanem gloriam' non la lode della storia, ma 'in tragoediis lamentationes'?" Croce, "Antonio de Ferrariis detto il Galateo," *Humanisme et Renaissance*, 4 (1937), 376.

44. Passero, *Giornali*, p. 108.

45. The present arrangement (the group is being restored) and possibly even the present number of the figures are not original (see below, n. 69; the note by Benedetto Croce, *NN*, 3, 1894, 43–45; and F. De Filippis, "Napoli—Restauro di una statua in terracotta di Guido Mazzoni," *Bollettino d'Arte*, 18 [1924–25], 576.

46. Cf. Causa, "Contributi," pp. 112–16.

47. Cf. A. Venturi, "Di un insigne Artista modenese del sec. XV," *Archivio storico italiano*, ser. 4, 14 (1884), 339–66; E. Pèrcopo, "Guido Mazzoni e le sue Opere in Napoli," *NN*, 3 (1894), 41–43; and note by B. Croce, loc. cit., 43–45; A. Venturi, "Una Pietà di Guido Mazzoni a Reggio Emilia," *L'Arte*, 17 (1914), 227–30; Francesco Malaguzzi Valeri, "Scultura dal rinascimento a Bologna," *Dedalo*, 3 (1922–23), 341–72; Arturo Petorelli, *Guido Mazzoni da Modena Plasticatore* (Turin, 1925), esp. p. 17; and Seymour, *Sculpture in Italy*, pp. 184–87. The connection of Mazzoni's art with the drama, and especially with the dummies used for festival

impulse behind his style came from Niccolo dell'Arca, whose Lamentation in Santa Maria della Vita, Bologna, is particularly relevant. From this source, particularly, comes Mazzoni's rejection of Florentine order, reticence, and harmony.

Before he arrived in Naples Mazzoni had had experience that was to stand him in good stead in Ferrante's capital. In 1477–80 he had created a splendid Deposition in San Giovanni Battista della Buona Morte, Modena, in which, it is said, some of the leading citizens, including Ser Gaspare de Longhi and Ser Francesco Pancera, were portrayed. In 1473 Mazzoni made theatrical properties, probably masks, for the marriage of Eleonora and Ercole I in Ferrara.[48] He also created a Lamentation for them in which Eleonora is clearly portrayed as Mary of Cleofa and Ercole as Joseph of Arimathea,[49] so that even before his arrival in Naples, the artist was associated with a kind of religious theater featuring portraits of the grief-stricken patrons.

Mazzoni is first recorded in Naples in 1489. Vasari tells us that he was a competitor of Benedetto da Maiano.[50] Considering Mazzoni's work, we might even take this statement in a double sense: the Modenese sculptor competed with the Florentine for the Duke's commissions; he also represented a rival, even antithetical, art. We hear of Mazzoni in Naples again in 1492, when he made various objects for a festival, including giants that were presumably carried in procession.[51] On October 31, 1492, Domenico Caleff was paid for making an altar and prie-dieu for one of the Duke's oratories and for supplying material to Mazzoni. This could conceivably mean that Mazzoni also made the "kneeling figure," a portrait of the Duke, which Sanudo saw in the chapel at Castel Capuano.[52]

Finally, on December 27, 1492, Mazzoni was paid for the "sepolcro," i.e. the Lamentation.[53] He was still in Naples later that month, and one indication of his position at the Ducal court is that he was given a house.[54] It is usually assumed that he remained through the French occupation and then traveled north with Charles VIII. In France he is known to have

tableaux, is suggested by early sources. For example there is De Lignamine's description of the festivals (in the 70s or earlier) at the court of Ferrante: "ut enim Christus noster passus, crucifixus, mortuus, sepultusque esset ac resurrexisset et coelos tandem relictis terris penetrasset, haec omnia, mira arte ingenioque Dedalici Alphonsi, fabri artificesque imitati sunt." Cited in Pontieri, *Per la storia,* p. 60.

48. A. Venturi, "Di un insigne Artista," pp. 347, 350. There are some Mazzoni groups that could bear further study, e.g. that in the town of Palazzo Pignano, near Cremona, in the parish church, or the one in the church at Medole, also near Cremona. Michiel (*Der Anonimo Morelliano,* p. 44) mentions two others, so far as I know untraced. Under the heading of San Lorenzo, Cremona, he lists "La pietà de terra cotta, simile a quella de S. Antonio de Venetia, fu de man del Paganino, ouer Turriano."

49. Arduino Colasanti, "Ritratti di principi estense in un gruppo di Guido Mazzoni," *Bollettino d'Arte, 15* (April 1922), 458–74. The Lamentation is now in the Church of the Gesù. Less convincingly he identifies the St. John the Evangelist as Acarino d'Este, founder of the dynasty.

50. Vasari, 2, 474, and C. von Fabriczy, "Toscanische und oberitalienische," pp. 108–11.

51. Ibid., and Barone, "Notizie," *ASPN, 10* (1885), 15–16 [April 15, 1492].

52. Barone, "Cedole," *ASPN, 10* (1885), 20. This material, also, was for giants. For the kneeling statue in La Duchesca's oratory, see Sanudo, "La Spedizione," p. 240.

53. Fabriczy, "Toscanische und oberitalienische," pp. 108–09. See also Pietro Summonte, in Nicolini, *L'Arte napoletana,* p. 168.

54. "Denante el Castello de Capuana." Fabriczy, "Toscanische und oberitalienische," p. 109.

executed several important works, among them the latter's tomb, which, interestingly enough, also included a portrait of the King kneeling before a prie-dieu.[55]

Essentially the Monteoliveto Lamentation is a modern-dress recreation of a historic event. Everything is done to make it immediate and unforgettable. The poses and gestures are full of unself-conscious abandon. There is not the slightest idealization: each wrinkle and scar is sculptured with almost sadistic emphasis. The figures, also, are separate and movable, i.e. rearrangeable around the lean body of Christ. There is thus no pre-established composition, no set of geometries within which the bodies are installed. The work is not only in an entirely different style, it constitutes a different use of art, one that makes it in some ways not art at all but rather a machine to elicit sorrow.

Mazzoni's Lamentation, like so many other plastic expressions of the renewal, has a possible literary echo. This is a fervid outpouring by Mazzoni's friend and admirer, Sannazaro, composed after the fall of the dynasty, called *Lamentatio de morte Christi domini ad mortales.*[56] The poem is a verbal pietà,[57] and concentrates like Mazzoni's sculpture on effects of naturalistic violence and on the sorrow of the beholders:

> Look upon him, his breast transfixed by the pitiless spear, his breast, his mutilated hands, his face wet with gore, his bloodied head, his torn hair; look, and shed brimming streams of tears. [ll. 11–14].

Even when the mourners' grief is generalized, when the whole universe weeps, there is still a sort of naturalism: "the sun . . . himself bears witness . . . marking his forehead with dusky blackness, and thou, too, O Moon, coverest thy ugly cheeks and pale face" (ll. 23–26).

Near the end Sannazaro seems to identify the dead Christ with a more recent monarch:

---

55. Ibid., pp. 110–11. Cf. also Anatole de Montaiglon, "Sur deux Statues de Louis XII par le sculpteur modenais Guido Paganino," *Archives de l'art français,* ser. 2, 2 (1862), 219–28. For the tomb of Charles VIII see Panofsky, *Tomb Sculpture,* pp. 75–78. It was made shortly after Charles' death in 1498 and destroyed during the Revolution. Panofsky reproduces a drawing of it. For another echo of the Naples Lamentation cf. G. Filangieri, *Documenti, 5,* 197 [24 April, 1552]. Here Antonio Ferrara, called Imbarracocina, of Giuliana (Gugliano in Campania?), receives payment for a freestanding group imitated from the Monteoliveto Lamentation and made for the Church of San Lorenzo in Caltabellotta, near Sciacca, Sicily. The T.C.I. Guide for Sicily (Milan, 1953, s.v.), describes a life-sized polychromed terra-cotta group in that church (which I have not visited) saying it is by Antonio Ferraro and dating from this same year, 1552. See also the useful table of Mazzoni groups in Seymour, *Sculpture in Italy,* p. 186.

56. Sannazaro actually commissioned a work of sculpture to illustrate another of his poems, the famous

De partu virginis. This is by Giovanni da Nola and is to be found in Sannazaro's own chapel, Santa Maria del Parto, in Mergellina. Pietro Summonte (*L'Arte napoletana,* p. 169) describes the relief as that "ch'el Sannazaro la have in versi dipincta nel divino suo libro 'De partu Virginis'." For Sannazaro's admiration for Mazzoni cf. the sonnet published and commented upon in E. Percopo, "Nuovi documenti," *ASPN, 18* (1893), 785–86.

57. Cf. Filippo Scolari, ed. and trans., *Il Parto della vergine de Azio Sincero Sannazaro* (Venice, 1844), p. 42, where he supposes it to have been based on a Good Friday sermon. He dates it after 1500. I quote the text from the Padua, 1719, edition, pp. 62–66. An Italian version by Sannazaro himself is printed in Alfredo Mauro, ed. *Opere volgari* (Bari, 1961), pp. 210–11, under the title "Lamentazione sopra al corpo del Redentor del mondo a' mortali." This is much shorter than the Latin original. Cf. also Vittorio Borghini, *Il più nobile Umanista del rinascimento* (Turin, etc. 1943), pp. 397–401.

This king of men, despoiler of the empty Avernus, forgetful of crimes, from love of his kindred and mindful of his promise, will enter friendly breasts, and he heals your hearts as temples that have been profaned.[58]

The "king of men" I think is both Christ and Alfonso. Christ cheated hell, i.e. the mythological Avernus, while Alfonso drained the real one: both were its despoilers. Both, moreover, resanctify profaned temples, Christ spiritually in building his Church in the hearts of the faithful, and Alfonso physically in the three church buildings he provided for in his will. Both, in Heaven, will greet the elect who have suffered for their sake.

Similar ideas were applied specifically to Mazzoni's Lamentation in an inscription, hitherto not noted and difficult to interpret, that was to be found in the chapel at least as late as the 1640s. It was transcribed, with an obvious mistake as to the date (and perhaps others), by Celano:

A.D. 1460. You see, wanderer, these simulacra of a half-dead and dying piety are the living, breathing images of the faith of Aragon. They live, but yet are dead of grief. And death, deceived, has passed them by [thinking them already dead]. Do not ask why they do not move: the authority of King Alfonso, now released into Heaven, is able to create immovable loyalty here, such as he could not find in the great projects for which he gave a shower of gold. He has commended himself in clay, as a witness to this faith of adamant, to his Olivetan brethren.[59]

Celano neither tells us where this inscription was in the chapel nor does he identify its author. But I assume it is coeval with the sculptures, and we can learn some important things from it. First, it seems to say that a terra-cotta portrait figure of their benefactor was commissioned by the monks at Alfonso's death. This supports the long-standing legend that Mazzoni added a figure of Alfonso to the original group,[60] which we would now therefore date 1492–94. The inscription also suggests certain ironies. For example, the group as a whole is a witness to loyalty to the Aragonese, but the king's image is also a witness to the scriptural event that is used to symbolize this loyalty. The words also stress the paradox that terra-cotta figures, suggesting mortal clay, can be the expression of eternal faith, made of adamant. The mere simulacra of grief can thus be a mode of immortality for him who has died.

Another aspect of Mazzoni's Lamentation connects it with funeral ceremonies. Just as the

---

58. "Sic Rex ille hominum vacui spoliator Averni, / Oblitus scelerum, cognatae stirpis amore, / Promissique memor, mentes intrabit amicas, / Vestraque posthabitis recolet praecordia templis (ll. 110–13).

59. Celano, *Notizie, 3,* 332: A D MCCCCLX / QUAE SEMIMORTUAE ET EXPIRANTIS VIDES HOSPES / SIMU-LACRA PIETATIS / VIVAE ET SPIRANTES SUNT ARAGO-NAE PIETATIS / IMAGINES / VIVUNT SED PRAE DOLORE EXANIMES [•] DECEPTA / MORS UT EXANIMATAS PRAE-TERIIT / CUR NON GRESSUS MOVEANT NE QUAERITO [•] / QUAE ENIM IAM AD COELOS AUFUGIT / REDDERE HIC PIETATEM IMMOBILEM POTIS / EST ALPHONSI RE-GIS AUCTORITAS / QUI NEC REPERETUR IN TOTUM QUIBUS / SE PLURIES [PLUVIUS?] AUREUM DEDERAT [•] HIC SE EX ARGILLA CONFECTUM ADAMANTINAE / FIDEI TESTIMONIUM / OLIVETANIS SUIS COMMENDA-VIT.

60. P. N. Signorelli, *Vicende della coltura nelle Due Sicilie, 3* (Naples, 1810), 518.

tomb of Maria of Aragon represents the body lying in state and the soul rising on the wings of the mass, so Mazzoni's figures represent an earlier stage in the funeral, when the body of the dead person was laid out in his house and his friends lamented. The supposed "Early Christian" method of celebrating this part of a funeral ceremony was later described and illustrated (Fig. 168) by Tommaso Porcacchi in *Funerali antichi* [1574]. He says: "[The mourners] stand about and weep over the dead person . . . and in weeping some raise their arms up high, tear their hair and their cheeks, bare their arms, and dress in black."[61] Seen as both a contemporaneous ceremony and a historical scene, therefore, Mazzoni's group depicts the lifeless simulacra of the king's friends kneeling before his departed soul, now become one with Christ.

There is another important parallel, or rather a kind of antithesis, to Mazzoni's Lamentation. Ferrante maintained an exhibition gallery of the corpses of his enemies. Paolo Giovio describes it in his *Historia:* "They say that their dried cadavers were displayed, pickled with herbs, a frightful sight, in the dress they wore when alive and with the same ornaments, so that by this terrible example of tyranny, those who did not wish to be similarly served might be properly afraid."[62] These simulacra achieved "immovable loyalty" of a sort quite different from that of the Monteoliveto statues. But similar paradoxes or ironies of death and life, of mortal clay and immortal substance, can apply to them.

Given all this is it not difficult to identify the figure of Joseph of Arimathea, kneeling on the left, as the portrait of himself that Alfonso commissioned through his Olivetan friends (Figs. 172, 173). The features correspond perfectly to those we have identified as the King's. Indeed the shorn hair and deforming web of wrinkles around the eyes are almost lovingly dwelt on by the artist. "Ha un' aria terribile," as Vasari says of it. Vasari adds that he himself copied this head for his portrait of Alfonso, standing next to Ercole d'Este, in the fresco depicting Ferrante welcoming Lorenzo to Naples in the Sala di Lorenzo of the Palazzo Vecchio (Fig. 174).[63]

As Joseph of Arimathea, the rich man who provided Christ's body with its sepulcher, Alfonso plays the right role for the patron of a Lamentation. It is the same role Ercole d'Este played in the Ferrarese group. But Alfonso's money pouch stands for the "shower of gold" of the renewal, mentioned in the inscription, as well as for Joseph's riches.[64] That Alfonso was a king, as well as being Joseph, is confirmed by Summonte, who writes that the figure

61. Tommaso Porcacchi, *Funerali antichi di diversi popoli et nationi* . . . (Venice, 1574), pp. 107–08. This is a précis of an oration given in Venice by Andrea Menichini da Castelfranco on Early Christian burial customs, quoting St. John Chrysostom in the *Homilies.*

62. Paolo Giovio, *Historia suis temporis, 1* (Florence, 1550), 11.

63. Vasari, *8,* 107.

64. Federigo, or whoever the other elderly kneeling figure is, also carries a pouch. On the literary sources of

Lamentation scenes see Wolfgang Stechow, "Joseph of Arimathea or Nicodemus?", *Festschrift für Ludwig Heydenreich: Studien zur Toskanischen Kunst* (Munich, 1964), pp. 298–99; and H. Aurenhammer, *Lexikon der christlichen Ikonographie*, pt. 4 (Vienna, 1962), pp. 357–74, esp. pp. 364–72. According to Stechow, Nicodemus is usually the nail extractor and carries pliers, hammers, pincers, or the like (p. 296). But none of the figures in Mazzoni's group carries implements.

grasped a scepter in its right hand. (Regrettably, almost all the hands have had to be restored.)[65] Meanwhile the mourner on the right, Nicodemus (Fig. 171), may portray Federigo. He has the gaunt, rather Ferrante-like features seen in Alfonso's brother (Fig. 38).[66]

Thus we can read Mazzoni's group, in the light of the inscription and in relation to the moment of its creation, as equating the renewal with the establishment of Christ's kingdom. Naples becomes a heavenly city, an earthly paradise transformed by Alfonso's love. The Lamentation scene is the tomb of Alfonso's hopes, and is at the same time his own tomb, at which he himself weeps. Meanwhile the theme of communion and the mass, present in stylized form in the marble chapels of Maria Piccolomini and Marino Curiale, is here re-presented in a naturalistic, "Early Christian" way, with the communicants gathered around the body of Christ. The renewal therefore ends with the marble body of Parthenope transformed into the Redeemer's clay, while the queen-siren's children unite with the King of Men.

65. G. A. Summonte, *Historia, 4,* 630. He also mentions the "maravigliosa pittura" of this portrait. The illustrations of the group in Leopoldo Cicognara, *Storia della scultura dal suo risorgimento,* 2 (Venice, 1813–18), pl. LI, show that any modification of the hands was carried out before this engraving was made.

66. Pompeo Sarnelli in his *Guida de' forastieri* (Naples, 1697), illustrates one more female figure than we see today (opp. his p. 280), and he then mentions four male statues. Like Signorelli (n. 60 above) D'Engenio, *Napoli sacra,* p. 510, lists four male statues in the group, and identifies them (but without saying which is which) as Sannazaro (conceivably because of some mixup with the latter's poem), Pontano, Ferrante, and Alfonso. Celano, too, mentions a fourth male statue, and identifies the front left-hand figure as Sannazaro, the right-hand figure as Pontano, and the young St. John as Alfonso (*Notizie, 3,* 332). None of these identifications is possible, but the combined testimony of D'Engenio, Sarnelli, Celano, and Signorelli in favor of four original male statues in the group makes it almost certain that such a fourth statue (probably of Ferrante) once existed. The identification of the Joseph with Pontano influenced later art. At present on the New York market is a group of four small bronze busts, probably made in the seventeenth century, one of which is labeled Pontano (Fig. 175). It is derived from the head in Figs. 172 and 173; and in its brisk, dramatic way it is an effective Baroque restatement of Mazzoni's portrait.

Schedule of Events

Historical and Literary Background	Art in Naples	Art Outside Naples
1414 King Ladislas dies	Tomb of Ladislas in San Giovanni a Carbonara commissioned	
1419		Florence, rebuilding of San Lorenzo begun
1427–28	Tomb of Rinaldo Brancacci, Sant'Angelo a Nilo	
1442 Conquest of Naples by Alfonso of Aragon (June)		
1443 Triumph of Alfonso (February)	Rebuilding of Castel Nuovo begun	
1445	Colantonio's St. Jerome (Capodimonte)	
1446–51		Florence, Palazzo Rucellai
1448 Alfonso of Calabria born (November 4)		
1449		Siena, Mariano di Jacopo writes De machinis libri decem (?)
1450		Rimini, Alberti's work on Tempio Malatestiano begun (?)
1452	Arch of Alfonso and Sala dei Baroni begun at Castel Nuovo	Rome (?) Alberti writes De re aedificatoria; plans Borgo Leonino (?)
1458 Alfonso I dies (June), Calixtus III revokes Ferrante's investiture, Jean d'Anjou prevents Ferrante from entering Naples (until 1465)		
1459		Pius II begins new center in Pienza; San Sebastiano, Mantua, begun
1461		Florence, San Miniato, Chapel of the Cardinal of Portugal begun
1462 Alfonso's first engagement against Jean d'Anjou		Florence, Giuliano da Maiano builds upper floors of Palazzo dello Strozzino (finished 1465), Palazzo Pazzi-Quaratesi (finished 1469?)

	Historical and Literary Background	Art in Naples	Art Outside Naples
1465	Isabella di Chiaromonte dies (March), Alfonso marries Ippolita Sforza (September)	Ferrante begins inner arch at Castel Nuovo	Urbino, Ducal Palace begun
1466		Marble bust of Ferrante (Louvre), piazza in front of Castel Nuovo and Palazzo of Diomede Carafa begun	San Gimignano, work at Collegiata begun by Giuliano da Maiano
1468			San Gimignano, Santa Fina Chapel begun by Giuliano and Benedetto da Maiano
1469		Rose window, cappella Santa Barbara, begun; Palazzo Sanseverino	
1470		Tombs of Malizia and Ferdinando Carafa, San Domenico Maggiore; Antonio Piccolomini commissions tomb for wife in Monteoliveto	
1472			Siena, Palazzo Spannocchi begun
1473	Eleonora marries Ercole I d'Este		
1474		Portal of the Cappella Santa Barbara, Castel Nuovo; Laurana's Castel Nuovo and Materdomini Madonnas	
1475		Laurana bust of Beatrice (Rockefeller Coll.)	Perugia, Porta San Pietro rebegun; Francesco di Giorgio in Urbino (?)
1476	Beatrice marries Matthias Corvinus		
1477	Ferrante marries the elder Giovanna of Aragon	Presepe in San Giovanni a Carbonara by the Alemanni (finished 1480)	Modena, San Giovanni, Deposition by Mazzoni (finished 1480)
1478	Siege of Castellina	Medallion of Alfonso by Francesco di Giorgio	
1479	Alfonso in Siena; Lorenzo de' Medici's voyage to Naples to sign peace		
1480	Turkish war begins, René of Anjou dies		Modena, Cathedral, Holy Family by Mazzoni
1481	Battle of Otranto; claims of French King (Louis XI) to Naples	Benedetto da Maiano works on Piccolomini tomb medallion of Alfonso by Andrea Guacialoti	Giuliano da Maiano visits Urbino

Historical and Literary Background	*Art in Naples*	*Art Outside Naples*
1482		Terminus post for San Bernardino, Urbino
1483 Lorenzo becomes Gran Camerario of Naples		
1484	Eastern walls begun, work at site of Poggioreale	
1485 Barons' Revolt	Giuliano da Maiano arrives in Naples, Porta Capuana designed, first campaign for eastern walls ends in November	Florence, *De re aedificatoria* printed, Poggio a Caiano designed by G. Sangallo (?); Cortona, Santa Maria del Calcinaio; Ferrara, Mazzoni Lamentation
1486 Engagement party of the second Maria Piccolomini and Marco Coppola (August), Alfonso's triumph (December)		
1487 Altilio's epithalamium for Isabella (?)	Laurana busts of Isabella and Ferrandino, Monteoliveto rebegun, Poggioreale rebegun, Giuliano returns from Florence, La Duchesca, eastern walls, Porta Capuana	
1488 Ippolita Sforza dies (August 18)	Giuliano da Sangallo arrives with Tribunali plan, Berlin and Washington busts of Ippolita, Palazzo Como begun	
1489 Isabella marries Giangaleazzo (January), terminus ante for *Lepidina,* Innocent VIII to revoke Ferrante's investiture	Fra Giocondo in Naples, Piccolomini and Terranuova Chapels finished, Frick bust of Ippolita	
1490 Matthias Corvinus dies, marriage of Isabella and Giangaleazzo consummated (April 25), wedding of il Moro with Beatrice d'Este	Third campaign for eastern walls, Otranto Chapel planned, Giuliano da Maiano dies	
1491	Francesco di Giorgio in Naples, works on Castel Nuovo water system	
1492 Charles VIII attains majority, Alexander VI to revoke Ferrante's investiture	Guido Mazzoni arrives, makes bronze bust of Alfonso in Capodimonte, Fra Giocondo again in Naples, Cappella Pontano and Sannazaro's villa (?),	Vigevano, new civic center begun; Ercole I d'Este begins extension of Ferrara

Historical and Literary Background	*Art in Naples*	*Art Outside Naples*
	Alfonso has copies of Francesco di Giorgio and Filarete's treatises made, Francesco returns to Naples, Benedetto da Maiano visits, Mazzoni begins Lamentation, SS Severino e Sossio rebegun	
1494 Ferrante dies, coronation of Alfonso II, Giangaleazzo Sforza dies, Pontano's *De magnificentia* (?)	New western defenses planned, Porta Reale re-designed, Porta Capuana finished, SS Severino e Sossio begun, salita Sant'Elmo begun	San Gimignano, San Bartolo altar in Sant'Agostino by Benedetto da Maiano
1495 Alfonso abdicates, Ferrandino succeeds, Charles VIII enters Naples, Ferrandino retakes eastern part of city, Alfonso dies in Messina, Francesco di Giorgio explodes mine, the French are driven from the city	Francesco di Giorgio arrives, Castel Sant'Elmo and Castel Nuovo rebuilding starts, Francesco di Giorgio visits Capua; Fra Giocondo and Mazzoni depart for France	
1496 Most of kingdom in Ferrandino's hands, he dies	Pere Marza decorates new apartments in Castel Nuovo alla catalana	
1497 Federigo crowned in Capua	Federigo asks Benedetto to Naples, also Francesco di Giorgio; Marchese estab-lished as royal architect, Soccorpo begun in Duomo	Florence, Benedetto da Maiano dies
1498 Charles VIII dies, Louis XII succeeds		
1499–1501	Western walls completed	
1502 Sannazaro's *Lamentatio*		
1503 Ferdinand the Catholic becomes Ferdinand III of Naples	Terminus post for Peruzzi's sketches of Poggioreale	
1516 Ferdinand III dies, Charles V succeeds		
1517	Decision to build polygonal bastion on Castel Nuovo, Santa Caterina a Formello begun	
1522 Naples and Sicily integrated in Spanish Empire		

Historical and Literary Background	Art in Naples	Art Outside Naples
1524 Pietro Summonte's letter to Marcantonio Michiel		
1528	Western city walls partly torn down	
1532 Don Pietro of Toledo becomes Viceroy of Naples		
1535 Charles V enters Castel Nuovo	Portraits of Ferrante removed from Porta Capuana and arch in Castel Nuovo	
1537	SS Severino e Sossio rebuilt according to 1494 plans, outer fortifications of Castel Nuovo finished	
1540	Other western defenses finished	
1565	Castel Capuano becomes Tribunali	

Bibliography

Except for two brief sections on catalogues and manuscripts, the bibliography is arranged alphabetically by author. I have not included every work mentioned in the text and notes; for example I have omitted standard reference works and texts, as well as well-known modern works which though consulted were not directly related to my arguments, e.g. Wittkower's *Architectural Principles in the Age of Humanism* and Ackerman's *The Architecture of Michelangelo*. I have also omitted certain works that were marginal to my topic; even so the bibliography is rather long. For further writings on Neapolitan art, see Giuseppe Ceci, *Bibliografia per la storia delle arti figurative nell'Italia meridionale*, 2 vols. Naples, 1937.

CATALOGUES

[Duveen Brothers, Inc.], *Duveen Sculpture in Public Collections of America,* New York, 1944.

Berlin, Staatliche Museen, *Die italienischen und spanischen Bildwerke der Renaissance und des Barock,* ed. Frida Schottmüller, Berlin, 1913.

London, Victoria and Albert Museum, *Catalogue of Italian Sculpture in the Victoria and Albert Museum,* ed. John Pope-Hennessy and Ronald Lightbown, 2 vols. London, 1964.

Naples, Capodimonte, *Notizie su Capodimonte,* ed. Bruno Molajoli, Naples, 1960.

——, *Sculture lignee nella Campania,* ed. Bruno Molajoli, Naples, 1950 (with contributions separately noticed under Bologna, F., and Causa, R.).

——, Museo Filangieri, *Il Museo civico Gaetano Filangieri,* ed. Francesco Acton, Naples, 1961.

Paris, Musée Jacquemart-André, *Catalogue itinéraire,* 6th ed. Paris, 1929.

Venice, Ca'd'Oro, Carlo Gamba, "La Ca'd'Oro e la collezione Franchetti," *Bollettino d'arte, 10* (1916), 321–34.

Washington, National Gallery of Art, *Preliminary Catalogue of Paintings and Sculpture,* Washington, D.C., 1941.

UNPUBLISHED MANUSCRIPTS

Florio, Vincenzo, "Memorie istoriche o siano annali napolitani," 1759–1820, MS XXVI.D.14 in Biblioteca Società Napoletana di Storia Patria, Naples.

Giordano, Fabio, "Historia neapolitana," MS Cod. lat. XIII.B.XXVI in Biblioteca Nazionale, Naples.

Maiano, Benedetto da, copy of will dated July 3, 1497, Bigallo no. 1219 (1497), 99–109, in Archivio di Stato, Florence.

Martini, Francesco di Giorgio, "Trattato sull'architettura," Cod. ital. II.1.141 in Biblioteca Nazionale, Florence.

OTHER WRITINGS

Ackerman, James S., "Sources of the Renaissance Villa," *Acts of the Twentieth International Congress of the History of Art, 2* (Princeton, 1963), 6–18.

Aeschlimann, E. See Bisticci.

Alberti, Leandro, *Descrittione di tutta Italia . . . ,* Bologna, 1550.

Alberti, Leon Battista, *An Autograph Letter from Leon Battista Alberti to Matteo de' Pasti, November 18, 1454,* ed. Cecil Grayson, New York, 1957.

Albino, Giovanni, *De gestis regum neapolitanorum ab aragonia qui extant libri quatuor,* Naples, 1589.

——, *Lettere, istruzioni ed altre memorie de' re aragonesi,* in Gravier, *Raccolta, 5,* Naples, 1749.

Alisio, Giancarlo, "La Cappella Pontano," *NN,* ser. 3, *3* (1963), 29–35.

Altamura, Antonio, *Jacopo Sannazaro,* Naples, 1951.

————, *L'Umanesimo nel mezzogiorno d'Italia,* Florence, 1941.

Altilio, Gabriele, *Epithalamium in nuptias Johanni Galeatii Sfortiae et Isabellae Aragoniae,* Padua, 1718.

Anon., *Cérémonial des réligieuses de l'abbaye de Notre-Dame de Montier-Villiers,* Paris, 1626.

Anon., *Cronaca di anonimo veronese* [1446–88], ed. G. Soranzo, in *Monumenti storici pubblicati della r. deputazione veneta di storia patria,* ser. 3, 4, Venice, 1915.

Anon., "Dell'Istoria del regno di Napoli d'incerto autore," in Gravier, *Raccolta, 4,* Naples, 1749.

Anon., "Francesco di Giorgio nel Montefeltro," *Il Marzocco, 32,* July 3, 1927.

Anon., Note on Ippolito and Pietro Donzello, in "Notizie," *Rassegna d'arte senese, 1* (1905), 87–91.

Arslan, E. See Morisani.

Ashby, T., "Sixteenth-Century Drawings of Roman Buildings Attributed to Andreas Coner," *Papers of the British School of Rome, 2* (1904), 23.

Astolfi, Carlo, "Quando è vissuto Antonio Solario detto lo Zingaro?" *Rassegna bibliografica dell'arte italiana, 10* (1907), 38–39.

Baccelli, A., "Ippolita Sforza Duchessa di Calabria," *Rassegna nazionale,* ser. 3, 52 (1930), 21–32.

Bacchelli, Riccardo, *La Congiura di Don Giulio d'Este,* Milan, 1931.

Badaloni, Nicola, "La Interpretazione delle arti nel pensiero di L. B. Alberti," *Rinascimento* [*La Rinascita*], 3 (1963), 59–113.

Barfucci, Enrico, *Lorenzo de' Medici e la società artistica del suo tempo,* Florence, 1945.

Barocchi, Paola, *Vasari pittore,* Milan, 1964.

Barone, Nicola, "Le Cedole di tesoreria dell'Archivio di Stato di Napoli dal 1460 al 1504," *ASPN, 9* (1884), 5–34, 205–48, 387–429, 601–37; *10* (1885), 5–47.

————, "Notizie storiche raccolte dai registri curia della cancelleria aragonese," *ASPN, 14* (1889), 5–16, 177–203, 397–409.

Baroni, G., *La Parrocchia di San Martino a Majano,* Florence, 1875.

Bauer, Hermann, *Kunst und Utopie. Studien über das Kunst und Staatsdenken in der Renaissance,* Berlin, 1965.

Beck, James H., "The Historical 'Taccola' and Emperor Sigismund in Siena," *Art Bulletin, 50* (1968), 309–19.

Beloch, Karl Julius, *Campanien* [1879], Breslau, 1890.

Bernard, Antoine, *La sépulture en droit canonique du décret de Gratien au Concile de Trente,* Paris, 1933.

Berzeviczy, Albert, *Beatrice d'Aragona,* ed. Rodolfo Mosca, Milan, 1931.

————, "Les Fiançailles successives de Béatrice d'Aragon," *Revue de Hongrie, 2* (1909), 146–65.

————, "Rapporti storici fra Napoli e l'Ungheria nell'epoca degli Aragonesi (1442–1501)," *Atti della Accademia Pontaniana, 58* (1928), 180–202.

————, "Les tristes Reines de la maison d'Aragon," *Revue de Hongrie, 5* (1910), 145–69.

Bianchini, Lodovico, *Della Storia delle finanze del regno di Napoli,* Naples, 1834.

Biringuccio, Vanuccio, *De La Pirotechnia,* Venice, 1540, ed. and trans. C. S. Smith and M. T. Gnudi, New York, 1942–43.

Bisticci, Vespasiano [da], *Vite di uomini illustri del secolo XV,* ed. P. d'Ancona and E. Aeschlimann, Milan, 1951.

Bloch, Marc, *Les Rois thaumaturges,* Strasbourg, 1924.

Bode, Wilhelm von, "Desiderio da Settignano und Francesco Laurana: zwei italienischen Frauenbusten des Quattrocento in Berliner Museum," *Jahrbuch der preussischen Kunstsammlungen, 9* (1888), 209–27.

————, *Italienische Bildhauer der Renaissance,* Berlin, 1887.

Bologna, Ferdinando, "Problemi della scultura del cinquecento a Napoli," in B. Molajoli, ed., *Sculture lignee nella Campania* (Naples, 1950), pp. 153–73.

Bombe, Walter, "Die Kunst am Hofe Federigos von Urbino," *Monatshefte für Kunstwissenschaft, 5* (1912), 456–74.

Borgatti, Mariano, *Castel Sant'Angelo in Roma,* Rome, 1931.

Borghini, Vittorio, *Il più nobile Umanista del rinascimento,* Turin, 1943.

Bori, Mario, " 'L'Annunciazione' di Piero del Donzello in una cappella Frescobaldi nella chiesa di Santo Spirito," *Rivista d'arte, 4* (1906), 117–23.

Bottari, Stefano, "Per Domenico Gaggini," *Rivista d'arte, 17* (1935), 77–85.

———, "Un'Opera di Francesco di Laurano," *Bollettino d'arte, 45* (July–Sept. 1960), 213–16.

Braghirolli, W., "Luca Fancelli, Scultore architetto ed idraulico del secolo XV," *Archivio storico lombardo, 2* (1876), 610–38.

Braunfels, Wolfgang, *Mittelalterliche Stadtbaukunst in der Toskana,* Berlin, 1953.

Brendel, Otto, "Laurana's Bust of Ippolita Sforza," *Art Quarterly, 7* (1944), 59–62.

Brenzoni, Raffaello, *Fra Giovanni Giocondo Veronese,* Florence, 1960.

———, "Una nuova Revisione della biografia fragiocondiana nelle 'Vite' del Vasari," *Studi storici veronesi, 12* (1961), 3–16.

———, *La Loggia del Consiglio veronese nel suo quadro documentario,* Venice, 1958.

Bresciano, Giovanni, "Documenti inediti concernenti artisti napoletani del quattro e cinquecento," *ASPN, 52* (1927), 366–78.

Brinton, Selwyn, *Francesco di Giorgio Martini of Siena. Painter, Sculptor, Engineer, Civil and Military Architect (1439–1502),* London, 1934–35.

Burchard, Jean, *Diarium,* ed. L. Thuasne, Paris, 1884.

Burger, Fritz, *Francesco Laurana: eine Studie zur italienischen Quattrocento-Skulptur,* Strasbourg, 1907.

———, *Geschichte des florentinischen Grabmals von den ältesten Zeiten bis Michelangelo,* Strasbourg, 1904.

Cagiati, Memmo, *Le Monete del reame delle Due Sicilie,* Naples, 1911–13. See also Volpicella.

Cangiano, Luigi, *Su le Acque potabili della città di Napoli,* Naples, 1843.

Capaccio, Giulio Cesare, *Il Forastiero. Dialoghi,* Naples, 1634.

Capasso, Bartolommeo, "Sull'Annedoto riguardante gli affreschi del cav. Calabrese sopra le porte di Napoli," *ASPN, 3* (1878), 597–605.

———, "Appunti per la storia delle arti in Napoli," *ASPN, 6* (1881), 531–42.

———, *Sulla Circoscrizione civile ed ecclesiastica e sulla popolazione della città di Napoli,* Naples, 1882.

———, "Le Denominazioni delle torri di Napoli nella murazione aragonese e viceregale," *NN, 2* (1893), 30–31.

———, "La Fontana dei Quattro del Molo di Napoli," *ASPN, 5* (1880), 158–94.

———, *Le Fonti della storia delle provincie napoletane,* Naples, 1902.

———, *Napoli greco-romana esposta nella topografia e nella vita,* Naples, 1905.

———, "Pianta della città di Napoli nel secolo XI," *ASPN, 16* (1891), 832–62.

———, "La Torre d'Arco e la casa del Pontano in Napoli," in *Strenna della r. tipografia Giannini, 4* (1892), 97–104.

———, "Sul vero Sito di Napoli e Palepoli," in A. Marcheri, *Il Risanamento di Napoli,* Naples, 1889.

———, "La 'Vicaria vecchia,' " *ASPN, 15* (1890), 388–433.

Caracciolo, Tristano, *Opuscula historica de Ferdinandi qui postea rex aragonum fuit eiusque posteris,* in Gravier, *Raccolta, 6,* Naples, 1769.

Carafa, Ferdinando, *Studi di letteratura storia ed arte,* Naples, 1876.

———, *Taluni Ricordi storici intorno alle chiese del duomo, San Domenico Maggiore, S. Filippo Neri, SS Severino e Sossio, S. Martino,* Naples, 1864.

Carletti, N., *Topografia universale della città di Napoli,* Naples, 1786.

Carli, Enzo, *Pienza: Die Umgestaltung Corsignanos durch den Bauherrn Pius II,* Basel and Stuttgart, 1964.

———, *Pienza, la città di Pio II,* Rome, 1966.

Carratelli, G. P., "Napoli antica," *La Parola del passato, 7* (1952), 243–68.

Carotti, Guido, *Ville e castelli d'Italia,* Milan, 1907.

Carrara, Enrico, *La Poesia pastorale,* Milan, 1909(?).

Cartwright, Julia, *Beatrice d'Este, Duchess of Milan,* London, 1905.

————, *Isabella d'Este, Marchioness of Mantua, 1474–1539,* London, 1903.

Carusi, Enrico, *Dispaccie lettere di Giacomo Gherardi nunzio pontificio a Firenze e Milano,* Rome, 1909.

Cassi Ramelli, A., *Dalle Caverne ai rifugi blindati,* Milan, 1964.

Castaldi, Giuseppe, "Il Palazzo di Giulio de Scorziatis," *NN, 12* (1903), 180–83.

Castelfranchi Vegas, Liana, "I Rapporti Italia-Fiandra," *Paragone,* n.s., no. 15 (May 1966), 9–24, and no. 21 (Nov. 1966), 42–69.

Catalani, L., *I Palazzi di Napoli,* Naples, 1845.

Catalani, N., *Le Chiese di Napoli, descrizione storica ed artistica,* Naples, 1845–53.

Causa, Raffaello, "Angiolillo Arcuccio," *Proporzioni, 3* (1950), 99–110.

————, "Contributi alla conoscenza della scultura del '400 a Napoli," in B. Molajoli, ed., *Sculture lignee nella Campania* (Naples, 1950), pp. 105–21.

————, *Pittura napoletana dal XV al XIX secolo,* Bergamo, 1957.

————, "Precisazioni relative alla scultura del '300 a Napoli," in B. Molajoli, ed., *Sculture lignee nella Campania* (Naples, 1950), pp. 63–73.

————, "Sagrera, Laurana e l'Arco di Castelnuovo," *Paragone,* n.s., no. 5 (1954), 3–23.

Ceci, Giuseppe, "Per la Biografia degli artisti del XVI e XVII secolo," *NN, 13* (1904), 45–47, 57–61.

————, "La Chiesa e il convento di Santa Caterina a Formello," *NN, 9* (1900), 49–51, 67–70; *10* (1901), 35–39, 101–05, 178–83.

————, "Nella Chiesa di Monteoliveto," *Rassegna storica napoletana, 2* (1934), 205–12.

————, "Due Architetti napoletani del rinascimento, Novello de Sancto Lucano, Gabriele D'Angelo," *NN, 7* (1898), 181–82.

————, "Una Famiglia di architetti napoletani del rinascimento: i Mormanno," *NN, 9* (1900), 167–72, 182–85.

————, "Nuovi Documenti su Giuliano da Maiano ed altri artisti," *ASPN, 29* (1904), 784–92.

————, "Nuovi Documenti per la storia delle arti a Napoli durante il rinascimento," *NN, 9* (1900), 81–84.

————, "Il Palazzo dei conti di Maddaloni poi di Colubrano," *NN, 2* (1893), 149–52, 168–70.

————, "Il Palazzo Gravina," *NN, 6* (1897), 1–4, 24–31.

————, "Il Palazzo dei Sanseverino principi di Salerno," *NN, 7* (1898), 81–85.

Celano, Carlo, *Notizie del bello dell'antico e del curioso della città di Napoli* [1692], ed. G. B. Chiarini, Naples, 1856–58.

Céndali, L., *Giuliano e Benedetto da Maiano,* Florence, 1926.

Ceva-Grimaldi, F., *Della Città di Napoli dal tempo della sua fondazione sino al presente,* Naples, 1857.

Chastel, André, "Cortile et théâtre," in *Le Lieu théâtral à la Renaissance,* Colloques internationaux du centre national de la recherche scientifique. Sciences humaines (Paris, 1964), pp. 41–47.

Chiarini, G. B. See Celano.

Chiappini, Luciano, *Eleonora d'Aragona prima Duchessa di Ferrara,* Rovigo, 1956.

Chioccarello, Bartolommeo, *Archivio della reggia giurisdizione del regno di Napoli . . . ,* Naples, 1721.

Chtedowski, Casimir von, *Neapolitanische Kulturbilder, XIV–XVIII Jahrhundert,* Berlin, 1920.

Ciaccio, Lisetta Motta, "Francesco Laurana in Francia," *L'Arte, 11* (1908), 409–18.

Ciaceri, E., *Storia della Magna Grecia,* Rome, 1924.

Ciapponi, Lucia, "Appunti per una biografia di Giovanni Giocondo da Verona," *Italia medioevale e umanistica, 4* (1961), 131–58.

Cibrario, G. A. L., *Descrizione storica degli ordini cavallereschi,* Turin, 1846.

Cicogna, Emmanuele A., "Intorno la vita e le opere di Marc Antonio Michiel," in *Atti del reale Istituto veneto di scienze lettere ed arti, 9* (1860), 359–425.

Cimber, M. L. See De Saint-Gelais.

Cirillo, Mastrocinque Adelaide, "Personaggi e costumi della Napoli aragonese," *Partenope, 1* (1960), 17–32.

Clausse, Gustave, *Les Sangallo,* Paris, 1900–02.

Cocchia, Enrico, "Napoli e il Satyricon di Petronio Arbitro," *ASPN, 18* (1893), 278–315.

Cohansen, August, "Zur Geschichte des Bastions," *Archiv für die Artillerie und Ingenieur-Offizieren des deutschen Reichsheeres, 102* (1895), 57–63.

Colasanti, Arduino, "Ritratti di principi estense in un gruppo di Guido Mazzoni," *Bollettino d'arte, 15* (April 1922), 458–74.

Colombo, Alessandro, "Il 'Grido di dolore' di Isabella d'Aragona duchessa di Milano," in *Studi di storia napoletana in onore di Michelangelo Schipa* (Naples, 1926), pp. 331–52.

Colombo, Antonio, "Il Palazzo e il giardino della Duchesca dal 1487 al 1760," *ASPN, 9* (1884), 563–74.

————, "Il Palazzo e il giardino della Duchesca," *NN, 1* (1892), 81–83.

————, "Il Palazzo e il giardino di Poggio Reale," *ASPN, 10* (1885), 186–209, 309–42.

————, "Il Palazzo e il giardino di Poggio Reale," *NN, 1* (1892), 117–20, 136–38, 166–68.

————, "I Porti e gli arsenali di Napoli," *NN, 3* (1894), 9–12, 72–74, 89–92, 105–08, 141–43.

Conforti, Luigi, "Le Fontane di Napoli. I. Mezzocannone," *NN, 1* (1892), 44–45.

Coniglio, G., *Il Regno di Napoli al tempo di Carlo V,* Naples, 1951.

Corio, Bernardino, *L'Historia di Milano,* ed. Egidio De Magri, Milan, 1855–57.

Corsi [Faustino?], *Principali Edifizii della città di Napoli,* Naples, 1859.

Corti, G. See Hartt.

Corvisieri, C., "Il Trionfo romano di Eleonora d'Aragona nel giugno del 1473," *Archivio della società romana di storia patria, 1* (1878), 475–91.

Cosenza, Giuseppe, "La Chiesa e il convento di San Pietro Martire. IV.," *NN, 9* (1900), 104–09.

Courajod, Louis, "Un Fragment du rétable de Saint-Didier d'Avignon, sculpté par Francesco Laurana au musée du Louvre," *Gazette des beaux-arts, ser. 2* (Feb. 1884), 182–87.

————, "Observations sur deux bustes du musée de sculpture de la Renaissance au Louvre," *Gazette des beaux-arts, ser. 2, 28* (July 1883), 24–42.

Croce, Alda, "Contributo a un'edizione degli scritti di Antonio Galateo," *ASPN, 62* (1937), 366–70.

Croce, Benedetto, "Antonio de Ferrariis, detto il Galateo," *Humanisme et Renaissance, 4,* fasc. iv (1937), 366–82.

————, "Antonio da Solario Autore degli affreschi nell'atrio di San Severino," *NN, 5* (1897), 122–24.

————, ["Don Ferrante"], "L'Incoronazione di Ferdinando d'Aragona," *NN, 12* (1903), 48.

————, "I Seggi di Napoli," *NN, n.s., 1* (1920), 17–19.

————, *La Spagna nella Vita italiana durante la rinascenza,* Bari, 1917.

————, *Storia del regno di Napoli,* Bari, 1925.

————, *Storie e leggende napoletane,* Bari, 1919.

————, "La Tomba di Jacopo Sannazaro e la chiesa di Santa Maria del Parto," *NN, 1* (1892), 68–76.

————, ["Don Fastidio"], "La Torre Spinella," *NN, 15* (1906), 57–58.

Cutolo, Alessandro, "La Nascita di Ferrandino d'Aragona," *ASPN, 67* (1945), 99–108.

Dalli Regoli, Gigetta, "Problemi di grafica crediana," *Critica d'arte, 12* (1965), 25–45.

D'Aloe, Stanislao, *Le Pitture dello Zingaro nel chiostro di San Severino in Napoli . . . ,* Naples, 1846.

D'Alos, R., *Documenti per la storia della biblioteca di Alfonso I,* Rome, 1924.

D'Ambra, Raffaele, *Napoli antica illustrata,* Naples, 1889–93.

D'Ancona, P. See Bisticci.

D'Ayala, Mariano, "Intorno alle Sculture nella chiesa di San Domenico ed in espezialità sulle tombe di Malizia Carafa . . . ," *Annali civili del regno delle Due Sicilie, 41* (1846), 99–105.

De Baroncellis, Francesco Bandini, "In laudem neapolitanae civitatis," ed. P. O. Kristeller in *Studies in Renaissance Thought and Letters,* ed. Kristeller (Rome, 1956), pp. 395–410.

De Cesare, Francesco, *Le più belle Fabbriche del millecinque cento ed altri monumenti di architettura esistenti in Napoli . . .*, Naples, 1845.

De Commines, Philippe, "Chroniques du roy Charles VIII . . . ," in Buchon, *Choix des chroniques, 7,* pt. 3, Paris, 1837.

De Filippis, Felice, *Castelcapuano, Reggia e fortezza,* Naples, 1956.

———, "Napoli—Restauro di una statua in terracotta di Guido Mazzoni," *Bollettino d'arte, 18* (1924–25), 576.

———, *Piazze e fontane di Napoli,* Naples, 1957.

De Fiore, Gaspare, *Baccio Pontelli, Architetto fiorentino,* Rome, 1963.

De Frede, Carlo, "Il Palazzo dei Sanseverino, principi di Salerno," *Partenope, 2* (1961), 19–28.

Dehio, Georg, "Die Bauprojekt Nikolaus V und L. B. Alberti," *Repertorium für Kunstwissenschaft, 3* (1880), 241–57.

Delaborde, H. F., *L'Expédition de Charles VIII en Italie. Histoire diplomatique et militaire,* Paris, 1888.

De la Croix, Horst, "The Literature of Fortification in Renaissance Italy," *Technology and Culture, 4* (1963), 30–50.

———, "Military Architecture and the Radial City Plan in Sixteenth-Century Italy," *Art Bulletin, 42* (1960), 263–90.

De la Sizeranne, Robert, *Béatrice d'Este et sa Cour,* Paris, 1920.

De la Vigne, André. See De Saint-Gelais.

De la Ville sur-Yllon, Lodovico, "La Chiesa di S. Barbara in Castel Nuovo," *NN, 2* (1893), 70–74, 118–22, 170–73.

———, "Di un Quadro attribuito ai fratelli del Donzello," *NN, 1* (1892), 120–22.

———, "Le Mura e le porte di Napoli," *NN, 12* (1903), 49–56.

———, "Il Sebeto," *NN, 11* (1902), 113–16.

De Lellis, Carlo, *Parte seconda ovvero supplemento a Napoli sacra,* Naples, 1654. See also D'Engenio Caracciolo.

De Lignamine, G. F., *Inclyti Ferdinandi regis vita et laudes* [1472], in E. Pontieri, *Per la Storia del regno di Ferdinando I d'Aragona re di Napoli,* Naples, 1946.

Della Chiesa, Francesco Agostino, *Theatro delle donne letterate,* Mondavi, 1620.

De Luca, Giuseppe, "Un Umanista fiorentino e la Roma rinnovata di Sisto IV," *La Rinascita, 1* (1938), 74–90.

De Magri, E. See Corio.

De Marinis, Tammaro, *La Biblioteca napoletana dei re d'Aragona,* 4 vols. Milan, 1947–52.

De Montaiglon, Anatole, "Sur deux Statues de Louis XII par le sculpteur modenais Guido Paganino," *Archives de l'art français,* ser. 2, 2 (1862), 219–28.

Demonts, Louis, "Maître de l'Annonciation d'Aix et Colantonio," *Mélanges Hulin de Loo* (Brussels, 1931), pp. 123–27.

D'Engenio Caracciolo, Cesare, *Napoli sacra,* Naples, 1624.

De Nicola, Giacomo, "Un Disegno della porta di Capua di Federigo II," *L'Arte, 11* (1908), 384–85.

De Petra, Giulio, "Nuovi Avanzi delle antiche mura di Napoli," *NN, 14* (1905), 113–14.

De Reiffenberg, F. A. F. T., *Histoire de l'ordre de la toison d'or,* Brussels, 1830.

De Rinaldis, Aldo, "Forme tipiche dell'architettura napoletana nella prima metà del quattrocento," *Bollettino d'arte, 18* (1924–25), 162–83.

———, *Santa Chiara. Il Convento delle chiarisse, il convento dei minori, la chiesa,* Naples, 1920.

De Rossi, G. B., *Le Piante iconografiche e prospettiche di Roma anteriori al XVI secolo,* Turin and Rome, 1902.

De Saint-Gelais, Octavien, and André de la Vigne, "Le Vergier d'honneur," in M. L. Cimber, *Archives curieuses de l'histoire de France,* ser. 1, 1, Paris, 1834.

[Desbordes, Henri], *La Mausolée de la toison d'or ou les tombeaux des chefs et des chevaliers du noble ordre de la toison d'or,* Amsterdam, 1639.

De Vigneulles, Philippe, *Journal,* ed. H. Michelant in *Bibliothek des litterarischen Vereins in Stuttgart, 24,* Stuttgart, 1852.

Di Costanzo, Angelo, *Istoria del regno di Napoli,* in Gravier, *Raccolta, 1,* Naples, 1749.

Di Cristoforo, Scipione, "Life of G. A. Summonte," in G. A. Summonte, *Historia, 1,* Naples, 1748.

Di Falco, Benedetto, *Antichità di Napoli* [1539], Naples, 1626.

Dina, Achille, "Isabella d'Aragona Duchessa di Milano e di Bari," *Archivio storico lombardo, 48* (1921), 273–457.

Di Sarno, Roberto, *J. J. Pontani Vita,* Naples, 1761.

Di Stefano, Pietro, *Descrittione dei luoghi sacri della città di Napoli . . . ,* Naples, 1560.

Di Stefano, R., "La Chiesa di Sant'Angelo a Nilo e il seggio di Nido," *NN,* ser. 3, 4 (May-Aug. 1964), 12–31.

———, "Napoli sotterranea," *NN,* ser. 3, *1* (1962), 101–12.

Dittrich, U., "Die vermeintlichen Bastione des Taccola," *Archiv fur die Artillerie und Ingenieur Offizieren des deutschen Reichsheeres, 89* (1891), 571–76.

Donati, F., "Francesco di Giorgio in Siena," *Bullettino senese di storia patria, 9* (1902), 149–85.

Doria, Gino, *Storia di una capitale,* 3d ed. rev. Naples, 1958.

———, *Le Strade di Napoli,* Naples, 1943.

Dupont, J., "Un Triptyque de Jean Bourdichon au musée de Naples" (Institut de France. Académie des inscriptions et belles-lettres), *Monuments et mémoires, 35* (1935–36), 179–88.

Dussler, Luitpold, *Benedetto da Maiano, ein florentiner Bildhauer des späten Quattrocento,* Munich, 1924.

———, "A Clay Model by Benedetto da Maiano for the Altar in Monteoliveto, Naples," *Burlington Magazine, 45* (1924), 21–22.

Eden, W. A., "Studies in Urban Theory. The 'De re aedificatoria' of Leon Battista Alberti," *Town Planning Review, 19* (1943), 10–28.

Egger, Hermann, "Entwürfe Baldassare Peruzzis für den Einzug Karl V. in Rom," *Jahrbuch des Kunsthistorischen Sammlungen, 23,* pt. 1, sec. 1 (Vienna, 1902), 1–44. See also Ehrle.

Ehrle, F., and Egger, H., *Piante e vedute di Roma e del Vaticano dal 1300 al 1676,* Rome, 1956.

Eichmann, Eduard, *Die Kaiserkrönung im Abendland,* Würzburg, 1942.

———, "Studien zur Geschichte der abendländischen Kaiserkrönung," *Historisches Jahrbuch, 45* (1925), 21–56.

Eimer Gerhard, *Die Stadtplanung im schwedischen Ostseereich, 1600–1715,* Lund, 1961.

Fabriczy, Cornel von, "Adriano Fiorentino," *Jahrbuch der preussischen Kunstsammlungen, 24* (1903), 71–98.

———, "Chronologischen Prospekt über Giuliano da Sangallo," *Jahrbuch der preussischen Kunstsammlungen, 23* (1902), supps. 1–42.

———, "Documenti su due opere di Antonio Rossellino," *Rivista d'arte,* ser. 1, 5 (1907), 162–65.

———, "Giuliano da Maiano in Siena," *Jahrbuch der preussischen Kunstammlungen, 24* (1903), 320–37, and supps. 137–76.

———, "Das Marmorrelief der Krönung eines Kaisers in Museo Nazionale zu Florenz," *Repertorium für Kunstwissenschaft, 26* (1903), 262–63.

———, *Medaillen der italienische Renaissance,* Leipzig, n.d.

———, "Summontes Brief an Marcantonio Michiel," *Repertorium für Kunstwissenschaft, 30* (1907), 143–68.

———, "Toscanische und Oberitalienische Künstler in Diensten der Aragonesen zu Neapel," *Repertorium für Kunstwissenschaft, 20* (1897), 85–120.

Falb, R. See Sangallo.

Faraglia, N. F., "I Dipinti a fresco dell'atrio del Platano in S. Severino," *NN, 5* (1896), 49–52, 135–37, 167–68; 6 (1897), 56–58, 103–05.

———, "Due Pittori per amore," *NN, 3* (1894), 113–17.

————, "Il Libro di Santa Marta," *NN*, 9 (1900), 17–19; and *10* (1901), 5–10, 26–30.

————, "Memorie artistiche della chiesa benedettina di SS Severino e Sossio di Napoli," *ASPN, 3* (1878), 236–52.

————, "Il Sepolcro di re Ladislao," *ASPN*, 7 (1882), 169–71.

————, *Storia della Lotta tra Alfonso V. d'Aragona e Renato di Angiò,* Lanciano, 1908.

————, *Storia dei prezzi in Napoli dal 1131 al 1860,* Naples, 1878.

Ferrajoli, Ferdinando, *I Castelli di Napoli,* Naples, n.d.

Ferrari, Oreste, "Per la Conoscenza della scultura del primo quattrocento a Napoli," *Bollettino d'arte, 39* (1954), 11–24.

Ferrier, George, "De Francesco Laurana," *Les Arts, 4* (June 1905), 41.

Fichard, Jean, "Italia," in August Schmarsow, ed., "Excerpte aus John. Fichard's 'Italia' von 1536. II," *Repertorium für Kunstwissenschaft, 14* (1891), 373–83.

Fiengo, Giuseppe, "La Chiesa e il convento di Santa Maria del Pozzo a Somma Vesuviana," *NN*, ser. 3, 4 (Sept.-Dec. 1964), 125–32.

Filangieri, Gaetano, *Documenti per la storia le arti e le industrie delle provincie napoletane,* 5 vols. Naples, 1883–97.

————, "Maestro Giovanni Mormando Organista ed architetto," *ASPN*, 9 (1884), 286–304.

————, "Prospetto cronologico della vita e delle opere di Maestro Giovanni Donadio de Mormanno organista ed architetto," *ASPN*, 9 (1884), 297–300.

Filangieri, Riccardo, "Antonio Marchese da Settignano, Architetto militare del rinascimento," *Rivista di artiglieria e del genio, 70* (1931), 473–79.

————, "L'Architetto della reggia aragonese di Napoli," *L'Arte, 31* (1928), 32–35.

————, "La Casa di Federigo d'Aragona in Castel Nuovo," *Studi di storia napoletana in onore di Michelangelo Schipa* (Naples, 1926), pp. 353–64.

————, *Il Castello di Capuana, fortezza e reggia,* Naples, n.d.

————, "Castelnuovo nel '400," *Il Fuidoro, 3* (1956), 3–15.

————, *Castelnuovo, Reggia angioina ed aragonese di Napoli,* Naples, 1934; rev. ed. Naples, 1964.

————, "La Citadella aragonese e il recinto bastionato di Castel Nuovo," *Atti dell'Accademia Pontaniana,* ser. 2, *34* (Naples, 1929), 49–73.

————, ed., *Una Cronaca napoletana figurata del quattrocento,* Naples, 1956.

————, "Les Origines de la peinture flamande à Naples," *Actes du XIIe congrès international d'histoire de l'art* (Brussels, 1930), pp. 560–76.

————, "La Peinture flamande à Naples pendant le xvième siècles," *Revue belge d'archéologie et d'histoire de l'art, 2* (1932), 128–43.

————, "Rassegna critica delle fonti per la storia di Castel Nuovo," *ASPN, 62* (1937), 267–333; *63* (1938), 258–342; *64* (1939), 237–322.

————, "La Scultura in Napoli nei primi albori del rinascimento," *NN*, ser. 2, *1* (1920), 65–69, 89–94.

————, "Il Tempietto di Gioviano Pontano in Napoli," *In Onore di Giovanni Gioviano Pontano nel V centenario della sua nascita* (Naples, 1926), pp. 13–49.

Fillon, Benjamin, "Ouvriers italiens employés par Charles VIII," *Archives de l'art français, 1* (1851–52), 273–76.

Fiocco, Giuseppe, "Giovanni Giocondo veronese," *Atti della r. Accademia d'agricoltura industria e commercio di Verona,* ser. 4, *16,* Verona, 1916.

————, *Introduzione e commento alla vita di Fra Giocondo e d'altri veronesi, 1,* Florence, 1915.

Firpo, Luigi, ed., *Leonardo Architetto e urbanista,* Turin, 1963.

Fontana, Paolo, "I Codici di Francesco di Giorgio Martini e di Mariano di Jacomo detto il Taccola o Archimede," *Actes du XIVe congrès international d'histoire de l'art, 1* (Berne and Basel, 1936–38), 102–03.

Foster, Philip E., "The Date of Lorenzo de' Medici's Villa at Poggio a Caiano," unpublished Master's thesis, Yale University, 1965.

Fra Giocondo. See Frontinus.

Francisco de Hollanda, Italian sketchbook, ed. E. Tormo as *Os Desenhos das antiqualhas que vio Francisco d'Ollanda,* Madrid, 1940.

Frimmel, T. See Michiel.

Frizzoni, G., *Arte italiana del rinascimento,* Milan, 1891.

Frommel, Christoph Luitpold, *Die Farnesina und Peruzzis architektonisches Frühwerk,* Berlin, 1961.

Frontinus, *De aqueductibus urbis romae,* ed. Fra Giovanni Giocondo, Florence, 1513.

Fulin, R. See Sanudo.

Fusco, Giuseppe Maria, *I Capitoli dell'ordine dell'armellino,* Naples, 1845.

———, *Intorno all'Ordine dell'armellino,* Naples, 1844.

———, *L'Iscrizione d'Artemidoro,* Naples, 1863.

Gàbrici, Ettore, "Contributo archeologico alla topografia di Napoli della Campania," *Monumenti antichi,* 41 (1951), cols. 553–674.

———, *Problemi di numismatica greca della Sicilia e Magna Grecia,* Naples, 1959.

Galassi, G., *La Scultura fiorentina del quattrocento,* Milan, 1949.

Galateo, Antonio, "In Alphonsum regem epitaphium," in *Delectus scriptorum rerum neapolitanarum,* ed. Domenico Giordano, Naples, 1735. See also Croce.

Gamba, Carlo. See under Catalogues, Venice.

Gareth, Benedetto [Cariteo], *Le Rime di Benedetto Gareth,* ed. Erasmo Percopo, Naples, 1892.

Garzilli, P. See Notar Giacomo.

Gaye, Giovanni, *Carteggio inedito d'artisti dei secoli XIV, XV, XVI, 1,* Florence, 1839.

Gerevich, Ladislas, "Le Maître des reliefs en marbre du roi Mathias et de sa femme Béatrice," *Bulletin du Musée hongrois des beaux-arts,* no. 27 (1965), 15–32.

Geymüller, Heinrich von, *Cento Disegni di architettura, d'ornato e di figure di Fra Giovanni Giocondo,* Florence, 1882.

Giglioli, O. H., "Tre Capolavori di scultura fiorentina in una chiesa di Napoli," *Rivista d'Italia, 5,* tome 2 (1902), 1030–44.

Giordano, Domenico. See Galateo.

Giordani, Paolo, "Baccio Pontelli a Roma," *L'Arte, 11* (1908), 96–112.

Giovannoni, Gustavo, "Il Palazzo dei Tribunali del Bramante in un disegno di Fra Giocondo," *Bollettino d'arte, 8* (1914), 185–95.

Giovio, Paolo, *Historia suis temporis,* Florence, 1550.

Gnoli, D., "Il Palazzo di Giustizia di Bramante," *Nuova antologia,* Apr. 16, 1914.

Gnudi, M. T. See Biringuccio.

Gothein, Eberhard, *Die Culturentwicklung Sud-Italiens in Einzeldarstellungen,* Breslau, 1886; Ital. trans. of second half of book, with added notes, Tommaso Persico, *Il Rinascimento nell'Italia meridionale,* Florence, 1915.

Gottschalk, H., *Antonio Rossellino,* Leignitz, 1930.

Grant, W. L., "An Eclogue of Giovanni Pontano," *Philological Quarterly, 36* (1957), 76–83.

Gravier, Giovanni, ed., *Raccolta di tutti i più rinomati scrittori dell'istoria generale del regno di Napoli,* 22 vols. Naples, 1769–72.

Grayson, Cecil. See Albèrti, L. B.

Grigioni, Carlo, "Antonio Solario, detto lo Zingaro, nelle Marche," *Arte e storia,* ser. 3 (Dec. 1906), pp. 177–79.

Grimaldi, Giulio, "Bernardo Dovizi alla Corte d'Alfonso II d'Aragona," *ASPN, 25* (1900), 218–37.

Gruyer, Gustave, "Les Monuments de l'art à San Gimignano," *Gazette des beaux-arts, 4* (July 1870), 26–37; 4 (Aug. 1870), 162–79.

Guerra, Camillo, "Dei Dipinti di recente scoperti nella cappella della famiglia Tolosa in Monteoliveto di Napoli," *Atti della r. accademia di archeologia lettere e belle arti di Napoli, 1* (1865), 213–22.

Guglielmotti, Alberto, *Storia delle fortificazioni nella spiaggia romana,* Rome, 1886–93.

Gukovskj, M. A., "Ritrovamento dei tre volumi di disegni attribuiti a Fra Giocondo," *Italia medioevale e umanistica, 6* (1963), 263–69.

Haeghen, Ph. van der, "Examen des droits de Charles VIII sur le royaume de Naples," *Revue historique, 28* (1885), 89–111.

Hahn, Hanno, *Hohenstaufenburgen in Süditalien,* Munich, 1961.

Hale, J. R., "The Development of the Bastion, 1440–1534," in J. R. Hale, J. R. L. Highfield, B. Smalley, eds., *Europe in the Late Middle Ages* (London, 1965), pp. 466–94.

Hamberg, P. G., "The Villa of Lorenzo il Magnifico at Poggio a Caiano and the Origin of Palladianism," *Figura,* ser. 1, 2 (1959), 76–87.

———, "Vitruvius, Fra Giocondo and the City Plan of Naples," *Acta archaeologica, 36* (1965), 105–25.

Hare, T. Leman, "Sculptured Marble Bust Presumed Portrait of Princess Beatrice of Aragon," *Apollo, 19* (Jan. 1934), 57.

Hartt, Frederick, Gino Corti, and Clarence Kennedy, *The Chapel of the Cardinal of Portugal, 1434–1459,* Philadelphia, 1964.

Hellmann, Gunter, "Proportionsverfahren des Francesco di Giorgio Martini," *Miscellanea bibliothecae hertzianae, 16* (1961), 157–66.

Hersey, George L., "Alfonso II Benedetto e Giuliano da Maiano e la Porta reale," *NN,* ser. 3, 4 (1964), 77–95.

Heydenreich, Ludwig H., "Bemerkungen zu den zwei wiedergefundene Manuskripten Leonardo da Vincis in Madrid," *Kunstchronik, 21* (1968), 85–96.

———, "Entstehung der Villa und ländlischen Residenz im 15. Jahrhundert," *Acta historiae artium, 1–3* (1967), 9–12.

———, "Leonardo da Vinci, Architect of Francis I," *Burlington Magazine, 94* (1952), 177–85.

———, "Pius II als Bauherr von Pienza," *Zeitschrift für Kunstgeschichte, 6* (1937), 105–46.

Highfield, J. R. L. See Hale.

Hofmann, Theobald, *Bauten des Herzogs Federico da Montefeltro als Erstwerke der Hochrenaissance,* Strasbourg, 1905.

Huelsen, C. See Sangallo.

Infessura, Stefano, *Diario della città di Roma . . . ,* ed. Oreste Tommasini, Rome, 1890.

Intravaja, Ignazio, *La Poesia di Giovanni Pontano,* Palermo, 1923.

Jahns, Max, *Geschichte der Kriegswissenschaften, 1,* Munich and Leipzig, 1889.

———, *Handbuch einer Geschichte des Kriegswesens von der Urzeit bis zur Renaissance,* Leipzig, 1880.

Kantorowicz, Ernst, *The King's Two Bodies,* Princeton, 1957.

Kardos, Tiberio, "Mattia Corvino, Re umanista," *La Rinascita, 3* (1940), 803–41; 4 (1941), 69–83.

Keller, Harald, "Die Entstehung des Bildnisses am Ende des Hochmittelalters," *Römische Jahrbuch für Kunstgeschichte, 3* (1939), 229–334.

Kennedy, Clarence. See Hartt.

Kennedy, Ruth Wedgwood, *Four Portrait Busts by Francesco Laurana,* n.p. [Northampton, Mass.?], 1962.

Klauser, Theodor, *Die Cathedra im Totenkult der heidnischen Antike,* Münster, 1927.

Kristeller, P. O. See under De Baroncellis.

Lalanne, Lud., "Transport d'oeuvres d'art de Naples au château d'Amboise en 1495," *Archives de l'art français, 3* (1852–53), 305.

Lavagnino, E., "L'Architetto di Sisto IV," *L'Arte, 27* (1924), 4–13.

Leostello, Joampiero, *Effemeridi delle cose fatte per il duca di Calabria* (1484–91), in Filangieri, *Documenti, 1,* Naples, 1883.

Lesueur, Pierre, "Fra Giocondo en France," *Bulletin de la société de l'histoire de l'art français* (1931), pp. 115–44.

Levi Pisetzky, Rosita, *Storia del costume in Italia,* Milan, 1964.

Liberatore, P., "Porta Capuana," *Poliorama pittoresco, 1* (1836–37), 6–7.

Lightbown, Ronald. See under Catalogues, London.

Lisini, A., "L'Architetto di Palazzo Spannocchi a Siena," *Miscellanea storica senese, 3* (1895), 59–60.

Lisner, Margrit, "Zu Benedetto da Maiano und Michelangelo," *Zeitschrift für Kunstgeschichte, 12* (1958), 141–56.

Loffredo, Ferrante, *Le Antichità di Pozzuolo e luoghi convicini,* Naples, 1675.

Loschiaro, Salvatore, "Una Scultura ignorata di Francesco Laurana a Napoli," *Il Rievocatore, 3* (1953), 3.

Lugano, Placido, "Origine e primordi dell'ordine di Monteoliveto," *Bullettino senese di storia patria, 9* (1902), 279–335; *10* (1903), 24–36, 206–57, 441–66.

Lukomski, G. K., *Les Sangallo,* Paris, 1934.

MacDougall, Elizabeth B., "Michelangelo and the Porta Pia," *Journal of the Society of Architectural Historians, 19* (1960), 97–108.

Maggiorotti, Leone Andrea, *Architetti e architetture militari,* Rome, 1933.

Magnuson, Torgil, "The Project of Nicholas V for Rebuilding the Borgo Leonino in Rome," *Art Bulletin, 36* (1954), 89–115.

———, *Studies in Roman Quattrocento Architecture,* Stockholm, 1958.

Maiuri, Amedeo, *La Cena di Trimalchione di Petronio Arbitro,* Naples, 1945.

Malaguzzi Valeri, F., *La Corte di Lodovico il Moro,* Milan, 1913–23.

———, "Scultura del rinascimento a Bologna," *Dedalo, 3* (1922–23), 341–72.

Maltese, C. See Martini.

Mancinelli, N., *Pietro Summonte, Umanista napoletano,* Rome, 1923.

Mancini, Girolamo, ed., *Vite cinque* [by Vasari], Florence, 1917.

Manfredi, M. See Percopo.

Marcheri, A. See Capasso.

Marchini, Giuseppe, *Giuliano da Sangallo,* Florence, 1942.

———, "Il Palazzo ducale d'Urbino," *Rinascimento* [*La Rinascita*], *9* (1958), 43–78.

Maresca, A., "Battenti e decorazione marmorea di antiche porte esistenti in Napoli," *NN, 9* (1900), 51–58.

Mariani, Valerio, "Roma in Leon Battista Alberti," *Studi romani, 7* (1959), 636–46.

Marini, Mario, *Atlante di storia dell'urbanistica,* Milan, 1963.

Martelli, Mario, "I Pensieri architettonici del Magnifico," *Commentari, 17* (1966), 107–11.

Martini, Francesco di Giorgio, *Trattati di architettura ingegneria e arte militare,* ed. Corrado Maltese, Milan, 1967; idem, ed. Cesare Saluzzo and Carlo Promis, Turin, 1841.

Mastroianni, E. Oreste, "Sommario degli atti della cancelleria di Carlo VIII a Napoli," *ASPN, 20* (1895), 48–63.

Masuccio del Salernitano, *Il Novellino,* ed. Alfredo Mauro, Bari, 1940.

Mauro, A. See Sannazaro.

Maxe-Werly, "Francesco da Laurana Fondeur-ciseleur à la cour de Lorraine," *Réunion des sociétés des beaux-arts des départements* (Paris, 1899), pp. 276–85.

———, *Le Vite dei re di Napoli,* Naples, 1594.

Mazzoleni, Iole, "Gli Apprestamenti defensivi nei castelli di Calabria ultra alla fine del regno aragonese," *ASPN, 69* (1944–46), 132–44.

———, *Il Monastero benedettino dei SS Severino e Sossio,* Naples, 1964.

Meller, Peter, "Physiognomical Theory in Heroic Portraits," *Acts of the Twentieth International Congress of the History of Art, 2* (Princeton, 1963), 53–69.

Michel, André, "La Question Laurana: lettres de MM André Michel, E. Müntz, E. Moliner," *Les Arts, 1* (May 1902), 37–47; *1* (Dec. 1902), 29–30.

Michelant, H. See De Vigneulles.

Michelini Tocci, Luigi, "Disegni e appunti autografi di Francesco di Giorgio in una codice del Taccola," in *Scritti di storia dell'arte in onore di Mario Salmi*, 2 (Rome, 1962), 202–12.

Michiel, Marcantonio, *Der Anonimo Morelliano: Marcantonio Michiel's Notizie d'opere del disegno*, ed. Theodor Frimmel, Vienna, 1888.

Middeldorf, Ulrich, and Martin Weinberger, "Unbeachtete Werke der Brüder Rossellino," *Münchner Jahrbuch der bildenden Kunst*, ser. 2, 5 (1928), 85–110.

Milanesi, Gaetano, *Nuovi Documenti per la storia dell'arte toscana dal XII al XV secolo*, Rome, 1893 and Florence, 1901.

———, *Sulla Storia dell'arte toscana*, rev. ed. Siena, 1873.

Millon, Henry, "The Architectural Theory of Francesco di Giorgio," *Art Bulletin*, 40 (1958), 257–61.

Minervini, "Il Mito di Frisso ed Elle, in un vaso dipinto," *Bullettino archaeologico napolitano*, n.s., no. 155, 7 (1858), 33–42.

Minieri-Riccio, Camillo, *Gli Artisti ed artefici che lavorarono in Castel Nuovo a tempo di Alfonso I e Ferrante I*, Naples, 1876.

Miola, A., "Il Soccorpo di San Gennaro descritto da un frate del quattrocento," *NN*, 6 (1897), 161–66, 180–88.

Modigliani, E., "A Madonna by Antonio da Solario and the Frescoes of SS Severino e Sossio at Naples," *Burlington Magazine*, 11 (1907), 376–82.

Molajoli, Bruno. See under Catalogues, Naples.

Moliner. See Michel.

Mommsen, Theodor, "Inschrift des Pollius Felix," *Hermes*, 18 (1883), 158–60.

———, "Trimalchios Heimath und Grabschrift," *Hermes*, 13 (1878), 106–21.

Montalto, Lina, "Vesti e gale alla corte aragonese," *NN*, ser. 2, 1 (1920), 25–29, 41–44, 70–73, 127–30, 142–47.

Morisani, Ottavio, "Considerazioni sui Malvito di Como," in Edoardo Arslan, ed., *Arte e artisti dei laghi lombardi*, 1 (Como, n.d. [1959]), 265–74.

———, "Considerazioni sulle sculture della porta di Capua," *Bollettino di storia dell'arte dell'istituto universitario di magistero, Salerno*, 3 (Jan. 1953), 1–20; 3 (Mar. 1953), 1–4; 3 (Sept.-Dec. 1953), 1–76.

———, *Letteratura artistica a Napoli*, Naples, 1958.

———, *Saggi sulla scultura napoletana del cinquecento*, Naples, 1941.

Mormile, Giuseppe, *Descrittione dell'amenissimo distretto della città di Napoli, et dell'antichità della città di Pozzuolo . . .*, Naples, 1617.

Mormone, Raffaelle, "Contributo ad una storia delle fontane napoletane," *Bollettino di storia d'arte dell'istituto di magistero, Salerno*, 3 (Sept.-Dec. 1953), 108–14.

Mosca, Rodolfo. See Brezeviczy.

Moscato, Arnoldo, *Il Palazzo Pazzi a Firenze*, Rome, 1963.

Müntz, Eugène, *Les Arts à la cour des papes pendant le XVe siècle*, Paris, 1878.

———, "Les dernières Années du sculpteur Laurana," *Chronique des arts*, année 1900, p. 152. See also Michel.

———, *Histoire de l'art pendant la renaissance*, Paris, 1891.

———, *La Renaissance en Italie et en France à l'époque de Charles VIII*, Paris, 1885.

Muñoz, Antonio, "Studii sulla scultura napoletana del rinascimento," *Bollettino d'arte*, ser. 1, 3 (1909), 55–73; 83–98.

Napoli, Mario, "Napoli antica," *La Parola del passato*, 7 (1952), 243–85.

———, *Napoli greco-romana*, Naples, 1959. See also Russo.

Negri, Paolo, "Studi sulla crisi italiana alla fine del secolo XV," *Archivio storico lombardo*, 50 (1923), 1–135; 51 (1924), 75–144.

Nicolini, Fausto, *L'Arte napoletana del rinascimento e la lettera di Pietro Summonte a Marcantonio Michiel*, Naples, 1925.

————, "Dalla Porta reale al palazzo degli studii," *NN, 14* (1905), 114–18, 129–35, 156–58.

Norberg-Schulz, Christian, "La Fortezza di Porto Santo Stefano e l'architettura militare," *Acta ad archae-ologium et artium historiam pertinentia* [Institutus romanum Norvegiae], 2 (1965), 253–60.

Notar Giacomo, *Cronica di Napoli,* ed. Paolo Garzilli, Naples, 1845.

Nunziante, Emilio, "Il Concistoro d'Innocenzo VIII per la chiamata di Renato duca di Lorena contro il regno (marzo 1486)," *ASPN, 11* (1884), 751–66.

Pächt, Otto, "René d'Anjou et les van Eyck," *Cahiers de l'Association internationale des études françaises,* 8 (1956), 41–67.

Panatelli, A., *Di Francesco di Giorgio Martini, Pittore, scultore, e architetto senese del secolo XV e dell'arte de' suoi tempi in Siena,* Siena, 1870.

Pane, Giulio, "La Villa Carafa e la storia urbanistica di Pizzofalcone," *NN,* ser. 3, 4 (1964), 133–48.

Pane, Roberto, *L'Architettura del rinascimento in Napoli,* Naples, 1937.

————, *Napoli imprevista,* Turin, 1949.

Panofsky, Erwin, *Tomb Sculpture,* New York, 1964.

Papini, Roberto, *Francesco di Giorgio Architetto,* Florence, 1946.

Parrino, Domenico Antonio, *Teatro eroico, e politico de' governi de' vicere del regno di Napoli . . . ,* Naples, 1692–94.

Passero, Giulio, *Giornali,* ed. Michele Vecchioni, Naples, 1785.

Patzak, Bernhard, *Die Renaissance- und Barockvilla in Italien,* Leipzig, 1908–12.

Pecchiai, Pio, *Il Campidoglio nel cinquecento sulla scorta dei documenti,* Rome, 1950.

Pedretti, Carlo, *A Chronology of Leonardo da Vinci's Architectural Studies After 1500,* Geneva, 1962.

Pepe, Ludovico, *Memorie storiche dell'antica Valle di Pompei,* Valle di Pompei, 1887.

————, *Storia della successione degli sforzeschi negli stati di Puglia e Calabria e documenti,* Bari, 1900.

Percopo, Erasmo, "Coronazione di Alfonso II d'Aragona," *ASPN, 14* (1889), 140–43.

————, "Nuovi Documenti su gli scrittori e gli artisti dei tempi aragonesi," *ASPN, 18* (1893), 527–37, 784–812; *19* (1894), 376–409, 560–91, 740–79; *20* (1895), 283–335.

————, "Per l'Entrata solonelle di Carlo VIII in Napoli," *Studi di storia napoletana in onore di Michelangelo Schipa* (Naples, 1926), pp. 347–52.

————, "Guido Mazzoni e le sue Opere in Napoli," *NN, 3* (1894), 41–43.

————, "Gli Scritti di Giovanni Pontano," *ASPN, 62* (1937), 57–234.

————, "Una Statua di Tommaso Malvico ed alcuni sonetti del Tebaldeo," *NN, 2* (1893), 10–13.

————, "La Villa del Pontano ad Antignano," in *In Onore di Giovanni Gioviano Pontano nel V centenario della sua nascita* (Naples, 1926), pp. 141–61.

————, "Ville ed abitazioni di poeti in Napoli. I. La Villa del Pontano ad Antignano," *NN,* ser. 2, 2 (1921), 1–7.

————, "La Vita di Giovanni Pontano," *ASPN, 62* (1937), 116–250.

————, *La Vita di Giovanni Pontano,* ed. Michele Manfredi, Naples, 1938.

Perito, Enrico, *La Congiura dei baroni e il conte di Policastro,* Bari, 1926.

————, "Uno Sguardo alla guerra d'Otranto e alle cedole di tesoreria aragonese di quel tempo," *ASPN,* 40 (1915), 313–35. See also Gareth.

Persico, Tommaso. See Gothein.

Petorelli, Arturo, *Guido Mazzoni da Modena Plasticatore,* Turin, 1925.

Petroni, Giulio, *Del gran Palazzo di Giustizia a Castel Capuano in Napoli,* Naples, 1861.

Petrovitch, Rastko, "Questi schiavoni: II. Luciano e Francesco Laurana," *Gazette des beaux-arts,* ser. 6, *31* (1947), 65–80.

Pieri, Piero, *Il Rinascimento e la crisi militare italiana,* Turin, 1952.

Planiscig, Leo, *Bernardo und Antonio Rossellino,* Vienna, 1942.

Pointner, Andy, *Die Werke des florentischen Bildhauers Agostino d'Antonio di Duccio,* Strasbourg, 1909.

Pontano, Giovanni Gioviano, *Carmina,* ed. Benedetto Soldati, 2 vols. Florence, 1902.

——, *De bello neapolitano,* in Gravier, *Raccolta, 5,* Naples, 1749.

——, *Opera omnia,* Venice, 1518.

——, *Poemata,* Naples, 1505–12.

——, *I Trattati delle virtù sociali,* ed. Francesco Tateo, Rome, 1965.

Pontieri, Ernesto, "L'Atteggiamento di Venezia nel conflitto tra papa Innocenzo VIII e Ferrante I d'Aragona (1485–1492). I.," *ASPN, 81* (1963), 197–324.

——, "Camillo Porzio Storico," *ASPN,* 75 (1957), 127–61; 76 (1958), 121–79.

——, "La Dinastia aragonese di Napoli e la casa de' Medici di Firenze," *ASPN, 65* (1940), 274–342; *66* (1941), 217–73.

——, "La Giovinezza di Ferrante I d'Aragona," in *Studi in onore di Riccardo Filangieri, 1* (Naples, 1959), 531–601.

——, *Per la Storia del regno di Ferrante I d'Aragona re di Napoli,* Naples, 1946. See also Porzio.

Pope-Hennessy, John, *Italian Renaissance Sculpture,* New York, 1958.

——, "The Martelli David," *Burlington Magazine, 101* (1959), 134–39. See also under Catalogues, London.

Porcacchi, Tommaso, *Funerali antichi di diuersi popoli, et nationi . . . ,* Venice, 1574.

Porzio, Camillo, *La Congiura de' baroni, del regno di Napoli . . . ,* ed. Ernesto Pontieri, Naples, 1964.

Promis, C. See Martini.

R. L. [Roberto Longhi], "Ancora sulla cultura del Fouquet," *Paragone,* n.s., no. 3 (1952), 56–57.

——, "Una 'Crocifissione di Colantonio," *Paragone,* no. 63 (1935), 3–10.

Ratti, Nicola, *Della Famiglia Sforza,* Rome, 1794.

Redtenbacher, H., "Beiträge zu Kenntniss des Lebens des florentinischen Architekt Giuliano da San Gallo," *Allgemeine Bauzeitung,* 44 (1879), 1–10.

Renda, Umberto, *Giovanni Pontano,* Turin, 1939.

Reymond, M., *La Sculpture florentine,* Florence, 1897.

Ricca, Erasmo, *La Nobilità del regno delle Due Sicilie,* Naples, 1859–89.

Rigoni, E., "Notizie di scultori toscani a Padova nella prima metà del '400," *Archivio veneto, 6* (1929), 118–36.

Rocchi, Enrico, "Le Artiglierie italiane del rinascimento e l'arte del getto," *L'Arte, 2* (1899), 347–72.

——, *Le Fonti storiche dell'architettura militare,* Rome, 1908.

——, "Francesco di Giorgio Martini nelle Tradizioni dell'ingegneria militaria italiana," *Bullettino senese di storia patria,* 9 (1902), 186–201.

——, "L'Opera e i tempi di Francesco di Giorgio Martini," *Bollettino senese di storia patria,* 7 (1900), 183–230.

——, *Le Origini della fortificazione moderna,* Rome, 1894.

Rolfs, Wilhelm, *Franz Laurana,* Berlin, 1907.

——, *Geschichte der Malerei Neapels,* Leipzig, 1910.

Romano, Elena, *Saggio d'iconografia dei reali angioini di Napoli,* Naples, 1920.

Rosi, Giorgio, "La Cinta bastionata cinquecentesca di Castel Nuovo," *Atti del V Convegno di storia dell'architettura* (1948) (Florence, 1957), pp. 317–26.

——, "Il Restauro di Castelnuovo di Napoli," *Le Arti, 4,* fasc. 4 (1942), 284–87.

Rotondi, Pasquale, *Appunti ed ipotesi sulle vicende costruttive del palazzo ducale di Urbino,* Urbino, 1942.

——, "Contributi urbinati a Francesco di Giorgio," *Studi artistici urbinati, 1* (1949), 85–135.

——, *Il Palazzo ducale di Urbino,* Urbino, 1950.

Russo, Giuseppe, "La Città di Napoli dalle origini al 1860," in Mario Napoli, ed., *Contributi allo studio della città,* Naples, 1960.

——, *Napoli come città,* Naples, 1966.

Saalman, Howard, "The Authorship of the Pazzi Palace," *Art Bulletin, 46* (1964), 388–94.

Salazar, Lorenzo, "Marmi di Porta Medina e di Porta Capuana," *NN, 10* (1901), 40–42.

————, ed., "Racconti di storia napoletana," *ASPN, 33* (1908), 474–548.

Salmi, Mario, "Arnolfiana," *Rivista d'arte, 22* (1940), 133–77.

————, *Disegni di Francesco di Giorgio nella collezione Chigi-Saraceni* (Siena. Accademia Chigiana. *Quaderni, 2*), Siena, 1947.

————, "Il Palazzo ducale di Urbino e Francesco di Giorgio," *Studi artistici urbinati, 1* (1949), 9–55.

Saluzzo, C. See Martini.

Sambon, Arturo, "I 'Carlini' e la medaglia trionfale di Ferdinando I d'Aragona re di Napoli," *Rivista italiana di numismatica, 4* (1891), 481–88.

Sangallo, Giuliano da, *Il Libro di Giuliano da San Gallo* (fac. ed. of Vatican MS Cod. barb. lat. 4424), ed. C. Huelsen, Leipzig, 1910.

————, *Il Taccuino senese di Giuliano da Sangallo* (fac. ed. of MS Cod. S.IV.8, Biblioteca Comunale, Siena), ed. Rodolfo Falb, Siena, 1902.

Sannazaro, Jacopo, *Opere volgari,* ed. Alfredo Mauro, Bari, 1961.

————, *Il Parto della vergine di Azio Sincero Sannazaro,* ed. and trans. Filippo Scolari, Venice, 1844.

————, *Poemata,* Padua, 1719.

Santoro, M., *Uno Scolaro del Poliziano a Napoli: Francesco Pucci,* Naples, 1948.

Sanudo, Marin, "La Spedizione di Carlo VIII in Italia," R. Fulin, ed., in *Archivio veneto, 3* (1873), supp.

Sarnelli, Pompeo, *Guida de' forastieri, curiosi di vedere, e intendere,* Naples, 1697.

Sassi, Giuseppe Antonio, *Historia literario-typographica mediolanensis,* Milan, 1745.

Savi-Lopez, Paolo, "Napoli nelle Descrizioni dei poeti. Le 'Selve' di Stazio," *NN, 6* (1897), 45–46.

Scaglia, Gustina, "Drawings of Machines for Architecture from the Early Quattrocento in Italy," *Journal of the Society of Architectural Historians, 25* (1966), 90–114.

Scandone, F., "Le tristi Reyne di Napoli, Giovanna III e Giovanna IV di Aragona," *ASPN, 53* (1928), 114–55; *54* (1929), 151–205.

Scherillo, Giovanni, "Delle Naumachie negli anfiteatri," *Atti della r. Accademia di archeologia lettere e belle arti di Napoli, 2* (1845), 217–36.

Schiavo, Armando, *Monumenti di Pienza,* Rome, 1942.

————, *Il Palazzo della Cancelleria,* Rome, 1964.

————, "I Progetti berniniani per il Louvre," *Emporium, 1* (1940), 15–26.

Schinosi, Francesco, *Istoria della compagnia di Giesu app. al regno di Napoli,* Naples, 1706.

Schipa, Michelangelo, "Alcuni Opinioni intorno ai seggi o sedili di Napoli nel medio evo," *NN, 15* (1906), 97–99, 113–15.

————, "Napoli greco-romana," *NN, 14* (1905), 97–101.

————, "Una Pianta topografica di Napoli del 1566," *NN, 4* (1895), 161–66.

————, "Porta Capuana, una Questione," *NN, 3* (1894), 49–51.

Schmarsow, August, "Die Kaiserkrönung in Museo Nazionale," *Festschrift zu ehren des Kunsthistorischen Instituts in Florenz* (Leipzig, 1897), pp. 54–74. See also Fichard.

Schottmüller, Frida. See under Catalogues, Berlin.

Schrader, Hermann, *Die Sirenen nach ihrer Bedeutung und kunstlerischen Darstellung im Alterthum,* Berlin, 1868.

Schreiber, Fritz, *Die franzözische Renaissance-Architektur und die Poggio-Reale Variationen des Sebastiano Serlio,* Halle, 1938.

Schroeder, G., "Martini und die bastionirte Front," *Archiv für die Artillerie und Ingenieur-Offizieren, 89* (1891), 360–88, 400–13.

————, "Nochmals Taccola," ibid., pp. 343–59.

————, "Taccola und die bastionirte Front," ibid., pp. 32–50.

Schubring, P., *Die Plastik Sienas im Quattrocento,* Berlin, 1907.

Scolari, F. See Sannazaro.

Scully, Vincent J., Jr., "Michelangelo's Fortification Drawings. A Study in the Reflex Diagonal," *Actes du XVIIe congrès international d'histoire de l'art* (The Hague, 1955), pp. 323–32. Part of this appeared in *Perspecta, 1* (1952), 38–45.

Sepe, Giovanni, *La Murazione aragonese di Napoli. Studio di restituzione,* Naples, 1942.

Serra, Luigi, *L'Arte nelle Marche,* Rome, 1934.

——, "Nota sugli affreschi dell'ex convento dei SS Severino e Sossio a Napoli," *NN, 9* (1906), 206–12.

——, "La Pittura napoletana del rinascimento," *L'Arte, 8* (1905), 340–54.

——, "Le Rocche di Mondavio e di Cagli e le altre fortezze di Francesco di Giorgio Martini nella Marca," *Miscellanea di storia dell'arte in onore di Igino Benvenuto Supino* (Florence, 1933), pp. 435–55.

——, "Due Scultori fiorentini del '400 a Napoli," *NN, 14* (1905), 181–85; *15* (1906), 4–8.

Seymour, Charles, Jr., *Italian Sculpture: 1400–1500,* Harmondsworth, Mddx, England, 1966.

Signorelli, Pietro Napoli, *Vicende della coltura nelle Due Sicilie,* Naples, 1810.

Smalley, B. See Hale.

Smith, C. S. See Biringuccio.

Soergel, Gerda, "Die Proportionslehre Albertis und ihre Anwendung an der Fassade von S. Francesco in Rimini," *Kunstchronik, 13* (1960), 348–51.

Soldati, B. See Pontano.

Soranzo, G. see Anon., *Cronaca di anonimo veronese.*

Soria, Francescantonio, *Memorie storico-critiche degli storici napolitani,* Naples, 1781.

Spadetta, Pietro, "La Lanterna del Molo," *NN, 1* (1892), 109–11.

Spinazzola, Vittorio, "Due Marmi figurati nel Museo nazionale di San Martino," *NN, 10* (1901), 97–101, 128, 143–44 (letters on the same subject).

——, "Il Nome di Napoli," *NN, 1* (1892), 33–35, 49–51.

——, "Porta Nolana," *NN, 10* (1901), 100; *15* (1906), 111.

Stechow, Wolfgang, "Joseph of Arimathea or Nicodemus?" in *Festschrift für Ludwig Heydenreich: Studien zur toskanischen Kunst,* Munich, 1964.

Strazzullo, Franco, "La Cappella Carafa del duomo di Napoli in un poemetto del primo cinquecento," *NN,* ser. 3 (Mar.-Apr. 1966), 59–71.

——, "Documenti sull'attività napoletana dello scultore milanese Pietro de Martino (1453–1473)," *ASPN, 81* (1963), 325–41.

——, "La Fondazione di Monteoliveto di Napoli," *NN,* ser. 3, *3* (1963–64), 103–11.

Summonte, Giovanni Antonio, *Historia della città e regno di Napoli 1601–43,* Naples, 1748.

Summonte, Pietro. See Nicolini.

Supino, I. B., *L'Incoronazione di Ferdinando d'Aragona,* Florence, 1903.

Swoboda, Karl M., "Palazzi antichi e medioevali," *Bollettino del Centro di studi per la storia dell'architettura, 2* (1957), 3–32.

——, "The Problem of the Iconography of the Late Antique and Early Medieval Palaces," *Journal of the Society of Architectural Historians, 20* (1961), 78–89.

Tallarigo, C. M., *Giovanni Pontano e i suoi tempi,* Naples, 1874.

Tateo, F. See Pontano.

Tesorone, G., "Una Porta del rinascimento a Napoli," *Arte italiana decorativa e industriale, 11* (1902), 61–62.

Thiem, Gunther and Christel, *Toskanische Fassaden-Dekoration in Sgraffito und Fresko, 14 bis 17 Jahrhundert,* Munich, 1964.

Thuasne, L. See Burchard.

Tietze-Conrat, Erica, "A Relief Portrait by Francesco Laurana," *Bulletin of the Allen Memorial Art Museum, 12* (Oberlin, Ohio, 1955), 87–90.

Tigler, Peter, *Die Architekturtheorie des Filarete,* Berlin, 1963.

Toffanin, G., Jr., "I Seggi di Napoli," *Il Fuidoro, 3* (1956), 16–27.

Toppi, Nicola, *De origine omnium tribunalium,* Naples, 1655–56.

Tormo, E. See Francisco de Hollanda.

Torraca, F., *Jacopo Sannazaro, Note,* Naples, 1879.

Torraja, Antonio, ed., *Estudios sobre Alfonso el Magnánimo,* Barcelona, 1960.

Tutini, Camillo, *Discorsi de' sette officii overo de' sette grandi del regno di Napoli,* Rome, 1666.

——, *Dell'Origine e fundation de' seggi di Napoli . . . ,* Naples, 1644; 2d ed. Naples, 1765.

Tyskiewicz, Maryla, *Bernardo Rossellino,* Florence, 1928.

Urban, Gunter, "Die Kirchenbaukunst des Quattrocento in Rom und Bau- und Stilgeschichtliche Untersuchung," *Römisches Jahrbuch für Kunstgeschichte* (Biblioteca Hertziana), 9 and *10* (Munich and Vienna, 1961–62), 74–287.

Valentiner, W. R., "Andrea dell'Aquila, Painter and Sculptor," *Art Bulletin, 19* (1937), 503–36.

——, "Andrea dell'Aquila in Urbino," *Art Quarterly, 1* (1938), 275–88.

——, "The Early Development of Domenico Gagini," *Burlington Magazine, 76* (Jan.-June 1940), 76–87.

——, "Laurana's Portrait Busts of Women," *Art Quarterly, 5* (1942), 273–98.

——, "A Madonna Statuette of Domenico Gagini," *Art in America, 25* (1937), 104–17.

——, "A Portrait Bust of Alfonso I, of Naples," *Art Quarterly, 1* (1938), 61–68.

Vecchioni, M. See Passero.

Venturi, Adolfo, *L. B. Alberti,* Rome, 1923.

——, "L'Ambiente artistico urbinato nella seconda metà del '400," *L'Arte, 20* (1917), 259–93.

——, *Architetti del XV dal XVIII secolo. Francesco di Giorgio,* Rome, 1925.

——, "Una ignota Opera di Colantonio a Sorrento," *L'Arte, 30* (Sept.-Oct. 1927), 224–26.

——, "Di un insigne Artista modenese del secolo XV," *Archivio storico italiano,* ser. 4, *14* (1884), 339–66.

——, "Un'Opera inedita di Francesco Laurana," *L'Arte, 20* (1917), 195–98.

——, "Una Pietà di Guido Mazzoni a Reggio Emilia," *L'Arte, 17* (1914), 227–30.

Vischer, Robert, *Studien zur Kunstgeschichte,* Stuttgart, 1886.

Volpicella, Luigi, "Le Artiglierie di Castel Nuovo nell'anno 1500," *ASPN, 35* (1910), 308–48.

——, *Federigo d'Aragona e la Fine del regno di Napoli nel MDI,* Naples, 1908.

——, "Le Imprese della numismatica aragonese di Napoli," in M. Cagiati, *Le Monete del reame delle Due Sicilie,* supp., Naples, 1911.

——, "Le Porte di Castelnuovo e il bottino di Carlo VIII," *NN,* ser. 2, *1* (1920), 153–60.

——, *Regis ferdinandi primi instructionum liber* (Società per storia patria. Monumenti storici, ser. 2: Documenti), Naples, 1916.

——, "Un Registro di ligi omaggi al re Ferdinando d'Aragona," in *Studi in onore di Michelangelo Schipa, 1* (Naples, 1926), 305–29.

Volpicella, Scipione, *Diurnali di Giacomo Gallo e tre scritture pubbliche dell'anno 1495,* Naples, 1846.

Wazbinski, Zygmunt, "La Maison idéale selon Alberti," *Acta historiae artium, 1–3* (1967), 13–16.

Weber, Henny, *Achsialität und Symmetrie im Grundriss des italienischen Profanbaus von der Frührenaissance bis zum Frühbarock,* Berlin, 1937.

Weinberger, Martin, "Bildnisbüsten von Guido Mazzoni," *Pantheon, 5* (1930), 191–94. See also Middeldorf.

Weller, Allen S., *Francesco di Giorgio, 1439–1501,* Chicago, 1943.

Welliver, Warman, *L'Impero fiorentino,* Florence, 1956.

Wittkower, Rudolf, "Sculpture in the Mellon Collection," *Apollo, 26* (Aug. 1937), 79–84.

——, "Transformations of Minerva in Renaissance Imagery," *Journal of the Warburg and Courtauld Institutes, 2* (1938–39), 194–205.

Zevi, Bruno, *Biagio Rossetti Architetto ferrarese, il primo urbanista moderna europeo,* Florence, 1960.

Index

ILLUSTRATIONS

Where not otherwise credited,
photographs were supplied by the
museum to which the object belongs.

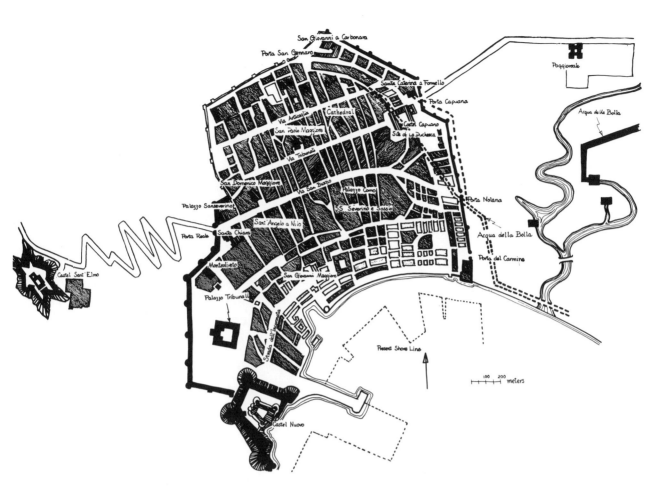

1. Alfonso of Calabria's projected rebuilding (in solid black) of Naples (Author)

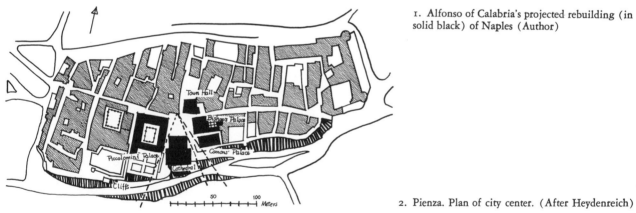

2. Pienza. Plan of city center. (After Heydenreich)

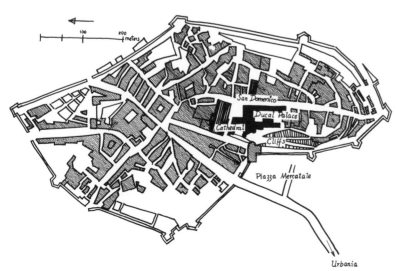

3. Urbino. Plan of city center. (After T.C.I. Guide)

4. Unknown artist. King Ferrante Returning to Naples
after the Battle of Ischia, 1465 (Tavola Strozzi) [c.
1465]. Detail. Naples, Museo Nazionale di San Martino.

5. Pienza. From the south. (Photo Alinari)

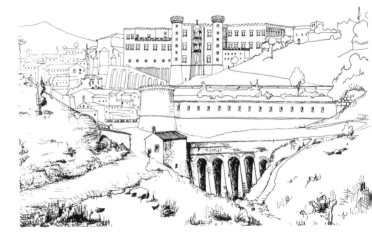

6. Urbino. Ducal Palace. Original facade as
reconstructed by Papini.

8. Castel Nuovo. Inner arch, 1465. (Author and Bernard M. Boyle)

9. Castel Nuovo. Cappella Santa Barbara, west front, 1469–74. (Photo Alinari)

7. Naples. Castel Nuovo, Arch of Alfonso I, c. 1453–65. (Photo author)

Pal nap

Metri

10. Naples. Palace of Diomede Carafa (now Palazzo Santangelo), 1466 ff. Portal. (Photo author)

11. Palace of Diomede Carafa. Courtyard. (Photo Author)

12. Naples. Palazzo Sanseverino (now Church of the Gesù Nuovo), 1470, by Novello de San Lucano. (Photo author)

13. Naples. Palazzo Como, 1488–90. (Photo Alinari)

14. Rome. Palazzo Caffarelli-Vidoni, lower two stories c. 1515. (Yale Photo Collection)

15. Florence. Palazzo dello Strozzino, lower floor, 1458, by Michelozzo; upper floors 1462–65, by Giuliano da Maiano. (Photo Alinari)

16. Florence. Palazzo Pazzi-Quaratesi, 1458–69? (by Giuliano da Maiano?). Courtyard. (Photo Alinari)

18. The same. Caryatid. (Photo author)

17. Naples. San Domenico Maggiore. Tomb of Malizia Carafa, c. 1470, by Jacopo della Pila (?). (Photo Alinari)

19. Naples. Church of Materdomini. Madonna
and Child, c. 1474, by Francesco Laurana.
(Photo Soprintendenza alle Gallerie, Naples)

20. The same. Detail.

21. Naples. Sant' Agostino della Zecca, Madonna and Child, c. 1487, by
Francesco Laurana. Detail. (Photo Soprintendenza alle Gallerie, Naples)

23. The same. Detail.

22. Naples. Castel Nuovo, Chapel of Santa Barbara, Madonna and Child, c. 1458(?), by Domenico Gagini. (Photo Soprintendenza alle Gallerie, Naples)

24. Anonymous Neapolitan. Adoration of the Shepherds. Central panel of a triptych. Naples, Gallerie
Nazionali di Capodimonte.

25. Girolamo Liparolo, medallion of Ferrante, obverse. (Hill 324). (From Hill)

26. Coronato of Ferrante, obverse. Naples, Museo Nazionale.

27. Girolamo Liparolo, medallion of Ferrante, obverse. Oxford, Ashmolean Museum (Hill 323)

28. The Triumph of Ferrante After the Barons' Revolt, 1486. (From Filangieri, *Una Cronaca figurata*)

29. Domenico Gagini(?), marble bust of Ferrante. Paris, Louvre. (Service de documentation photographique)

30. The same. Front view.

31. Carlino of Alfonso II, obverse.
Naples, Museo Nazionale.

32. Andrea Guacialoti, medallion of
Alfonso of Calabria, 1481. (Hill 745).
Oxford, Ashmolean Museum.

33. Francesco di Giorgio, medallion of
Alfonso of Calabria, 1479. (Hill 311).
Oxford, Ashmolean Museum.

34. Coronation procession of Alfonso II, 1494. (From Filangieri)

35. Guido Mazzoni, bronze bust of Alfonso of Calabria, c. 1489–92. Naples, Gallerie Nazionali di Capodimonte. (Photo Alinari)

36. The same. Front view.

37. Adriano Fiorentino, Medallion of Ferrandino, before 1494 (Hill 335). New York, Kress Collection.

38. Francesco di Giorgio, Medallion of Federigo, c. 1477 (Hill 312). London, British Museum.

39. Adriano Fiorentino (?), bronze bust of Pontano. Genoa, Palazzo Bianco. (Photo Direzione Belle Arti, Genoa)

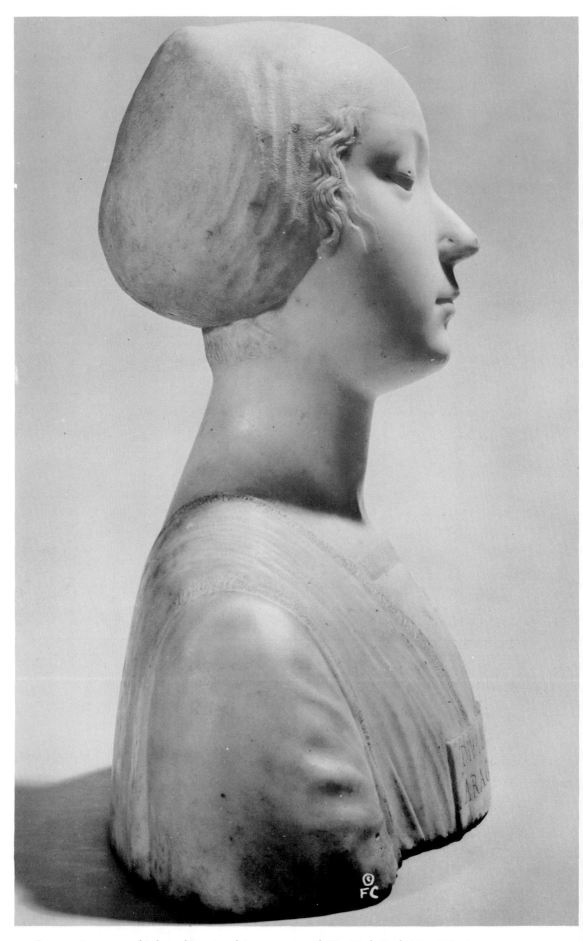

40. Francesco Laurana, marble bust of Beatrice of Aragon, 1474–76. New York, Rockefeller Collection.

41. The same. Front view.

42. Marble relief of Beatrice of Aragon, c. 1489. Budapest, Museum of Fine Arts.

43. Bernardino da Conti, pencil drawing of Isabella of Aragon, c. 1489. Florence, Uffizi, Gabinetto Disegni 1919. (From Malaguzzi Valeri, *La Corte di Lodovico il Moro*)

44. Francesco Laurana, marble bust of Isabella of Aragon, c. 1487–89. Palermo, Galleria Nazionale. (Photo Alinari)

45. Francesco Laurana, marble bust of Isabella of Aragon, c. 1487–89. Paris, Louvre.

46. Francesco Laurana, marble bust of Isabella of Aragon, c. 1487–89. Paris, Musée Jacquemart-André.

47. Miniature portrait of Ippolita
Sforza, in MS Servius, 1476.
Valencia, Biblioteca Universitaria.
(Photo Mas)

48. Another miniature portrait of
Ippolita in the same manuscript.
(Photo Mas)

49. Francesco Laurana, marble bust of Ippolita Sforza(?), c. 1482. Vienna, Kunsthistorisches Museum.

50. Francesco Laurana, marble bust of Ferrandino(?), c. 1474. Palermo, Galleria Nazionale.

51. Francesco Laurana, marble bust of Ippolita Sforza, 1488–89. Berlin, Staatliche Museen. (Photo before damage of 1945)

52. Neapolitan Greek stater,
obverse, "Parthenope"; reverse,
Acheloos. Berlin, Staatliche
Museen.

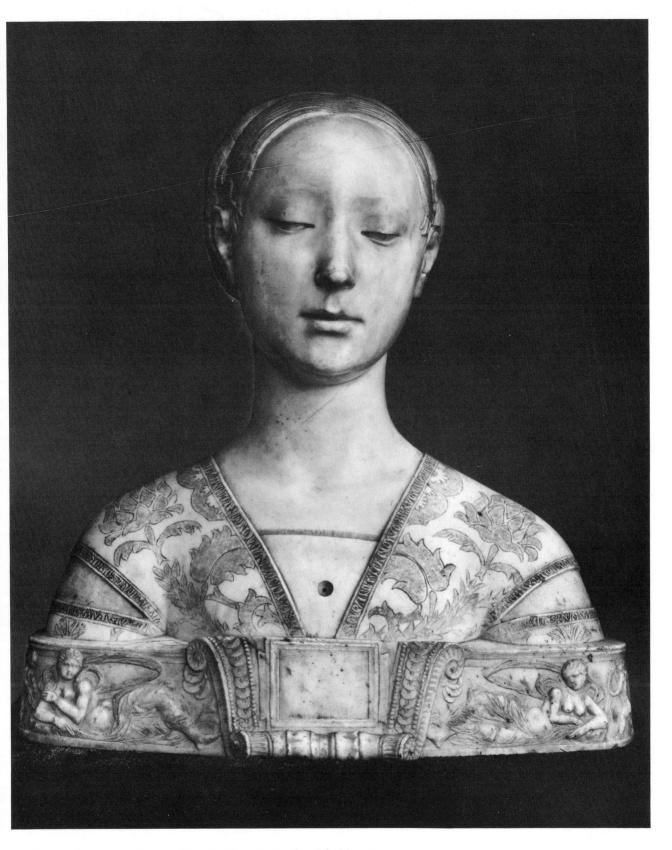

53. Francesco Laurana, marble bust of Ippolita Sforza. Berlin, Staatliche Museen.

54. Francesco Laurana, marble bust of Ippolita Sforza, c. 1488–89. Washington, D.C., National Gallery of Art.

55. Francesco Laurana, marble bust of Ippolita Sforza, c. 1488–89. New York, Frick Collection.

56. The same. Right profile.

57. The same. Left profile.

58. The same. Detail, left side of base.

59. The same. Detail, right side of base.

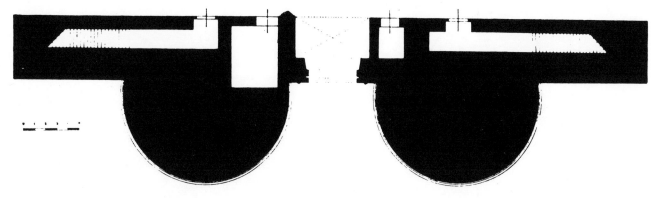

61. Naples. Porta Nolana, 1485–90. Plan. (From Sepe, *La Murazione aragonese*)

63. *Cavallo* of Ferrante, obverse. New York, American Numismatic Society.

60. Naples. New eastern walls, 1484–90. (From Antonio Lafrery, *Ritratto della nobile città di Napoli*)

62. Naples. Porta Nolana. (Photo Cotogni)

64. The arms of the Seggio al Nido. (From S. Mazzella, *Descrittione di Napoli*)

65. The arms of the Seggio di Capuana. (From Mazzella)

66. Naples. San Giovanni a Carbonara. Tomb of Ladislas, 1414(?)–28, by Andrea di Nofrio da Firenze and others. Detail, equestrian statue of King. (Photo Alinari)

67. Naples. Porta Nolana. Detail, marble relief of Alfonso of Calabria. (Photo Cotogni)

68. Naples. Formerly Porta del Carmine. Detail, marble relief of
Alfonso of Calabria. Museo San Martino. (Photo Alinari)

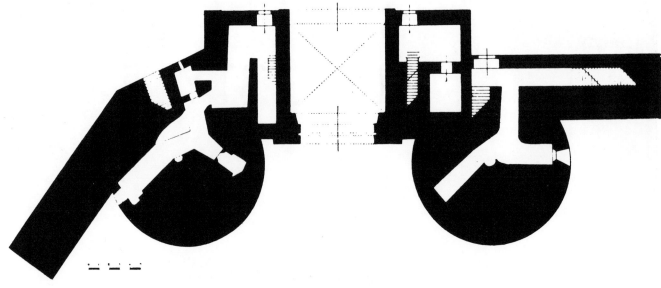

69. Naples. Porta Capuana, 1485–92, by Giuliano da Maiano. Plan. (From Sepe)

70. Naples. Porta
Capuana. (Photo
Cotogni)

71. Florence. San
Lorenzo, designed c.
1419 by Filippo Brunel-
leschi. Lateral bay. (Yale
Photo Collection)

72. Florence. Facade of
Palazzo Rucellai, 1446–
51, designed by Alberti.
Drawing of bay.
(From Stegmann and
Geymüller, *Die Archi-
tektur der Renaissance
in Toscana*)

73. Perugia. Porta San Pietro. Outer part, 1475 ff. by Agostino di Duccio. (Photo Alinari)

74. Naples. San Giacomo degli Spagnuoli. Tomb of Don Pedro of Toledo, 1539–70, by Giovanni da Nola. Detail, marble relief, Don Pedro welcoming Charles V to Naples, 1535. (Yale Photo Collection)

77. Naples. Porta Capuana. Detail, Victory on left spandrel by Jacopo della Pila (?) (Photo Cotogni)

81. Poggioreale. View. (From P. Petrini, *I Palazzi più cospicui . . . di Napoli*)

82. Poggioreale. View, by Bastiaen Stoopendael. (From Johann Blaeu, *Novum italiae theatrum*)

79. Naples. Poggioreale. Sketch plan, by Baldassare Peruzzi. Florence, Uffizi, Gabinetto Disegni A363a.

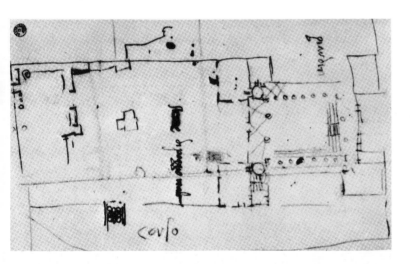

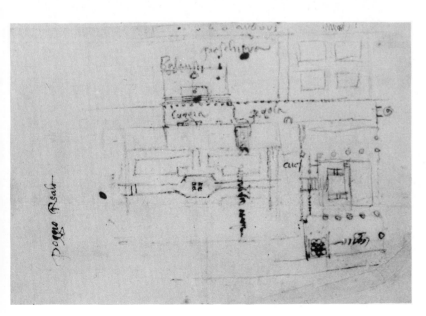

80. Poggioreale. Sketch plan of gardens, by Peruzzi. Florence, Uffizi, A363v.

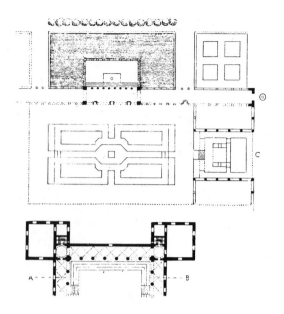

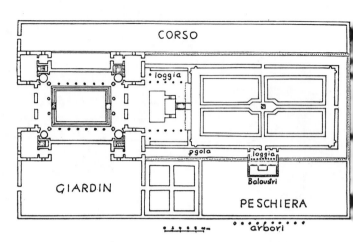

84. Reconstruction of the same. (From C. L. Frommel, *Die Farnesina*)

83. Poggioreale. Reconstruction of the plan of house and gardens. (From Stegmann and Geymüller)

85. Florence. Santo Spirito, Cappella Frescobaldi, Annunciation, 1497–98, by Pietro Donzello. (Photo Alinari)

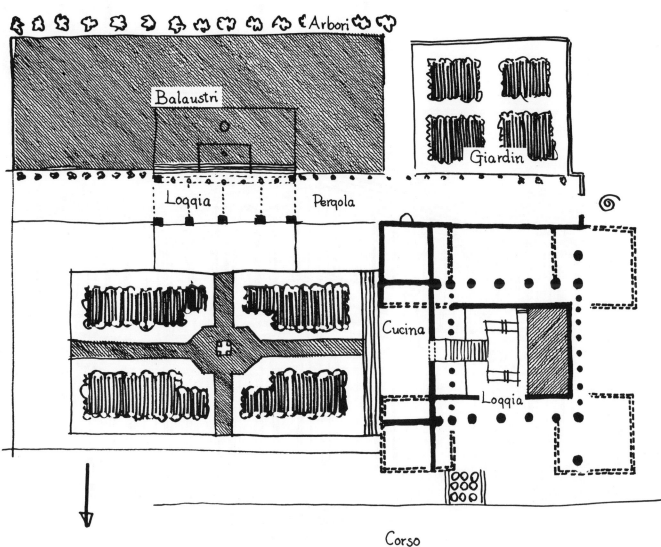

Arbori

Balaustri

Giardin

Loqqia   Pergola

Cucina

Loqqia

Corso

86. Naples. Poggioreale. Site plan as reconstructed by the author.

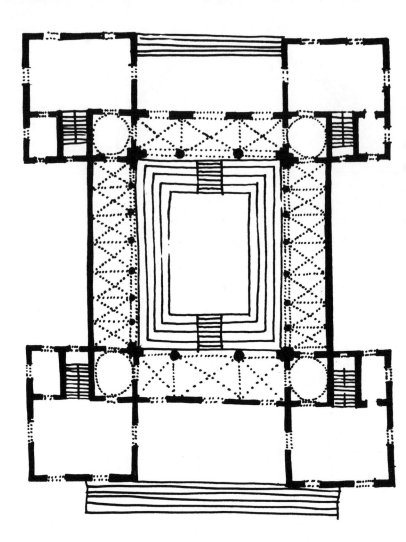

89. The same, main floor plan as reconstructed by author.

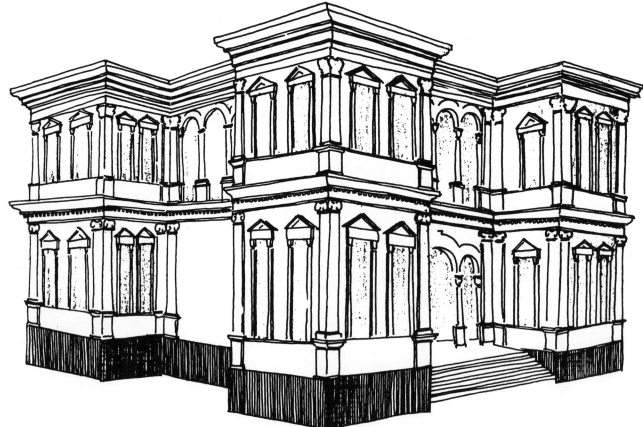

88. Poggioreale. View of villa as reconstructed by author.

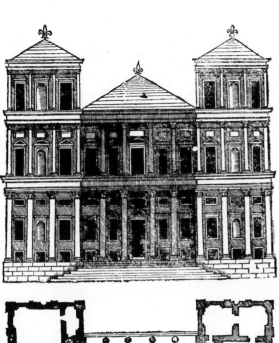

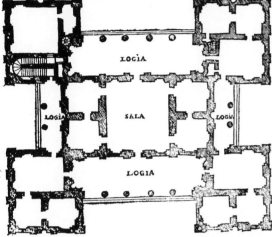

91. The same, second version. (From Serlio)

PIANTA DEL POGGIO REALE DI NAPOLI.

90. Poggioreale. Plan and elevation. (From Sebastiano Serlio, *Quattro Libri d'architettura*)

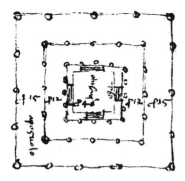

93. Pozzuoli. "Serapeum" or market. Plan. Possibly drawn by Francesco di Giorgio. Florence, Uffizi. (From Papini, *Francesco di Giorgio*)

92. Gyulafiratót Pogánytelek, Hungary. Reconstruction of villa no. 3. (From Thomas, *Römische Villen in Pannonien*)

94. Siena. Castello dei Quattro Torri, XIV–XV Century. (Photo Alinari)

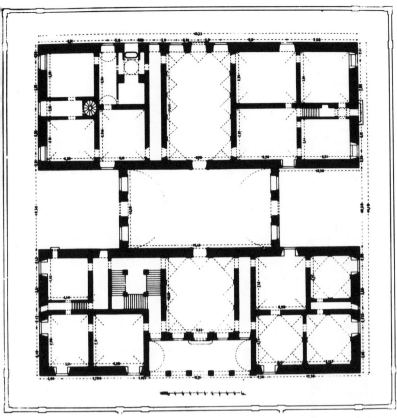

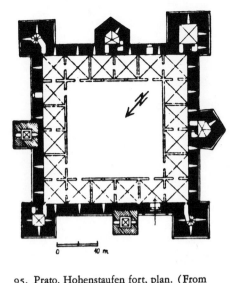

95. Prato. Hohenstaufen fort, plan. (From Hahn, *Hohenstaufen-Burgen in Suditalien*)

97. Poggio a Caiano. Plan. (From Stegmann and Geymüller)

96. Florence. Poggio a Caiano, begun 1485, by Giuliano da Sangallo. (Photo author)

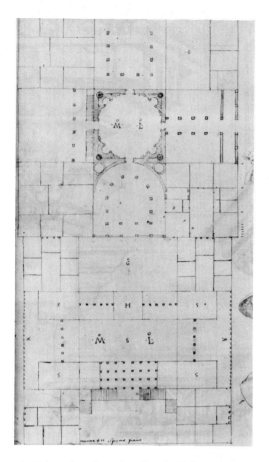

98. Palace plans from the *Libro di Giuliano da San Gallo,* Rome, Vatican.

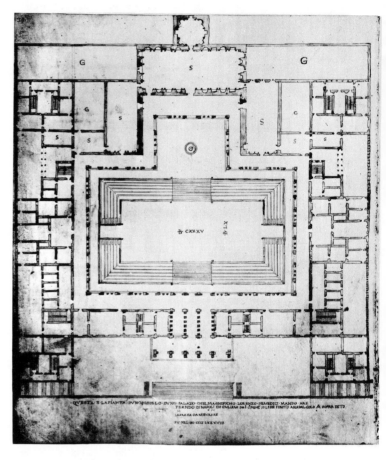

99. Naples. Palace for Ferrante. Plan, 1488, by Giuliano da Sangallo. Vatican *Libro*.

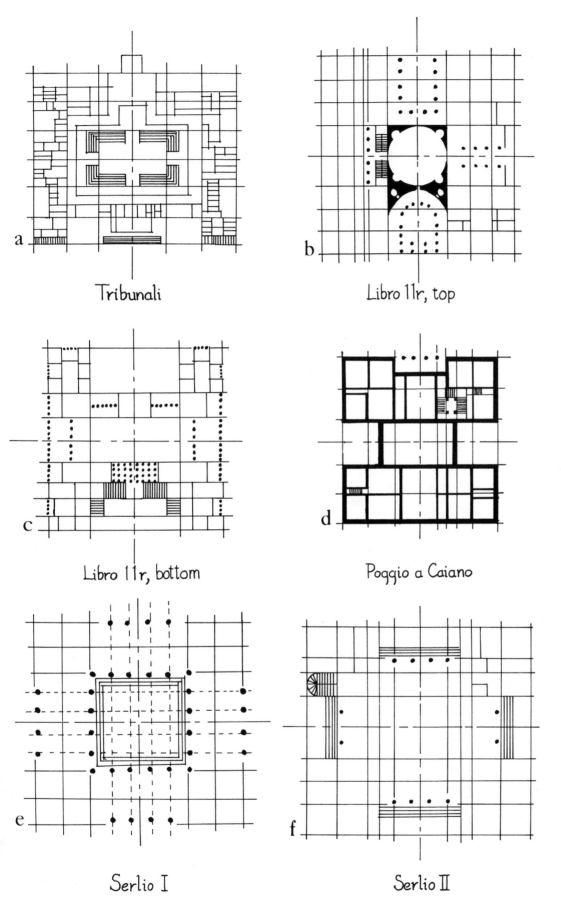

a Tribunali

b Libro 11r, top

c Libro 11r, bottom

d Poggio a Caiano

e Serlio I

f Serlio II

100. Plans: (a) Ferrante's Palazzo dei Tribunali. (b) Giuliano da Sangallo's Vatican *Libro*, fol. 11r. Upper building. (c) The same. Lower building. (d) Poggio a Caiano. (e) First Serlio variation of Poggioreale. (f) Second Serlio variation of Poggioreale. (Author)

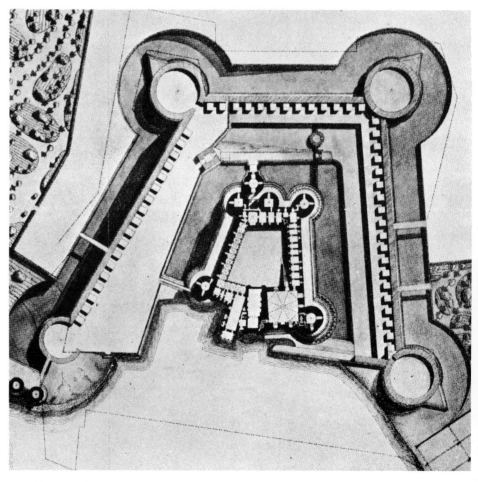

101. Francesco di Giorgio, new Fortifications at Castel Nuovo, c. 1492. (From Achille Stella, *Il Restauro di Castel Nuovo*)

102. San Leo (Urbino). Fort, c. 1450, probably by Francesco di Giorgio. (From Papini)

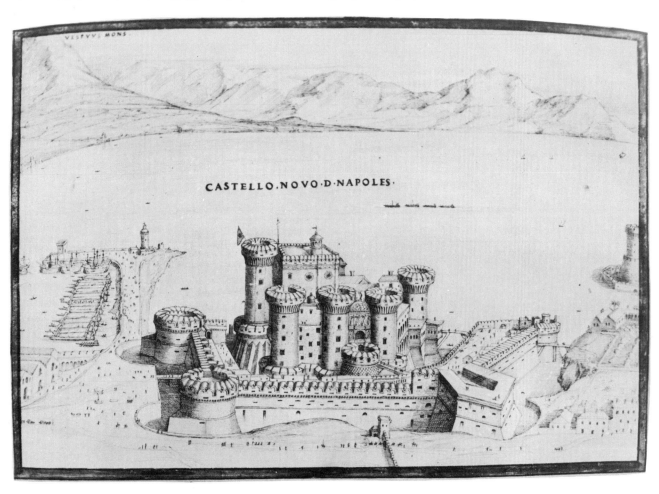

103. Francisco de Hollanda, drawing of the Castel Nuovo c. 1540. Escorial, Library.

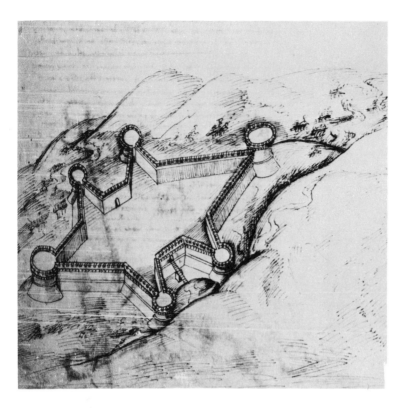

104. Drawing of a fort. From Francesco di Giorgio's *Trattato*. (Florence, Biblioteca Nazionale.

106. Naples. Castel Nuovo and Castel Sant' Elmo in c. 1566. (From Lafrery)

105. Castel Sant' Elmo at the beginning of the eighteenth century. (From Blaeu)

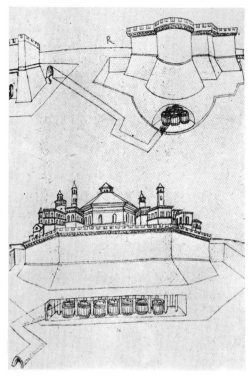

108. Francesco di Giorgio(?), sketch of
explosive mine. From M. Salmi, *Disegni di
Francesco di Giorgio nella collezione Chigi-
Saraceni*)

109. Fra Giocondo, ed. (a) a "castellum" with (b) "triplex
immissarium" [storage tank at city walls], and (c) "fornix" [conduit].
(From Frontinus, *De aqueductibus*)

107. Drawing of a fort, bound with Francesco di Giorgio's *Trattato*. Florence, Biblioteca Nazionale.

110. Benedetto da Maiano. Unfinished marble relief here identified as the coronation of Alfonso II, 1494–97. Florence, Bargello. (Photo Cotogni)

111. The same. Detail.

112. The same. Left profile of Alfonso II.

115. Benedetto da Maiano.
Marble bust of Onofrio di
Pietro, 1493. San
Gimignano, Museo dell'
Arte Sacra. (Photo author)

113. San Gimignano.
Church of Sant' Agostino.
Altar of San Bartolo, 1492–
94, by Benedetto da
Maiano. Detail, genuflect-
ing angel. (Photo Alinari)

116. Engraving of statue of
Frederick II Hohenstaufen,
formerly on the Porta
Romana, Capua. (From
J. B. L. J. Séroux d'Agin-
court, *Histoire de l'art par
les monuments*)

114. The same. Detail,
Charity. (Photo Alinari)

117. Arnolfo di Cambio, marble statue of Charles I of Anjou, King of Sicily, c. 1273. Rome, Palazzo dei Conservatori. (Photo Alinari)

118. Naples. Santa Chiara. Tomb of King Robert, 1342–45, by Pace and Giovanni Bertini da Firenze. Detail, statue of king. (Photo Alinari)

119. Naples. San Giovanni a Carbonara. Tomb of Ladislas, 1414(?)–28, by Andrea di Nofrio da Firenze and others. Detail, statues of Ladislas and Giovanna. (Photo Alinari)

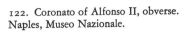

122. Coronato of Alfonso II, obverse. Naples, Museo Nazionale.

120. Naples. Castel Nuovo. Arch of Alfonso I, 1452–65. Detail, the King in Triumph. (Photo Alinari)

121. Castel Nuovo. Inner arch. (Photo author)

123. Naples. Church of SS Severino e Sossio. Chiostro del Platano, fresco series of 1494 ff. by Antonio Solario and others. St. Benedict Being Welcomed to Affile. (Photo Alinari)

124. The same. Detail. (Photo Alinari)

125. Naples. Old Church of SS Severino e Sossio, designed c. 1494 by Giovanni Mormando and built after 1537. Nave. (Photo author)

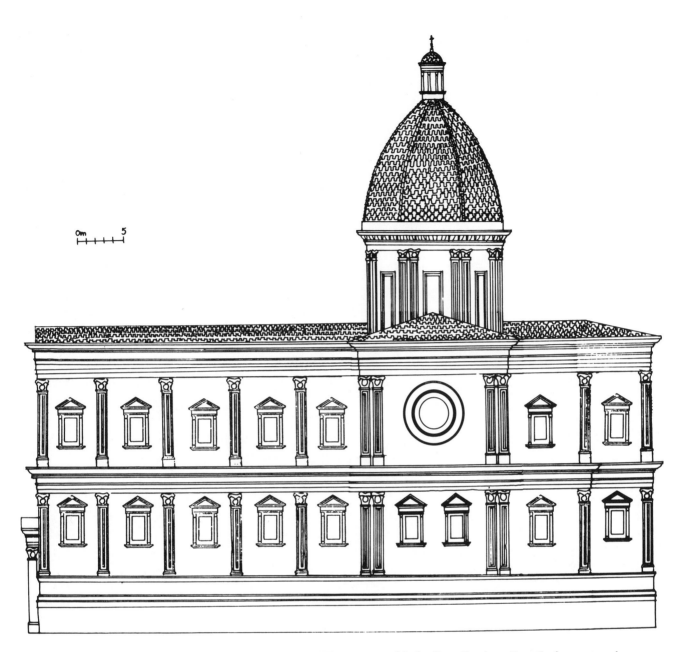

127. Naples. Santa Caterina a Formello, begun 1519, by
Antonio Marchese (?). Side elevation. (Adapted from Pane)

126. Naples. Cappella Pontano, 1492, by Fra Giocondo(?).
(From Pane, *Architettura del rinascimento*)

129. Anonymous, sheet of drawings of the Chapel of the Cardinal of Portugal, San Miniato, Florence. London, British Museum. (From Hartt, et al., *The Chapel of the Cardinal of Portugal*)

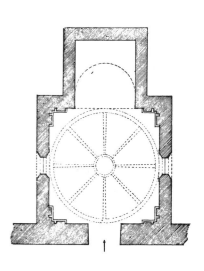

128. Naples. Church of Monteoliveto (Sant' Anna dei Lombardi). Cappella Tolosa, 1487–99, by Giuliano da Maiano(?). (From Pane)

130. Church of Monteoliveto. Chapel of Maria Piccolomini, c. 1470–89. Architect: Giuliano da Maiano. Sculptors: Antonio Rossellino
and Benedetto da Maiano. (Photo Alinari)

131. The same. Tomb of Maria Piccolomini, begun c. 1470 by Rossellino and completed 1481–89 by Benedetto da Maiano. (Photo Alinari)

132. Florence. San Miniato. Tomb of the Cardinal of Portugal, 1461–66, by Antonio Rossellino. (Photo Alinari)

133. Church of Monteoliveto. Tomb of Maria Piccolomini. Detail, sarcophagus and effigy. (Photo Alinari)

134. The same. Detail, base. (Photo Alinari)

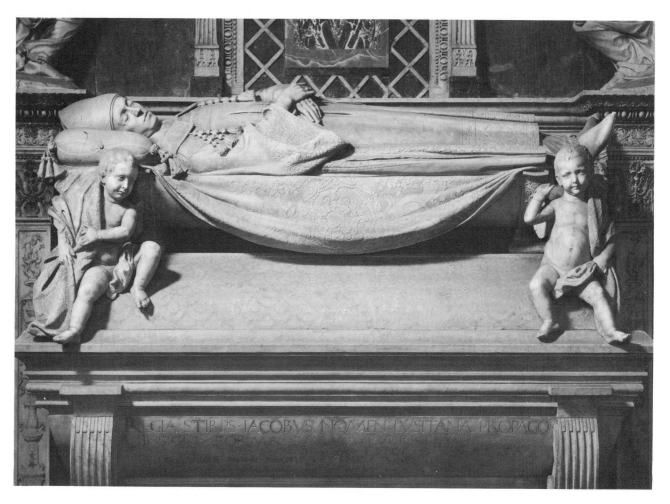

135. Florence. San Miniato. Tomb of the Cardinal of Portugal. Detail, effigy. (Photo Alinari)

136. The same. Detail, base. (Photo Alinari)

137. Naples. Church of Monteoliveto. Tomb of Maria
Piccolomini. Detail, left putto.

138. The same. Detail, right putto. (Photo Cotogni)

139. The same. Detail, left angel. (Photo Cotogni)

140. The same. Detail, right angel. (Photo Cotogni)

141. The same.
Detail, Virgin
and Child.
(Photo
Cotogni)

142. The same.
Detail, Ascen-
sion. (Photo
Cotogni)

143. Church of Monteoliveto. Altar of Piccolomini Chapel. (Photo Alinari)

144. The same. Detail, St. James the Apostle. (Photo Cotogni)

145. The same. Detail, St. John the Evangelist. (Photo Cotogni)

146. The same. Detail, left prophet. (Photo Cotogni)

147. The same. Detail, right prophet. (Photo Cotogni)

148. The same. Detail, Nativity. (Photo Alinari)

149. The same. Detail, Virgin from the Nativity, Fig. 148. (Photo Cotogni)

150. The same. Detail, angels from the Nativity, Fig. 148. (Photo Cotogni)

151. The same. Detail, left putti. (Photo Cotogni)

152. The same. Detail, right putti. (Photo Cotogni)

153. Church of Monteoliveto. Terranuova Chapel. Altarpiece, in place, 1489, by Benedetto da Maiano. (Photo Alinari)

154. Lorenzo di Credi(?), drawing of an altarpiece. Florence, Uffizi, Gabinetto Disegni, 1436e.

155. Naples, Church of Monteoliveto. Altar of Terranuova Chapel. Detail, St. John the Baptist. (Photo Cotogni)

156. The same. Detail, St. John the Evangelist. (Photo Cotogni)

157. The same. Detail, Annunciation scene. (Photo Cotogni)

158. The same. Detail, upper left putto. (Photo Cotogni)

159. The same. Detail, upper right putto. (Photo Cotogni)

160. The same.
Detail, predella:
(I) Adoration
of the Shep-
herds. (Photo
Cotogni)

161. The same.
Detail, predella:
(II) Adoration
of the Magi.
(Photo
Cotogni)

162. The same.
Detail, predella:
(IV) Entomb-
ment. (Photo
Cotogni)

163. The same. Detail, predella: (V) Appearance of Christ to the Virgin and Apostles. (Photo Cotogni)

164. The same. Detail, predella: (VI) The Pentecost with the Virgin. (Photo Cotogni)

165. The same. Detail, predella: (VII) Death of the Virgin. (Photo Cotogni)

166. Naples. San Domenico Maggiore. Cappella Saluzzo (formerly Carafa di Santa Severina), 1512–16, by Romolo di Antonio da Settignano. (Photo Alinari)

167. Florence. Santo Spirito. Altar of the Sacrament, c. 1490, by Andrea Sansovino. Detail. (Photo Alinari)

168. Funeral ceremonies of the Christian rite. (From Tommaso Porcacchi, *Funerali antichi*)

169. Naples. Church of Monteoliveto. Chapel of Alfonso II and Gurello Orilia (now Cappella del Sepolcro). Lamentation, 1492–94, by Guido Mazzoni. (Photo Alinari)

170. The same. Detail, left half. (Photo Alinari)

171. The same. Detail, Federigo(?) as Nicodemus. (Photo Cotogni)

172. The same. Detail, Alfonso II as Joseph of Arimathea. (Photo Cotogni)

173. The same. Detail, Alfonso II. (Photo Alinari)

175. Unknown seventeenth-century artist.
Bronze bust (labeled as Pontano but
taken from the Mazzoni portrait in Figs.
172 and 173). New York, Paul Drey
Gallery. (Photo John D. Schiff)

174. Florence. Palazzo Vecchio. Sala di
Lorenzo. Detail, The Arrival of Lorenzo
de' Medici in Naples, 1479, fresco,
1556–67, by Giorgio Vasari. Detail.
(Photo Alinari)